THE RISE-AND FALL?
OF MONTREAL

**A Case Study of Urban Growth,
Regional Economic Expansion
and National Development**

BENJAMIN HIGGINS

Institut canadien de recherche sur le développement régional
Canadian Institute for Research on Regional Development
Moncton

© Institut canadien de recherche sur le développement régional/
Canadian Institute for Research on Regional Development

ISBN 0-88659-004-3 (paper)

Legal deposit 2nd quarter 1986
National Library of Canada

Printed and bound in Canada by
La Compagnie de l'Éclaireur Limitée

CONTENTS

AVANT-PROPOS

Voici la première d'une série de monographies publiées par l'Institut canadien de recherche sur le développement régional. Ces monographies ont pour but de présenter les résultats et les analyses des recherches entreprises dans le domaine du développement régional. Seront explorés divers sujets allant de questions spécifiques au développement régional à des études de cas, en passant par le processus de formulation des politiques de développement régional et l'impact économique qu'exercent certaines collectivités sur les régions.

Dans la présente étude, Ben Higgins se penche sur des questions fondamentales concernant le rôle de Montréal et, plus particulièrement, son impact économique sur le Québec et ses liens économiques avec d'autres grands centres urbains. Il fait la critique des principales théories de développement régional, notamment celle des centres de croissance. En empruntant à diverses théories et approches, il élabore une nouvelle stratégie de planification urbaine, régionale et nationale. Cette monographie constitue une importante contribution à l'étude du développement régional.

Au nom du personnel de l'Institut, je tiens à remercier Ben Higgins d'avoir donné le coup d'envoi à notre série de monographies. Nous sommes très heureux de l'accueillir à titre de chercheur invité, le premier à se joindre à l'Institut. Sa sagesse, sa bonne humeur, son dévouement et, surtout, son vif intérêt pour l'avenir de l'Institut sont fort appréciés de tous.

Donald J. SAVOIE
Directeur général

v

FOREWORD

This is the first in a series of monographs published by the Canadian Institute for Research on Regional Development. The monographs are designed to present research results and analysis to advance our understanding of regional development issues and problems. These policy monographs will explore a variety of topics ranging from specific regional development policy issues, to case studies, to how regional development policies are defined, and to the economic impact of selected communities on regions.

In this study, Ben Higgins examines some fundamental questions about the role of Montreal, its economic impact on Quebec and about economic linkages between it and other major urban centres. He provides an important critique of some prominent theories of regional development, notably the growth centre theory. Skillfully weaving different theories and approaches, he develops a new strategy for urban, regional and national planning. The monograph constitutes an important contribution to the development process.

The staff at the Institute joins me in thanking Ben Higgins for launching our policy monograph series. We are also very grateful to him for having joined us at the Institute as our first visiting fellow. His wise counsel, his good humor, his dedication, and his strong interest in the Institute's future are greatly appreciated.

Donald J. SAVOIE
Executive Director

PREFACE

This book has several facets, perhaps too many for so slim a volume. One of these facets is a love poem. My family history is inextricably interwoven with Montreal's. I have spent more years of my adult life in Montreal than in any other city. Those years were among the richest and most rewarding I have known. My acquaintance with the city has been both personal and professional, and spans five decades. Inevitably, some of the affection I feel for Montreal shines through, even when I am trying to present a scholarly analysis of its past, present, and future. I make no apologies for that; I am merely forewarning the reader.

When discussing the future of Montreal, my personal concern for it has led me go beyond prognosis and to suggest a prescription, designed to assure that Montreal will remain the throbbing and charming city that it is today, and that it will continue to play a leading role in the economic, social, and cultural life of Quebec and of Canada. The recommended treatment is long lasting and arduous, the pills are not sugar coated. It is not likely to be readily accepted by all concerned. Some may accept the broad strategy but prefer different tactics. I will be happy if I get that far with a large proportion of my readers. The final chapter of the book argues for an *approach* to urban, regional, and national planning which is quite different from those normally adopted, either in industrialized countries or in developing ones. It is essentially a strategy designed in terms of interactions in space, with particular kinds of intervention in certain places in order to achieve a desired effect in another place. If this book encourages some urban and regional economists and planners, and others, to start thinking along these lines, it will have achieved one of its major objectives.

"Rise and Fall" was not the original title of the book. Some of my colleagues have objected to it as "exaggerated and theatrical." I don't mind it being that if it has the desired effect. Of course, Montreal has not yet "fallen" in the sense of total collapse. It is not a ghost town and shows no signs of becoming one. It has "fallen" only in the sense that it has been displaced as Canada's leading metropolitan centre in the terms of population, industry, commerce, transport, and finance. But the title was deliberately chosen to suggest a particular kind of theoretical framework in which cities are treated as social organisms, subject to almost biological laws of birth, growth, maturity, stagnation and decay. I wanted to indicate that I am dealing with the subject in a way that links it to theories of socio-economic evolution and to theories of history, as when one speaks of "The Rise and Fall of Rome (or Athens)"; or better, as when people speak of "The Rise and Fall of Capitalism." Many social scientists do speak of the rise and fall of capitalism, although capitalism has not yet fallen. They mean that the seeds of the fall of capitalism are planted in the causes of its rise, that their analytical models lead to the conclusion that capitalism must eventually fall, has started to fall, that it may possibly fall, or that something must be done to prevent it from falling. It is in this sense that I speak of "the Fall of Montreal." It has fallen from its pinnacle of 1967, it could easily fall further if nothing is done to prevent it, and something should be done to prevent it. Frankly, the title is designed to shock people into worrying about the fate of Montreal.

The main facet of the book, however, is a modest, but in my view significant and somewhat original, contribution to the literature on urban, regional and national development. These are the fields which have occupied my attention for the last thirty-five years, in reverse order. I started with national development, mainly in developing countries. It took nearly a decade for that concern to lead me to regions, and several years more for my interest in regional development to lead me to urban centres. Meanwhile I had come to recognize that in some respects the industrialized countries are in worse shape than the developing countries, and that they share many of the same problems; but that each group of countries, and ultimately each country, has its own problems or its own version of more general ones. One cannot avoid taking a close look at the society concerned if one wants to formulate effective policies and construct successful plans for it. My involvement in development planning and policy-making in both industrialized and developing countries has led me to two convictions: first, that interactions among urban centres, regions, and national economies are at the core of the development process; and second, that the most effective way to study such interactions is through case studies. This book is a study of Montreal as a case of such interactions. The subtitle is perhaps a more accurate indication of its content than the title.

I have made no attempt to cover all the literature on the history of Montreal or on urban and regional economics. The book is neither a Ph.D. dissertation nor a textbook. It is essentially a presentation of my own ideas regarding the evolution of Montreal, as a case of urban, regional and national interactions, based on my long involvement in the former and my long study of the latter.

If I were to list all the people who have assisted me, stimulated me, or influenced my ideas through the years in ways that are reflected in this book, I would end up with a directory nearly as long as the book itself. I shall therefore confine myself to the very few who have had a direct impact during the period when the book was being written, with the usual pronouncement that anything good in the book is due to them and anything bad is due to me.

At the Institut canadien de recherche sur le développement régional:
Donald J. Savoie, Executive Director
Rodolphe Lamarche, Coordinator of research
Jean Gagnon, Agent de recherche
Bernard Babineau, Assistant de recherche
Louise C. Robichaud, Coordinator of publications
Jacqueline Robichaud, Secrétaire

At the Centre de recherche en développement économique at the Université de Montréal:
Fernand Martin, Professeur titulaire en sciences économiques
André Raynauld, Professeur titulaire en sciences économiques (former Président du Conseil économique du Canada and Directeur du C.R.D.E.)

At the United Nations Centre for Research on Regional Development (during the period of my most intensive association with it):

Dr. Masahiko Honjo, Director

Dr. R.P. Misra, Deputy Director

At the Development Studies Centre, Australian National University:

Dr. Helen Hughes, Director

At the Centre for Research in Federal Financial Relations, Australian National University

Dr. Russell Mathews, Director

CHAPTER 1

INTRODUCTION:
MONTREAL AS CANADA'S METROPOLIS

The interactions between urban growth and regional economic expansion are among the most important phenomena in the whole process of national economic development and social change. From ancient times until today the rise, stagnation, and decline of nations has been closely associated with the fate of particular cities. There is an abundant literature on the history of cities, to which economic historians have contributed a great deal. Within the field of economics, we have the vast literature on growth poles, central places, location theory, regional disparities, base industries, transport and communications. Regional science has contributed such constructs as gravity models, rank size rules, polarization reversal, and regional convergence. Yet when all is said and done, our understanding of the way in which the growth and decline of cities interacts with the social and economic development of their own peripheral regions, with other regions in the same country, with development of the nation as a whole, and with other countries, is still imperfectly understood.

The mechanism of "transfer of spread effects" in both directions between cities and various other parts of the world — including other cities — has not yet been analyzed in a way that provides a solid basis for policy and planning. One reason for this state of affairs is that the methodology applied by social scientists, and especially by economists, has been unsuited to its task. The tendency has been to look always for "laws" that are true always and everywhere, after the manner of physics. Of course, we must look for such laws, but we cannot expect to find them with respect to all aspects of development, any more than a biologist should expect behaviour of all species to be identical in all respects, or a medical doctor expect all patients to respond identically to the same treatment. We need case studies as well as econometrics.

Many if not most of the neo-classical economists who have studied urban economics have tried — naturally enough — to apply methods and constructs with which they are familiar. Accordingly they have tried to treat cities as a kind of market, and have analyzed the development of cities and impact on other regions as the result of individual, rational, marginal decisions, designed to maximize utility. Marginal changes in wage rates, expectations of finding employment, tax rates, transport costs, rents, are supposed to determine people's choices as to where they live, and what they do; these choices determine the geographical and occupational distribution between town and country, between town and town, region and region, and among nations. Such factors certainly have some effect on individual choices; but when we examine closely the cases of particular cities we find that such choices play a minimal role in determining what happens to them, and what happens elsewhere as a result. Sometimes, single individuals have enough wealth and power for their decisions to have a significant impact, as when the King of France sent Jacques Cartier to North America, or when Wolfe climbed the cliffs to the Plains of Abraham. Usually, however, the important choices are made by groups or collectivities of one sort or another. The choices are not "marginal", but "lumpy" and discontinuous. They are not market choices in the usual sense. They may be made hundreds or thousands of miles from the city where their impact is felt. Politics, geography, geopolitics, wars, revolutions, major innovations, cultural change — all these are part of the story of any particular city.

While the neo-marxists may start a little ahead of neo-classical economists in their understanding of interactions among cities, regions, and nations, because their analytical units are collectivities or groups rather than individuals, and because their models involve history and social evolution, they too have failed to provide a solid basis for policy and planning. They too are looking for universal laws, and the "classes" that comprise their analytical units are not always the groups that determine what happens in every society of the real world, and are almost never the only influential groups. Their models as well as the neo-classical ones are over-simplified and leave out too many important factors.

Once we abandon the hope of finding simple "laws" of urban, regional and national development that are true always and everywhere, and which together explain everything, we are led naturally to case studies. The practice of medicine is based upon solid knowledge of certain principles and uniformities in the fields of anatomy, physiology, biochemistry, neurology, endocrinology, etc. But the practitioner does not rely on these alone in treating individual patients. He examines each patient carefully, and before arriving at his diagnosis, prognosis and prescription, calls upon knowledge of other cases which, because of their similarities to *or* their differences from the case in hand, cast light upon it. In the social sciences, including urban and regional economics, we must learn to do the same.

Here then is one such case study. It does not pretend to be a history of Montreal, or even a complete economic history. As the subtitle suggests, it concentrates on *interactions* among urban growth, regional expansion, and national development. It shows how varied and how dispersed were the forces, events, groups and individuals that shaped the development of Montreal — both in time and in space. The book's organization is not strictly chronological. Chapter 1 presents a snapshot, focussed on Montreal at the height of her glory at the time of Expo '67, but with a lens wide enough to include in the picture the mid-1960s and data from the 1971 Census. Chapter 2 is a flashback, telling the story of the growth of Montreal from the early seventeenth century up to the late 1960s. Chapter 3 tells of the city's subsequent decline. Chapter 4 is concerned with the role of Montreal in the Quebec economy (and society) as such. Chapter 5 is intended to be more analytical and historical, and looks at inter-relationships among growth and change in Montreal, in Quebec, in other provinces, and in Canada as a whole. It lays considerable stress on structural change, especially change in occupational structure; and since census data on occupational structure began in 1911, this story begins in 1911 and ends in 1981. Chapter 6, with the story told, we consider several major theories of interactions among urban growth, regional expansion and national development. Our purpose there is to see to what extent the Montreal story confirms or denies these theories, and to seek whatever light these theories may cast on the future development of Montreal. The final chapter presents a diagnosis, prognosis, and prescription for Montreal, involving not only the metropolis itself, but Quebec, Ontario, and ultimately the whole of Canada.

As stated in the preface, use of the expression "rise and fall" in the title does not imply that Montreal is already finished. Rather we want to suggest a biological approach to the study of the evolution of cities, and the importance of historical precedent, as when one speaks of "The Rise and Fall of Rome" or "The Rise and Fall of Capitalism". So far Montreal has "fallen" only in the sense that it is no longer Canada's leading city in terms of population, industry, commerce, and finance. The question is whether or not there are forces so strong that, once even relative decline of a city sets in, nothing can prevent its ultimate collapse; and then the question is whether the eclipse will be permanent, as in the case of Carthage or Damascus, or whether there will be a limited resurgence, as in the case of Rome, Athens, or Vienna, or a return to position of world importance like Beijing. Finally, there is the most important question of all: even if forces tending towards further decay are at work, can they be offset by astute policy and planning?

Urban Growth and Regional Development In Canada

There are few industrialized countries where policy and planning with respect to urban growth and regional development have played a more important role than in Canada. The main reason for the concern with these matters has been the continued presence of regional disparities, which were unusually recalcitrant for a country having attained so high a level of overall national development, plus the fact that "regions" were identified with provinces or groups of them, within a federation with a constitution according a good deal of power to the provinces. In 1976 and again in 1981, this resentment was expressed in the election to the provincial government of a party dedicated to the achievement of Quebec independence, the Parti Québécois. The grievance felt in the Atlantic provinces, which have trailed development in the rest of the country even more markedly than Quebec, is more recent, dating from Confederation in 1867, but it is scarcely less deep, and

4

the ties of the Atlantic provinces to "the Boston states" are still strong. More recently still, oil-rich Alberta and minerals-rich British Columbia and Saskatchewan have grown restive because of federal limitations on their freedom to dispose of and price their natural resources as they wish. Regional development and reduction of regional disparities have come to be seen as crucial to the very survival of Canada as a nation, and consequently have been at the top of the list of objectives of national economic policy.

At the federal level, a whole series of agencies appeared in the early sixties, concerned with rural poverty and distressed industrial areas. These included the Agricultural Rehabilitation and Development Agency (1961, Ministry of Lands and Forestry); the Atlantic Development Board (1962, outside the formal government structure); the Area Development Agency (1963, Ministry of Industry); the Federal Fund for Rural Economic Development (1965, Ministry of Forestry and Rural Development, as it had then become); the Cape Breton Development Corporation (1967), concerned mainly with rehabilitation of the coal mining and the iron and steel industries in Nova Scotia. As their titles suggest, these were all *ad hoc* programs undertaken in response to particular economic and political situations. Some of them aroused a good deal of support and had some intellectual impact, especially ARDA in the province of Quebec, but they did not add up to a systematic attack on regional and local development problems. In 1969 they were brought together in, and replaced by, the new Department of Regional Economic Expansion (DREE).[1]

The establishment of DREE was the major event which shaped local and regional development policy and planning from 1969 to 1982. Great importance was attached to the new ministry by the Trudeau government. The legislation establishing the new department was called The Organisation of Government Act. The wording of the Act suggested that the government had in mind making DREE a kind of super-ministry; its minister was empowered to make plans in cooperation with other departments and agencies and to coordinate the work of all of them in implementing these plans. The minister was also required to assure the cooperation of the provinces in the planning and implementation of regional development programs. The powers to push and pull enterprises from one region to another were sweeping. In addition to providing infrastructure of all kinds, DREE could provide or arrange for training and retraining of workers, transport to their new jobs, and housing; for outright capital grants which could reach

5

50 percent of capital costs of new plant or extension and improvement of existing plant, under a formula that gave an implicit subsidy to the more labour-intensive undertakings; guarantees of bank loans to remove any difficulties in raising working capital, etc. To obtain these benefits the private enterprises had to operate in designated areas; but eventually the whole of Quebec and the Atlantic provinces were designated, plus smaller trouble spots in other provinces.

DREE's powers were never fully used. The incentives for relocating or expanding in designated areas were not a right under the law but a matter of negotiation between DREE and the respective firms. In the first years the incentives were used sparingly and DREE concentrated on providing standard infrastructure. The incentives were never used to the degree that the law permitted. DREE did not become a "super-ministry." Old line departments and agencies like the Ministry of Finance, the Bank of Canada, and the Ministry of Industry, Trade and Commerce continued to exercise a good deal more power than DREE.

DREE's strategy was urban based from the start. As in the United States and elsewhere during the late sixties and early seventies, the basic underlying theory was one of growth poles generating spread effects to their own hinterland. But growth poles could be anything from a major metropolitan centre like Montreal to a decaying small town like Moncton, New Brunswick, or even smaller centres. It seemed not to matter what was chosen as a growth pole so long as it was in a designated area. The results have been much the same as those obtained with the strategy elsewhere. While there has been keen debate on the impact of DREE on the spatial distribution of economic activity, the most careful studies indicate that it achieved some success in redistributing economic activity from cities in more prosperous regions to cities in designated areas. It is much less clear that the stimulus to cities in designated areas has generated significant spread effects to their own hinterlands, or that the long-term growth of poorer regions has been significantly accelerated by DREE's efforts.

In the face of growing dissatisfaction with the functioning of DREE, based in some cases on the feeling that it should do much more and in others on the conviction that it should do much less, the Trudeau administration scrapped the department early in 1982. Its general functions were taken over by a new central agency, the Ministry of State for Economic and Regional Development (MSERD) and its industrial incentives programs transferred to a newly created Department of Regional Industrial Expansion (DRIE). Before it had become clear what differences in regional policy and planning might have emerged from this reorganization, the Liberal regime was swept away in a crushing victory for the Progressive Conservative party under Brian Mulroney, in September 1984. During his election campaign Mr. Mulroney had attacked the Liberals for the ineptness of their regional development policy, and promised to do a better job of reducing regional disparities. At the time of writing it appeared that he intended to rely mainly on tax incentives to fulfill that promise.

Indeed, it seems clear that Canada is at a crossroads with regard to the whole matter of regional development. In developing countries, the period covered by the lifetime of DREE was one in which regional planning and development was seen increasingly as the most effective way of improving national development planning, bringing the planners into close touch with the target population and their problems, permitting disaggregation of national planning in space, and the subsequent assembly of national plans as an aggregation of regional and local plans.[2] In developing countries, regional planning and development is viewed as a device for improving the allocation of resources, assuring their full utilization, and speeding adjustment to change. In Canada, because of the special way in which regional policy evolved, regional development is inextricably interwined with redistribution of income and of economic activity from rich to poor regions, revenue sharing, and transfer payments to the disadvantaged regions. It therefore becomes possible to attack the whole concept of "regional development" as a program which lures industries and other activities to places where they ought not to be, misallocates resources, and delays readjustment by making it possible for people to stay where they are and doing what they are doing — including doing nothing — through subsidies of one kind or another. It is argued that regional development programs delay regional development by supporting cost structures that are too high to attract capital.

Donald Savoie, Executive Director of the Canadian Institute for Research on Regional Development, notes that in introducing the new legislation, Prime Minister Trudeau made no reference to regional disparities, and continues:

> Others, including scholars and practitioners of regional development, have also moved away from an emphasis on gap-closing or on

removing regional disparities... Few can deny the validity of Cour-
chene's argument that many federal transfer payments and programs
have served to blunt economic adjustment. In fact it has been
persuasively argued that the present system of federal transfers in
support of current consumption and services is actually hindering
the goal of regional growth and self-reliance.[3]

Thus it has become common to speak of a "trade-off" between
reduction of regional gaps and "national efficiency." Savoie also
points out, however, that within the Canadian political context
there is no question of abandoning regional development as a
major aim of policy, including reduction of regional gaps. Some
economists, and others too, would turn the whole business back to
the market. Others are fearful of any withdrawal of federal and
provincial governments from the effort to overcome the relative
poverty of Quebec and the Atlantic provinces.

In the whole debate about urban growth and regional development in Canada there is no doubt that the fate of Montreal is a
crucial issue. Montreal has been Canada's leading city, and then
her major metropolis, throughout almost all of Canada's history.
In terms of statistics, Montreal has recently lost its position of
primacy in many fields. But the interactions between the growth
of Montreal and the development of other regions have been a
major factor in Canada's development in the past, and they still
are. A healthy Quebec economy — even a healthy Canadian
economy — is hardly thinkable without a strong and vigorous
Montreal.

What is a metropolis ?

We have referred to Montreal as "Canada's major metropolis." But
what is a "metropolis"? Some thirty years ago Columbia University
in New York City celebrated its bicentennial. As part of these
celebrations the university organized a series of seminars, one of
them on "The Metropolis." It fell to John Burchard, then Dean of
the Faculty of Humanities and Social Sciences at the Massachusetts
Institute of Technology, to define "the metropolis" for the distinguished scholars and city planners who participated in the
seminar. After rejecting a series of possible definitions he said, in
effect:

> The best definition I can give of a metropolis is that it is a large city
> most of whose residents would accept substantially lower incomes in

8

order to stay there rather than move to a higher income somewhere else. In this country there are only three — or possibly four, depending on how you feel about New Orleans.[4]

The three, of course, were New York, Boston, and San Francisco. Today some people might argue for adding Los Angeles or Houston to the list. There is even a song from a hit musical, "My kind of town — Chicago is." But few would deny that if we were speaking of North America, and not just of the United States, Montreal must be included among the cities conforming to Dean Burchard's definition. There could be arguments about Toronto or Vancouver, but not about Montreal. Indeed, few cities anywhere in the world engender fiercer loyalty among residents who were not born and bred there than does Montreal. Not only members of long established Québécoise families, but "wasps" from Ontario or Nova Scotia, Italians, Greeks, Germans, Poles, Haitians, Arabs and Jews shudder at the thought of leaving Montreal — especially for some other city in Canada. Many residents of other Canadian cities make a point of "getting to Montreal" from time to time, to share in the city's special fascination and charm.

Montreal's peculiar appeal springs in large measure from the fact that *all* of Canada's major ethnic, linguistic, religious and cultural groups are substantially represented there. More than any other Canadian city Montreal represents Canada's ideal of "the mosaic," a country where all people can retain their culture, their language, and their religion, while remaining loyal and enthusiastic Canadians. Toronto and Vancouver do not compare well in this respect because, despite their cultural and ethnic diversity, these cities do not adequately reflect "le fait français." While the present Quebec government wishes to extend the use of French in business and education, no one expects Montreal's half million anglophones to speak French to each other in their homes, their churches, and their clubs. Moreover, Montreal was once predominantly English-speaking, while no large city outside of Quebec was ever predominantly French. Historically, Montreal has been the gateway to Canada — from Jacques Cartier's arrival until the recent opening of Toronto's international airport to transatlantic flights — but it is more than that. It is the synapse of Canadian society and the Canadian economy, a nerve centre which both responds to economic and social change and which transmits change to the rest of the country. In these respects, it is the most "Canadian" of Canadian cities.

9

The story of Montreal is more thoroughly meshed with the history of Canada than that of any other city since Jacques Cartier found the Indian settlement of Hochelaga on the site of the present city of Montreal in 1535. Sixty-six years later Champlain established a post there. This post became the centre of the fur trade, which gave the Canadian economy its first wave of growth. It was the jumping-off place for the exploration of the west, and even, via the Great Lakes and the Mississippi, for the south as well. It was transformed from an Indian village into a French city, then into a predominantly British city. It later reverted to being a predominantly French-speaking city, with an economy dominated by anglophones. From trading post it grew into a major port, and later to a general transport centre. It also became Canada's leading commercial, financial, industrial, and cultural centre. At the time of Expo '67 Montreal was still, in the eyes of most Canadians, Canada's leading metropolitan centre.

Montreal and "the Spirit of Expo '67"

It was therefore obvious that when Canada sought the 1967 World Fair to help Canadians celebrate their one hundredth anniversary of confederation it was Montreal that was proposed — and accepted — as the site. Many Canadians recall with nostalgia that glamorous year when Canada seemed for a while to be grown up, confident, and united, when all things seemed possible for our adolescent nation. Montreal especially, as the setting for that splendid family party, seemed ebullient, effervescent, dynamic, sophisticated, cultivated and creative, Mecca for the moment, not only for the distinguished and the curious of North America, but for those the world over.

The wiser visitors to Expo '67 did not spend all of their time on the exhibition grounds, but instead sampled the charms of the city itself. Montreal was a city with first class symphony concerts, opera, and ballet. Those who were fortunate enough to be bilingual could enjoy both English and French theatre, the latter presenting plays written and directed, as well as acted, by French Canadians. There were dozens of excellent restaurants, hundreds of good ones. Intellectuals among the visitors may have included the three major universities in their itinerary. The religious seldom had to walk far to find a church of their faith. There was a large art gallery and innumerable small commercial galleries. There were vast department stores, and a host of elegant small boutiques. One of the characteristics of a city that makes it a metropolis in Burchard's sense is the existence of areas where one can see interesting people on the streets and walk from café to night club to discotheque to bar to boutique and back again, preferably at all hours of day and night. Montreal had two such areas: the old town to the East, and the area from Peel Street to Côte de Neiges and from Sherbrooke to Dorchester. The "boîtes de chanson" provided the flavour of Paris but with Quebec nationalist overtones.

The diversity and high quality of cultural and entertainment activities reflected the fact that Montreal was still Canada's largest city, although its margin over Toronto was diminishing: 16 percent in 1961, 12 percent in 1966, 4 percent in 1971. This narrowing of the gap occurred, not because Montreal was growing slowly, but because Toronto was growing very fast. Of all the metropolitan centres on the North American continent, only the "sunbelt" cities of Atlanta, Dallas and Houston, together with Washington D.C. and Toronto, were growing faster than Montreal.

Seeds of decay

Despite the glitter, signs of the weakness of the Montreal economy — and society — were already appearing in the late 1960s. To begin with, Montreal's superiority in terms of population was already something of a statistical accident, depending on where the boundaries of the "metropolitan region" are drawn. The Higgins-Martin-Raynauld Report of 1970 (henceforth HMR Report)[5] showed that if the administrative region of Montreal were taken as the standard of comparison, and enough counties grouped around Toronto to arrive at the same area, the "Toronto region" would have 50 percent *more* people than the Montreal region.

Hamilton alone, which by then was contiguous with Toronto and clearly part of its metropolitan region, added some 450,000 people to its population. To get a city of that size in Quebec one would have had to go the whole way to Quebec City, which was quite clearly well outside the Montreal region. Neither Trois Rivières nor Sherbrooke were, strictly speaking, in the adminis-trative region of Montreal; but even if they were included as part of Montreal's "zone of influence," they added, in 1971, only 97,930 and 84,570 people, respectively. Montreal's "Hamilton," the steel town Sorel, had only 34,479 people in 1971.

The Economic Council of Canada, carrying further the analysis of the HMR Report on the basis of the 1971 census, measured population for "urban systems" and metropolitan regions.[6] An urban system was defined as a "group of cities close to each other with a more or less intensive and frequent exchange of goods, people, or ideas." A regional metropolis must have a population of at least 100,000; the distance between two regional metropolises must be at least 200 miles except when a city that is not one of the largest centres attracts at least 10 percent of the automobile traffic within a radius of 500 miles (a criterion permitting the isolation of the Quebec City and Ottawa urban systems, but compelling the linking of Hamilton, St. Catharines, Oshawa and London to Toronto and Victoria to Vancouver); and only urban agglomerations located less than 250 miles from a regional metropolis are considered part of its urban system. The Council also constructed a "spatial interaction index," derived from a "gravity model" based on the total population of the urban system, the population of the city at each rank in the hierarchy of the system, the number of cities at each rank in the hierarchy, and road distances between cities.

The results of this analysis are shown in Table 1. We see that Montreal in 1971 had 3.5 million people in its urban system and 4.1 million in its region, while Toronto had 4.8 million in its system and 5.7 million in its region. Vancouver, the third large metropolitan area, was still very much smaller, although growing much faster than Montreal or Toronto. Toronto's urban system was also growing more slowly between 1961 and 1971 than the average for all urban systems in Canada. The population of the region and of the urban system was much more concentrated in the metropolitan centre of Montreal than in either Toronto or Vancouver, both in 1961 and in 1971. It was also, not unexpectedly, higher than for the total of urban systems in Canada. Finally, the index of interaction, while significantly higher than for Vancouver, was far below that of Toronto.

Why does all this matter? The answer is simple: a city lives and grows primarily through interactions with other cities. If a metropolitan centre can serve as a "central place" for its own urban structure and region, providing sophisticated services and hi-tech industrial products to other nearby cities, which are themselves technologically advanced and dynamic, it becomes less dependent on national and international markets for the sale of such goods and services. In these markets, where the centre does

12

TABLE 1

Demographic characteristics and spatial interaction index of Urban Systems in Canada, 1961-1971

	Population				Population in the regional metropolis as a proportion of:		Spatial interaction index[2]	
	Urban system		Surrounding region[1]		(Percent)			
	1971	Variation 1961-71 (Percent)	1971	Variation 1961-71 (Percent)	Surrounding region 1971	Urban system 1971	1961	1971
St. John's (Nfld.)	159,304	18.0	347,750	10.5	37.9	82.7	8,22	4,84
Halifax	451,432	8.1	900,601	7.0	24.7	49.3	10,24	10,16
Saint John (N.B.)	287,193	12.2	634,557	6.1	16.8	37.2	6,15	5,42
Chicoutimi	231,599	27.9	398,222	12.0	33.6	57.7	7,89	7,65
Quebec City	649,058	22.2	1,127,060	9.4	42.6	74.0	11,51	16,60
Montreal	3,459,615	20.8	4,105,125	18.2	66.8	79.3	77,46	90,72
Ottawa	692,294	27.5	930,256	20.4	64.8	87.0	9,25	10,01
Toronto	4,839,856	30.4	5,721,741	27.5	45.9	54.3	113,10	152,23
Sudbury	356,079	17.6	582,379	8.8	26.7	43.6	6,10	6,82
Winnipeg	635,619	12.7	906,125	6.9	59.6	85.0	7,99	8,63
Regina-Saskatoon	401,075	21.4	904,421	0.0	29.5	66.6	5,41	5,76
Edmonton-Calgary	1,042,036	36.7	1,627,874	22.2	55.2	86.3	5,61	4,73
Vancouver	1,494,207	35.3	1,721,612	32.8	62.9	72.4	48,75	61,46
Total	14,699,307	25.6	19,907,723	18.6	50.2	68.0	—	—

1. The continuous region, whose boundaries include only those agglomerations making up the urban system, as estimated from census divisions, the population corresponds to the provincial total in Nova Scotia (including Prince Edward Island), in New Brunswick, in Saskatchewan, and in Alberta.

2. Computed from the gravity potential of each urban agglomeration, as determined by population masses and distances between the agglomerations in each urban system. This index increases with the number and the size of urban agglomerations but diminishes with the distance between them.

SOURCE: Estimates by the Economic Council of Canada, based on 1961 and 1971 Census data.

TABLE 2

Manufacturing industries, 1961 and 1971
Metropolitan Regions of Montreal and Toronto

	Montreal		Toronto		Montreal in percentage of Toronto	
	1961	1971	1961	1971	1961	1971
Number of establishments	5,088	5,448	5,011	6,019	101.5	90.5
Value added (millions of dollars)	1,880	3,656	2,076	4,770	90.6	76.7
Number of employees	245,245	267,935	235,387	309,107	104.2	86.7
Salaries and wages (millions of dollars)	978	1,829	1,028	2,350	95.1	77.8
Value added per employee ($)	7,664	13,645	8,819	15,430	86.9	88.4
Wages per employee ($)	3,989	6,828	4,366	7,601	91.4	89.8

SOURCE: Statistics Canada, Manufacturing industries of Canada.

TABLE 3

Investment in the manufacturing sector
1951-1974

Metropolitan Regions of the Census

Year	Montreal in percentage of Toronto	Year	Montreal in percentage of Toronto
1951	125	1964	92
1952	121	1965	76
1953	98	1966	73
1954	112	1967	90
1955	138	1968	97
1956	141	1969	86
1957	123	1970	75
1958	140	1971	87
1959	170	1972	83
1960	146	1973	84
1961	114	1974*	82
1962	85	1975**	87
1963	80		

* Temporary data.

** Planned estimation by Statistics Canada.

SOURCE: Statistics Canada, Private and Public Investments.

TABLE 4

Relative Importance of the Port of Montreal amongst Canadian Ports
(in percentage)

	Total traffic	International traffic	Bulk Merchandise	General Merchandise
1961	38.2	37.5	38.7	36.2
1962	36.8	36.2	36.9	35.3
1963	34.9	33.2	35.1	33.0
1964	32.8	31.1	32.3	34.5
1965	32.5	31.4	32.3	33.5
1966	33.1	30.5	33.8	30.4
1967	29.4	28.0	28.8	31.7
1968	28.5	25.9	28.0	30.0
1969	28.5	24.5	27.6	32.2
1970	29.6	23.0	28.9	32.7
1971	24.9	20.3	24.0	29.0
1972	21.6	17.1	21.5	21.8
1973	16.2	12.1	15.4	22.0

SOURCES: Government of Canada. Annual Report. Council of National Harbours-Cargo Tonnage Handled at Selected National Harbours, 1961–1970. Council of National Harbours, 1971.

not have the advantage of proximity, the centre may find it more difficult to compete against other large metropolitan centres throughout the world. Moreover, if the metropolitan centre is surrounded by sizeable and thriving cities, performing the less technologically demanding operations, the centre can specialize more narrowly in the most advanced services and manufactures. In that way, to the degree that it must compete in world markets, it will be in a stronger position to do so.[7]

A closer look at the Montreal of the late 1960s shows that there was indeed a relationship between the relative size, growth, and interaction of the urban system of Montreal in comparison to that of Toronto and the volume and quantity of economic activity in each of the two regions. As an industrial centre Montreal was already in second place. Even in 1961, while Montreal still had slightly more manufacturing establishments than Toronto, and a few more wage earners, it was already lagging in terms of value added, salaries paid, value added per employee, and salary per employee. (See Table 2) From 1951 to 1961 investment in manufacturing was higher in Montreal than in Toronto in every year except 1953, when it was about the same. From 1962 on it was lower than in Toronto (Table 3). Some indication of what was happening in the commercial sector is provided by figures of traffic through the Port of Montreal (Table 4). From 1961 on there was a sharp decline in Montreal's share of traffic through all Canadian ports, and the decline in share of international traffic was particularly sharp.

The relative decline of industry and commerce inevitably affected the financial sector as well, and vice versa, in a negative feedback mechanism. In 1952 Montreal had 20 percent more head offices of financial institutions than Toronto; in 1972 it had 36 percent less. As pointed out in a recent study, head offices like to be close to their principal market. The Toronto region is in the centre of the Canadian market and at the gates of the American market. Already in 1961 the value of industrial shares transacted in Toronto was a bit more than double that in Montreal. By 1971 the ratio had risen to 2.7.

The picture is even more disturbing if one looks at the structure of economic activity, as the HMR Report did. The study asked two questions: what would have been the growth of employment in manufacturing in Montreal if all of its industries had grown at the same rate as the national average for all industries, and how does that hypothetical rate compare with the average rate? What would have been the growth of each industry in Montreal if it had grown at the same rate as the national average for that industry? The difference between the first rate and the actual rate reflects the impact on Montreal's growth of its structure of manufacturing activity. The difference between the second hypothetical rate and the actual rate is a measure of the impact of regional factors.

Montreal turned out to be at a disadvantage on both counts. Between 1961 and 1965 Montreal gained 27,600 fewer jobs in manufacturing than it would have done if it had had an industrial structure as dynamic as the Canadian average, and if the industries it did have had grown as fast as their counterparts in Canada as a whole. Most of the relative loss was due to the inferior structure of Quebec industry, but losses due to regional factors were also substantial. Since the bulk of manufacturing in Quebec was concentrated in the Montreal region, it is obvious that similar conclusions can be drawn for Montreal manufacturing. Meanwhile, in the same period, Ontario gained 34,183 workers more than if its industrial structure and performance in each sector had conformed to the national average. Most of Ontario's relative gains were due to the superiority of her industrial structure. It is interesting to note that no other province but Ontario made relative gains during the period, but that Quebec's relative losses were far greater than those of any other province.

The study made similar comparisons for the administrative regions of Montreal, Trois Rivières, and Quebec. These show that the relative losses, due both to industrial composition and to regional factors, were far greater in Montreal than in the other two cities.

TABLE 5

Relative Losses of Employment
in Manufacturing by Administrative Region

Region	Loss due to Industrial Composition	Loss due to Regional Factors
Montreal	– 10,160	– 8,209
Trois Rivières	– 1,151	– 680
Quebec	– 2,196	– 2,453

SOURCE: *HMR Report*, pp. 61, 63.

A detailed examination in terms of individual industries yielded more bad news. Industries in which Quebec predominated tended to be those with both low productivity per manyear and low rates of growth. For example, Quebec in 1965 accounted for 72 percent of total Canadian employment in cotton thread and cloth production, a low-productivity industry which grew by only 4 percent between 1961 and 1965. On the other hand, in the manufacture of aircraft and parts, a high productivity and high growth industry, with 41 percent of its total employment in Quebec in 1965, the province lost 3 percent of its employment between 1961 and 1965. In this case the loss was entirely Montreal's, since the whole industry was located there. Moreover, even in relatively traditional industries with comparatively low output per manyear in Canada as a whole, such as textiles, leather, clothing, wood, paper and paper products, Quebec (and thus Montreal) had lower than average productivity.

Again, if one looks at industries where Montreal made relative gains because of regional factors, they turn out to be traditional, low-productivity industries: bakeries, stockings and socks, other knitwear; and the industries where losses were suffered due to relatively low growth were those where productivity is comparatively high: metal framework, aircraft and parts, electronic components for radio and television. There was during this period, to be sure, one tendency which might be regarded as healthy, which will be discussed in more detail below: a tendency for the city of Montreal to deconcentrate its industrial activity in favour of satellite towns within its region. But in the case of the more sophisticated industries like aircraft and parts, it is clear that Montreal's losses were the Toronto region's gain. Indeed York county's gains in this field (4,021) were almost precisely equal to Montreal's losses (4,840). In general, one could say that the more sophisticated the industry, the more likely it is that Montreal will register losses.

For those able to look beneath Montreal's glittering surface, then, the symptoms of threatened decay were already apparent on the occasion of the 100th birthday of the Confederation. The port, while active, no longer played a major role in the city's economic life. The financial centre of the country was no longer Montreal's St. James Street but Toronto's Bay Street. Montreal was also losing out in terms of technologically advanced, high-productivity, rapid-growth manufacturing and sophisticated high-productivity services. These trends may have been somewhat

19

accelerated later on by the election of a Parti Québécois government in Quebec in November 1976, but they certainly were not started by those elections.

The signs of trouble were not only economic. They were social and political as well. Even during 1967 there were jarring notes within the harmony: President Charles de Gaulle's "vive le Québec libre" speech from the balcony of Montreal's Hotel de Ville and Mayor Drapeau's emotional reply, in which he pointed out that Quebec is not tantamount to French Canada and that even the Québécois — most of them, at any rate — love "their vast country," meaning all of Canada, not Quebec. If it was no accident that Montreal was chosen as the site of Expo '67, it was also no accident that three years later Montreal was the site of "les événements," the kidnapping of United Kingdom Trade Commissioner, James Cross, and the kidnapping and subsequent murder of Quebec Cabinet Minister Pierre Laporte, by the Front de Libération du Québec: events which plunged the whole of Canada into an abyss of gloom, fear and anger. The very crosscurrents which make Montreal so exciting a city make it at the same time a city of tensions, confrontations, frictions, even of neuroses. (In the 'forties and 'fifties, in the polite English society of Montreal, when someone said "I met John coming down the hill today as I went up the hill," everyone understood that "John" was coming down from a session with his psychoanalyst at the Allan Memorial Institute while the speaker was on the way to his). But the conflicts in Montreal are symptoms of unresolved *Canadian* problems; they are not intrinsically *Montreal* problems. They appear more strikingly in Montreal because in that city, as Canada's metropolis, all aspects of Canadian life are concentrated and magnified, as if Montreal were a biological slide bearing a cross-section of Canadian life, viewed under a powerful microscope. No Canadian city offers such diverse and cosmopolitan living as Montreal; and if the country's problems cannot be solved in Montreal, there is little hope of their being solved in Canada at all.

Conclusion

Thus we see that on the occasion of Canada's 100th birthday as a Confederation, Montreal resembled a young man on his twenty-first birthday, grown up at last, replete with vigour and charm, cultivated and amusing, reasonably prosperous. Meeting him casually, almost anyone would be entranced, and predict for him a brilliant future. But the doctors in the clinic knew something that did not show on the surface. The youth had a malady, a disease had set in, an infliction which to be sure had not stunted his growth and did not threaten his early demise, but one which nonetheless raised questions about his future. Some of the doctors who analyzed his case doubted that the youth's early promise would ever be fulfilled.

Let us now introduce our "flashback" and look more closely at the youth's childhood and adolescence, to see if we can trace the origins of his malady. By analyzing Montreal's case history, we may better understand its present condition. Improved understanding of the present should assist in arriving at a prognosis and prescribing a cure. What happened? Why has Montreal fallen from its top position as Canada's leading industrial, commercial and financial centre? What does the decline of Montreal mean for Quebec, and for Canada? Could Montreal survive Quebec independence? Could an independent Quebec survive without a vigorous, dynamic Montreal? Can Montreal be reinvigorated with or without independence of Quebec? If so, how? To understand the reasons for Montreal's "fall," we must first analyse the reasons for its rise.

CHAPTER 2

THE RISE OF MONTREAL

> L'île de Montréal se trouve donc située à
> l'un des carrefours les plus importants
> du continent nord-américain.
>
> Relations des Jésuites
> 2e année 1642, p. 36.

Metropolitan centres the world over are born of geography and shaped by history. Montreal is no exception. Human habitation at the site of the present city of Montreal was assured by the confluence of three rivers, and a barrier to continuous transport to the west in the form of the Lachine rapids. Once there, the settlement became the gateway to Canada and the west and the main point of confluence of all crosscurrents of Canadian history. Sometimes events occurred which retarded the growth of Montreal; but for the most part, the stream of events up to the 1960's generated growth of the city.

The rivers: transportation crossroads

Where major transport arteries cross, a city is likely to grow up. For more than two centuries after Jacques Cartier landed at

MAP 1

Situation of Montreal

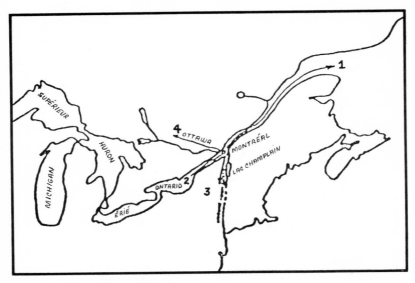

Montreal is situated at natural crossroads.
1. The route to the Atlantic by the lower St. Lawrence.
2. The route to the Great Lakes by the upper St. Lawrence.
3. The south route by the Richelieu-Hudson.
4. The northwest route by the Ottawa river.

Hochelaga the main transport arteries in Canada were the rivers
and lakes. Montreal stands at the crossroads of the main arteries
of water transport in North America. The city is often depicted as
the queen city of "The Empire of the St. Lawrence." Certainly the
St. Lawrence played a major role in the founding and subsequent
growth of Montreal: but it was not the St. Lawrence alone, nor
even the St. Lawrence plus the Lachine rapids to the west, making
Montreal a trans-shipment point, which explains the early growth
of Montreal. A glance at Map 1 will show that Montreal had more
going for it than the St. Lawrence. There was also the Ottawa, a
mighty river in its own right, and for generations a more important
"highway" to the west than the St. Lawrence itself. There was also
the Richelieu, leading to Lake Champlain and Lake George, and
finally to the Hudson and New York City. From the southern tip of

24

MAP 2

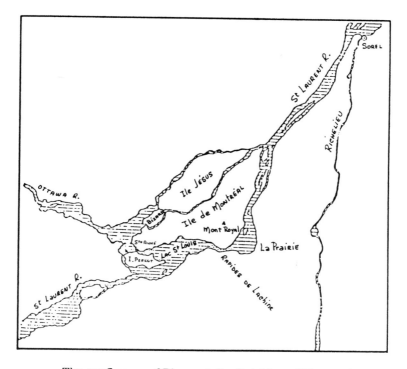

The confluence of Rivers at the Outskirts of Montreal

Lake Michigan it was not too far to the entire Mississippi system. Given such a situation at a time when only water transport counted, Montreal could not fail to become an important city. (See Maps 1 and 2)

We should not, however, exaggerate the advantage to Montreal of standing at these particular crossroads. The truth is that in their natural state, compared to the Rhine or the Thames, Montreal's rivers were rather inferior highways. To begin with, they were frozen for many months in each year. Below Montreal in the St. Lawrence, Lac St. Pierre was shallow and difficult to navigate, so much so that many ocean-going vessels preferred to unload at Quebec City rather than risk the trip to Montreal. The Lachine rapids to the west may have been an advantage in the sense that they made trans-shipment necessary (by portage when the canoe was the normal vessel and later by transfer of cargoes from ocean-going freighter to lakeboats or railroad) and thus made Montreal a natural stopping point. But an obstacle to continuous journeys is a strange kind of "advantage" and the rapids had to be bypassed somehow or other. Further along the Great Lakes route to the west was a still more formidable obstacle: Niagara Falls. In the Ottawa River the rapids were less fearsome than those at Lachine and were further upstream, but they were there; there were thirty-six of them between Lachine and the Lakehead. Indeed, the rapids at Bytown (Ottawa) helped to create a potential rival city there. And the "highway" to the south provided by the Richelieu could accommodate only small craft and did not join the Hudson directly.

It is obvious that an urban economy based on a site convenient for water transportation is in a precarious situation if for some reason water transport becomes less important. A good deep water port is still an advantage, of course; many of the world's major metropolitan centres are ports. Others are military bastions or capital cities, and some of the biggest are or have been all three (London, Tokyo, Athens, Rio de Janeiro, Buenos Aires, Montreal). But port cities that do not develop other functions do not continue to grow and thrive, and if their importance as ports wanes as well, they may very well "decline and fall."

But there is more to the story than that. For geography can be changed by mankind, notably by building canals, roads, and railways. For two centuries men in North America tried to improve upon the natural waterways by building canals. Later came railways, the roads, and finally airlines and airports. Some of these gave Montreal's economy a boost, but others dealt it a severe blow.

Montreal as a Fur Trade Capital

A situation at a waterway crossroads — even if "improved" by a barrier to the west making transhipment necessary — cannot generate growth of a city unless people have reason to use the waterways. For a century and a half after Champlain set up his trading post, the main reasons for using the waterways which came together at Ville Marie were to engage in the fur trade and to save souls. A third reason was to explore the west; but the numbers involved in this activity were few indeed. Champlain himself appreciated the fact that Hochelaga, as a rendez-vous for large numbers of Indians, provided an excellent site for trade in furs (especially beaver) and for converting the natives. As Raoul Blanchard puts it:

> Il prévoit donc la réalisation d'un poste de trafic où se négocieront les peaux de castors apportées par les indigènes. L'objectif est double : gagner l'argent par un honnête commerce, mais profiter du contact avec les Sauvages pour contribuer à la gloire de Dieu, en les convertissant à la vraie foi. ... Assurément la naissance de Montréal n'est pas, comme celles de Québec et de Trois-Rivières, la prosaique mise en place d'un poste de traite ; elle baigne dans le divin.[1]

Religious zeal, lust for gain, and the fascination of the unknown were forces not powerful enough, however, even in combination, to transform Montreal from a trading post to a truly urban centre by the time of the conquest in 1760. Population estimates vary, as is to be expected. The most authoritative, perhaps, are those of the 1871 census:

Year	Population
1665	625
1685	724
1698	1,468
1706	2,025
1739	4,210
1760	5,700

In percentage terms, then, the rate of growth was rapid enough, 1000 percent in a century. But the character of the settlement had not fundamentally changed. In retrospect, fur-trading and soul-saving seem to have been "leading sectors" with somewhat limited capacity to generate "spread effects," at least so far as Montreal was concerned.

In any case, during the eighteenth century Montreal became the North American centre of the fur trade. But in this period, for the most part, the Indians brought their furs to the French, rather than Frenchmen chasing Indians to find furs. To be sure, the French *coureurs des bois* were already demonstrating their prodigious strength, courage, and skill. As Hugh MacLennan points out, the Paul Bunyan stories were based largely on their exploits.[2] But the bulk of the trade took place at Montreal itself, at fairs lasting several months, to which thousands of Indians brought furs. The Indians did not stay, and not many Frenchmen were needed to handle the trade.

Nor would anyone wish to deny the importance of the Church in the growth of Montreal. Moreover, the Church in its wisdom took heed of man's physical as well as spiritual needs. Maisonneuve and his fellow Messieurs de Saint Sulpice took care to establish, in addition to their seminary and their hospital, a flour mill and a brewery. (It was Protestant Toronto, not Catholic Montreal, that was known between the wars as "the city of the good." The residents of Montreal seem from the beginning to have been bent on enjoying life as well as on their particular missions.) Be that as it may, up to the conquest the activities of the Church brought only limited "development" in the sense of "growth and change."

No doubt the constant terror of the Iroquois inhibited growth in the early years. As late as 1689 an Iroquois raid claimed 200 victims at Lachine. But the failure of Montreal to develop during the eighteenth century to the same extent as Boston, New York, or New Orleans, had something to do with the nature of the main stimuli to growth and change. Even as late as 1825, when a census of sorts was taken, there was little in the way of industry. There were carpenters and masons, kept busy rebuilding after fires and Iroquois raids; there were tanners, bakers, tailors, artisans serving a local need, not industrialists serving a larger region.

To some degree, of course, Montreal grew as a "central place," serving its agricultural hinterland. The rich plain surrounding Montreal, especially to the south and southeast, attracted farmers well before the conquest. The population on the land in Montreal's peripheral region exceeded that of the city itself. But the agriculture was self-sufficient in large measure, and the market provided by the population of Montreal for such agricultural surpluses as there were may have been more significant than the market for services and manufactures provided to Montreal by the residents of its hinterland.

The truth is that from the beginning, Montreal was much more an international than a regional centre. The market for furs was in Europe. The exploration of the west was aimed at expansion of international trade. In this respect, the limited development of Montreal up to the conquest laid the foundations for the city's future.

Conquest and Revolution

Two traumatic events of the late eighteenth century triggered the transformation of Montreal into a metropolitan centre, and at the same time released forces that were to bring the city to its current phase of relative decline. These were, of course, the conquest of Quebec by the British, and the American War of Independence. The first opened Quebec, and above all the city of Montreal, to British enterprise. The second sent loyalists to Montreal, accelerating its transformation into a British city. Even more important in the long run, it sent migrants into Ontario, started the settlement of what is now called "western Ontario" or "the Golden Triangle," and launched the long process leading to the economic dominance of Toronto.

Montreal Becomes British

On 8 September, 1760 the British grenadiers captured Montreal's only battery and took the city without firing a single shot. The rest of Quebec followed quickly enough. The British victory meant, among other things, that Montreal, and Quebec, were under the same colonial rule as the "thirteen colonies" to the south. General Amherst, once in control of the city, was quick to invite the merchants of New England, New York, and Pennsylvania to share in "the new market open to British adventure," as one such merchant, Alexander Henry, put it. They came, not only from the thirteen colonies of America, but directly from England, Scotland, and Ireland as well. Within one generation these British immigrants had taken over the economy of Montreal, and within three generations they had become the majority population of the city. And this despite the *revanche de berceau*. Raymond Tanghe states that the people of Quebec established a record for birth rates for the whole white race — sixty-five per thousand — but that achievement did not prevent Montreal from becoming a British city.[3]

Not that the conquest of Montreal was followed immediately by a flood of British immigration. Raoul Blanchard reports that in 1765 there were only 136 protestants in Montreal, 37 Irish, 30 English, 26 Scotch, the others German and Swiss. There were already a few Jews as well. (In 1777 Montreal had its first synagogue). Nor does he have a very high regard for those early

British settlers: "Les vivandiers qui suivaient les armées semblent avoir été fort médiocres sujets."[4] It was otherwise with the loyalists who came after 1775, as the American Revolution unfolded. These were often men of some education and some capital — or at least, as Tanghe suggests, with knowledge of how to get capital — the McGills, the Mackenzies, the Frobishers, the Molsons, the McTavishes. Among the loyalists were army officers, government officials, lawyers, doctors, merchants of some stature. Such men would stand out in their new city. James McGill wrote to the governor of Lower Canada in 1800 that not one boy in five in the Montreal area could sign his own name; the canoemen engaged in the fur trade signed with an "x."[5] In any case, Mr. I Weld reported after his visit to Montreal in 1795 that, while the great majority of the population was French, the eminent merchants and other distinguished citizens were all British.[6] Moreover, Weld noted, the French did not care to learn the language of their conquerors; they did not speak English. On the contrary, the majority of the British spoke French. They also intermarried with the French. McGill, MacTavish, Frobisher, lords of the fur trade, all had French wives. Of 553 British marriages between 1760 and 1787, Blanchard notes, 150 were mixed. Nor had the city divided itself into distinct French and English neighbourhoods as it did later. The two groups lived peaceably side by side. Blanchard adds, "Bref, c'est l'époque de la bonne entente, et il faut reconnaître que de cette entente, les Anglais sont entièrement responsables."[7]

In 1820 Montreal was 37 percent British, in 1825, 43 percent. For 1831 the figures are a bit hazy, but almost certainly the majority was British in that year. There are good figures for 1844: 19,041 French, 25,232 British, 212 "others," which included some of the great Jewish commercial and financial families. For the next three census years the figures are as follows:

	Numbers		Percent	
	French	British	French	British
1851	26,153	31,157	45	54
1861	43,679	45,941	48.4	51
1871	56,856	48,221	53	45

Thus in the half century between 1820 and 1871 the curves of total population crossed twice. By the time confederation came along, Toronto and the smaller cities of western Ontario were booming, and the prairies were opened up. Most British immigrants chose to go west of Montreal. But the British (and Jewish) stranglehold on the Montreal economy was not released; indeed it became tighter than ever. In some ways worse, perhaps, it became not only British but anglophone. Somewhere along the line the situation had become reversed; it was the French Canadians who learned English, not the other way around. As Montreal moved towards becoming the commercial, financial, and industrial metropolis of Canada, just as surely the language of commerce, finance and industry in the city became English.

The Retreat from Competition

How did the British manage to take over the Montreal economy so quickly and so thoroughly, particularly big industry, large-scale commerce, and finance? The British had the military power after the conquest, to be sure. But how was that power exercised? French and British were equal before the law, and in the beginning the French were in the majority. It is easy to speak of exploitation and discrimination, but to exploit and discriminate, there must be some power base from which to exploit and discriminate. We have seen that in the first decades after the conquest the British lived side by side with the French, intermarried with them, and spoke French because the French would not speak English. It also seems that there was a good deal of good will on the part of the conquerors to get along with the vanquished; and those French Canadians with some wealth and education who chose to go into finance, commerce and industry — or into politics — were not debarred from doing so.

The loyalists were better educated and better financed than the average French citizen of Montreal; but as Blanchard points out, tough, well-informed, competent and prosperous entrepreneurs were not lacking among the French Canadians. Where did they go? They cannot all have returned to France, although certainly some of the better educated and wealthier Frenchmen did so. It seems that those who stayed withdrew more or less voluntarily from the world of affairs, cloaking themselves in their religion, their culture, their language, all of which they regarded as superior to those of the crass, materialistic British. Some may have returned to the land.

One cannot escape the analogy with the "Old South" of the United States after its defeat by the north, a century after the conquest of Quebec by the British. There the Yankee "carpet-baggers" came down from New England and the mid-Atlantic states and took over the industry, commerce and finance, just as the British "carpetbaggers" took over Quebec. The defeated "southern gentlemen" retreated into their "superior culture," regarding the Yankee invaders as crass, materialistic, uncultured, and ill-mannered creatures, whom no gentleman would want in his house. They struggled along on the land, kept to themselves, intermarried amongst themselves, and argued that Man is closest to God on the land. They supported their churches and did little to support their schools, except for some elitist military academies for the sons of gentlemen, and a few very bad universities.

Professor William H. Nicholls of Vanderbilt University, himself an ardent southerner, describes the situation in the old south after the war between the states:

> In the South as in most underdeveloped countries, the dominant agrarian values long supported a scale of social prestige which placed the land owner, the religious leader, the military leader and the political leader on the top and the man of business down the line. As a result, much of the South's business leadership has been furnished, if at all, from such minorities as the migratory Yankees, and the South Highlanders who have been reared in other traditions.[8]

Nicholls goes on to describe the reaction of the southerners to their defeat by the Yankees, and particularly the agrarian movement:

> The Agrarian's indictment of Industrialism charges that through it science was applied to make labour intense, mercenary, servile, and insecure, instead of something to be performed with leisure and enjoyment; to create overproduction, unemployment, and greater inequality in the distribution of wealth which could lead only to the superstate; to destroy that relation of man to nature which is conducive to a flourishing religion and vital creative arts and to developing such amenities of life as good manners, hospitality, family life, and romantic loves; and to accelerate the tempo and threaten the stability of life by a never-ending race between material goods, human wants, and human efforts.[9]

He quotes "twelve southerners" in a volume entitled *I'll Take My Stand* as declaring "the culture of the soil is the best and most sensitive of vocations and... therefore... should have the economic preference and enlist the maximum number of workers.[10] Southern leaders complained of "the regional imperialism of the Northeast" and ascribed "all the ills to the outcome at Gettysburgh and Appomattox."[11] Nicholls also quotes the southern leader Cash with respect to the tendency for the south to "wrap itself in contemptuous superiority, to snear down the Yankee as low-bred, crass, money grubbing, and even to beget in his bourgeois soul the kind of secret and envy of all."[12]

In the American south the invasion by Yankee entrepreneurship turned the southeast region, which had been rather stagnant before the war, into the fastest growing region in the United States, a position it has held ever since, only recently to be rivalled by the southwest. As a consequence, both the economy and the society have been transformed, and most social groups have benefited in the process.

In Quebec a similar retreat seems to have taken place after the conquest, but with less favourable results. No doubt some of the richer and better educated French retreated the whole way back to France, depriving French Canada of much of its economic and political élite. France itself showed little concern for the fate of her former colonists once the colony itself was lost. Far from helping them to rebuild their economy after a damaging war, France even renounced its debts to the colony. But the impact of defeat seems to have been more profound. No longer in control of their own land, and finding themselves for one reason or another at a disadvantage in competition with the British conquerors, the French seem to have withdrawn from competition as the American southerners were to do a century later. Like them, they withdrew into their traditions and cultivated a local nationalism, consoling themselves for their failure to participate fully in the economic life of the province by assuring themselves that they did not wish to do so anyway. They preferred the gentility and humanity of their own life, their own faith, values, and culture to the vulgar materialism of the victors. As time went by these attitudes became formalized and ritualized. Ideologically, if not in fact, there was a "return to the land," as there was in the American south. Thus in 1895 a major bishop wrote that agriculture is the normal state of man on earth ; only when man is on the farm can he hope to attain a direct relationship with God, and only thus could the Québécois achieve "the great destiny which has undoubtedly been reserved for them by Providence." Monsignor Paquet reiterated this idea in 1902, maintaining that "notre mission est moins à allumer les feux de nos usines que de maintenir et déléguer les feux lumineux de la religion et de la pensée."[13]

So persuasive was this ideal of a serene, agrarian society led by the Church and a cultivated élite indifferent to wealth that many French Canadians began to think that Quebec really was like that. Thus in 1898 Sir John Bourinet, Clerk of the House of Commons in Ottawa, Honourable Secretary of the Royal Society of Canada, Doctor of Letters of Laval University, wrote:

> "In commercial and financial enterprise the French Canadians cannot compete with their fellow-citizens of British origin, who practically control the great commercial undertakings and bank institutions of Lower Canada, especially in Montreal. Generally speaking, the French Canadians cannot compare with the English population as agriculturalists. Their province is less favoured than Ontario with respect to climate and soil. The French system of sub dividing farms among the members of a family has tended to cut up the land unprofitably, and it is a curious sight to see the number of extremely narrow lots throughout the French settlements. It must be admitted, too, that the French population has less enterprise and less disposition to adopt new machines and improved agricultural implements, than the people of the other provinces.
>
> As a rule, the *habitant* lives contentedly on very little. Give him a pipe of native tobacco, a chance for discussing politics, a gossip with his fellows at the church door after service, a visit now and then to the county town, and he will be happy. It does not take much to amuse him, while he is quite satisfied that his spiritual safety is secured as long as he is within the sound of the church bells, goes regularly to confession, and observes all the fêtes d'obligation. If he or one of his family can only get a little office in the municipality, or in the 'government,' then his happiness is nearly perfect." [14]

J.P. Beaulieu of the Quebec Department of Industry wrote in a similar vein in 1952, although showing more appreciation of the industrialization which was then taking place:

> "Quebec, barely half a century ago, a picturesque region in a vast country, over most of its extent farm lands alternated with forest, rivers, villages and freshly cleared colonization centres. This was Quebec little changed from pioneer days with the old ways kept alive from one generation to the other by the rural population. Quebec today is a dominant factor in the Canadian nation. On its skyline the tall chimneys have increased in number and intense activity overflows from plants, factories and workshops." [15]

A year later Senator Maurice Lamontagne, with Albert Faucher, described the "neo-colonial" pattern of Quebec develop-ment as dualistic in structure, with a modern sector controlled by "foreigners," although indigenous peasants were being increasingly drawn into it as the pressure of population on the land became excessive:

> "These conditions are apt to breed such grievances as were expressed by the voice heard by Maria Chapdelaine forty years ago; 'Strangers have surrounded us whom it is our pleasure to call foreigners: they have taken into their hands most of the rule, they have gathered to themselves much of the wealth, but, in this land of Quebec, nothing has changed...' The message gathered by Maria Chapdelaine further reads: 'In this land of Quebec naught shall die and naught shall suffer change. ... The voice of Peribonka echoes now as a challenge to the spirit of scientific investigation and it suggests that perhaps, in the last forty years, more change has been wrought over this land of Quebec than many local philosophies may dream of; and in vivid contrast to it'." [16]

And here, finally is Prime Minister Pierre Trudeau, writing at the time of the asbestos strike in 1956, in which he was deeply involved:

> "C'est pourquoi, contre une ambiance anglaise, protestante, démocratique, matérialiste, commerciale et plus tard, industrielle, notre nationalisme, élabora un système de défense ou primaient toutes les forces contraires: la langue française, le catholicisme, l'autoritarisme, l'idéalisme, la vie rurale et plus tard le retour à la terre." [17]

This French-Canadian philosophy, complete with its "back to the land" component, did not prevent Montreal from becoming Canada's major industrial centre, nor did it prevent Quebec from industrializing just as fast as Ontario. But it may well have had something to do with the underrepresentation of French Canadians in Montreal's industrial, commercial, and financial activities. It has something to do too with the fact that until after World War II Quebec had no real trade unions but had instead *syndicats catholiques*; and why instead of a Chamber of Commerce devoted to expansion of business enterprise, francophone Montreal had an Association des Patrons devoted to the philosophical principles of *Rerum Novaraum* and *Quadragesimo Anno*.

The Ascendency of Montreal

We are interested in Montreal's past, we have said, in order to gain a better understanding of its present and thus improve our capacity to predict, and perhaps even to guide, its future. What we have seen thus far, and what we shall continue to see as we move towards the present, is a vast feedback system in which the development of Montreal reacts to changes in Quebec, in Ontario, in the Atlantic provinces, in the United States, in Europe, ultimately in the whole world. Our interest is centred on those basic forces and events which have had a major impact on growth and change in the city. We shall not, therefore, report in any detail the more or less continuous process of expansion of Montreal's industry, commerce, and finance. Rather we shall analyze those happenings and trends which have altered the basic structure and character of the city, and which have thus influenced its position in the North American urban hierarchy.

The War of the Ports

Furs were a product with relatively high value in relatively low bulk. The physical deficiencies of the St. Lawrence route, centred on Montreal, were a handicap, but a handicap worth surmounting, and surmountable, by portages. But by the early nineteenth century, developments in North America and in Europe were such that if Montreal were to survive as a port, in competition with Boston, New York, Portland, Halifax, and Quebec City, something would have to be done to improve the St. Lawrence system and overcome the major obstacles to navigation. Of these, in Blanchard's words, "Le premier, et le plus cruellement ressenti de tous, est celui de Montreal même. La ville lui doit la vie, c'est entendu ; mais maintenant qu'elle existe, elle trouve pesante cette obligation d'effectuer pour chaque transit deux déchargements, deux rechargements, en transport sur route." [18]

The growth of the North American population and the advance of the industrial revolution in Europe made North America an increasingly interesting market for European manufactured goods. These were items with relatively low value and high bulk, such as textiles and iron and steel products. Transport by canoe with multiple portages became almost prohibitively inconvenient and expensive. Second, the fur trade was declining and was being replaced by trade in other North American products which were low in value and high in bulk; lumber (processed or not), potassium, grain, flour. Once again, a less cumbersome waterway was required. Third, the age of steam had begun. Molson launched a regular service between Montreal and Quebec, with a small

36

steamship called *l'Accommodation* in 1809. Ten years later there were seven Montreal steamships on the river. Delays were even more expansive with steam than with sail.

The idea of constructing a canal from Lachine to the port of Montreal, using the bed of the Saint Pierre River, was at least as old as 1689, when the Sulpiciens first proposed it. They proposed it again in 1700 and in 1814. But it was not until 1821 that the work actually began, and it was 1825 before it was finished. Even then, it had a depth of only five feet, and required six locks to cope with the 42 feet difference in level between Lake St. Louis and the port. It was widened and deepened between 1843 and 1849, and the number of locks was reduced. Unfortunately for Montreal, the Erie Canal was also finished in 1825, linking Lake Erie to New York via the Hudson River. This canal gave New York the advantage over Montreal for virtually all traffic originating from the west and especially for trade between Europe and North America.

The Rideau Canal, completed in 1832 and linking Ottawa with the St. Lawrence had somewhat ambiguous effects on Montreal. The canal was started with the memory of the War of 1812-14 still fresh, and with military objectives in mind. By the time it was finished the military purpose had faded. Its main effect was to strengthen for a while the industrial towns of eastern Ontario, making that region the industrial centre of Ontario, and helping to make Kingston the biggest city of the province. The canal also offered an alternative route from the Ottawa to the west. On the other hand, eastern Ontario might well be regarded as within the zone of influence of Montreal. Had eastern Ontario remained the industrial heartland of Ontario, Montreal might well have benefited, and Toronto may never have asserted its superiority. As we shall see, however, eastern Ontario's supremacy was short lived, and today the Rideau system is used almost entirely by pleasure craft.

The Lachine rapids were far from being the only handicap faced by Montreal in the Battle of the Ports. To begin with, the port itself left much to be desired. For 200 years the port was nothing but the riverbed just above the city, between the bank and a small island called Normandin. Stephen Leacock, writing in 1942, posed the question, "What natural advantages has the port of Montreal?" — and answered his own question — "none, except to be less bad than the others." [19] However, it was reasonably deep; vessels drawing fifteen feet could come very close to the bank. The installations were simple. Apart from a muddy beach there was in

1920 only a narrow wooden quay 1100 feet long. Upstream, in addition to the Lachine rapids, there were more rapids above Lake St. Louis at Cascades, at Cedres, at Coteau. Governor Haldimand constructed four small canals, with a draft of two feet, between 1779 and 1783. They were deepened to three feet in 1917. Barges were hauled through these canals by horses or oxen. The regions of Cornwall and the Thousand Islands also offered difficulties for vessels of any size, not to speak of the Niagara Falls.

Upstream too there were problems. These began with the rocks around l'isle Sainte Hélène. The currents above that island were so strong that without a truly strong wind sailing vessels could not reach the port; they could be stalled for weeks within sight of the wharf. Thirty miles further downstream ships had to contend with the shallow waters and narrow channels of Lac St. Pierre. It was for reasons such as these that so many seagoing vessels chose to unload at Quebec rather than risking the upper St. Lawrence. In 1825, of 613 ships entering the Gulf, only 55 went on to Montreal.

One by one these obstacles were overcome. By 1849 the Lachine Canal was a sophisticated affair whose locks were used to provide water power for industry, and it was along this canal that modern industrial enterprises were first established. Growing traffic led to further improvements in 1875. The Beauharnois Canal, finished in 1854, took care of the rapids at Coteau, Cedres, and Cascades. The Welland Canal was started in 1847. In 1861 a fresh attack was made on Lac Saint-Pierre, to provide for ocean-going vessels a through channel of twenty feet, then of thirty feet. Towards the end of the century, an extraordinarily dynamic minister of public works, Israel Tarte of the Laurier cabinet, finally tackled the Port of Montreal itself in a grand-scale and systematic fashion. The final move in this gigantic chess game in space was, of course, the St. Lawrence Seaway itself, permitting ocean ships to bypass Montreal altogether if they so chose.

Thus we see that events occurring far from Montreal — including the Chicago Drainage Canal, linking Lake Michigan to the Mississippi and offering to the cities of the midwest an alternative route to the sea — have influenced Montreal's development. By the time the St. Lawrence Seaway and the Port of Montreal were perfected, it scarcely mattered any more. The roads and railroads and later, air traffic, were replacing shipping anyway, and Montreal's prosperity no longer depended on the relative advantages or disadvantages of her port.

Manufacturing Industry

During the nineteenth century, and indeed up to World War II, industrial location in the western world was determined mainly by half a dozen considerations: (1) proximity to markets; (2) access to transport and communications; (3) availability of skilled or cheap labour; (4) availability of raw materials; (5) cost of land and buildings; (6) cost of energy. Sometimes other factors entered into the decisions; branch plants, for example, were located partly in terms of proximity to the parent company. Access to complementary industries was sometimes important. No doubt elements relating to the quality of life for managers and workers, such as physical attractiveness of the city, appeal of residential districts, availability of schools, hospitals, and recreation facilities, cultural activities, played some role even then. But the six factors listed were paramount.[20]

It is important also, in analyzing industrial location, to remember what kind of industries served as "industries motrices" (propulsive industries) or leading sectors during this period. Most of them were heavy industries, producing output with relatively low value in relatively high bulk: iron and steel, metal products, transport equipment, textiles, pulp and paper, other wood products, cement, agricultural implements, fertiliser, flour, sugar, heavy chemicals. Proximity to markets, cost of raw materials, even cost of energy at a time when coal was its major source, all of these boiled down to transportation costs. It is for this reason that the neo-classical "theory of location" consisted so much of analysis of costs of transport. Being close to sources of raw materials and markets for products was very largely a matter of cost of transportation.

When all this is understood, it is clear why Montreal was destined to become Canada's leading industrial city, and why Montrealers and economic historians attached so much importance to the Port. For with all the disadvantages of the St. Lawrence system, it nonetheless made Montreal "close" in terms of cheap water transportation, to all of North America, to Europe, and ultimately to the whole world. And as the railways were built, and later the highways, with a consequent relative decline in importance of water transport, Montreal became a major railway centre and a crossroads of major highways.

But Montreal in the latter half of the nineteenth century was close to markets, raw materials, and energy in a sense beyond that

TABLE 6

Movement of the Centre of Population of Canada, Quebec and Ontario, expressed
in Miles North of Latitude 42° and West of Longitude 60°, 1851–1931

Years	Canada		Quebec		Ontario	
	N. of 42°	W. of 60°	N. of 42°	W. of 60°	N. of 42°	W. of 60°
1851	231	692	290	593	139	941
1861	224	700	292	591	138	952
1871	223	710	295	589	137	960
1881	226	730	297	588	139	965
1891	238	784	295	586	142	964
1901	258	845	296	593	148	964
1911	315	1,042	295	594	158	969
1921	334	1,113	297	597	157	973
1931	342	1,143	298	605	158	978

SOURCE: Vol V of the 1931 Census, pp. 105-106. The centre of gravity of Canada's population was carefully established at each census from 1851 to 1931 and shows a very definite shift towards the northwest up to 1911, then towards the west during the following decade and finally towards the north in 1931. At the 1851 and 1881 census, the centre was located near Valleyfield, Quebec; in 1891, 25 miles west of Ottawa; in 1901, near Pembroke; in 1911, 45 miles west of Sudbury; in 1921, 50 miles northeast of Sault Sainte-Marie, and in 1931, 35 miles north of Sault Sainte-Marie (Canada Yearbook, 1939, p. 87). Moreover, this table shows that the province of Quebec is in no way responsible for the translation of the population centre and that Ontario is responsible in only a small measure.

TABLE 7

Evolution of the Manufacturing Centers of Montreal and Toronto from 1922 to 1938, according to the number of establishments, invested capital and raw value of production

Years	Number of establishments		Invested capital		Raw value of production	
	Montreal	Toronto	Montreal	Toronto	Montreal	Toronto
				(thousands of dollars)		
1922	1,500	1,829	467,097	408,717	413,396	406,443
1923	1,492	1,959	484,330	414,724	467,788	427,439
1924	1,599	1,952	488,366	430,498	457,602	417,171
1925	1,717	1,988	542,955	463,458	480,264	478,982
1926	1,781	2,043	564,764	486,077	572,889	535,226
1927	1,880	2,127	602,646	513,502	579,241	565,991
1928	1,901	2,261	543,721	550,440	601,146	616,841
1929	1,917	2,279	653,583	593,011	731,360	650,773
1930	1,938	2,359	599,676	566,531	608,500	560,037
1931	2,095	2,485	574,531	561,649	498,399	542,030
1932	2,194	2,410	465,978	454,541	359,196	341,339
1933	2,328	2,651	468,333	427,829	366,728	327,200
1934	2,459	2,687	459,658	428,533	423,218	382,074
1935	2,444	2,747	466,035	421,332	454,996	413,432
1936	2,457	2,820	466,124	434,388	506,908	451,408
1937	2,571	2,857	497,090	464,231	614,964	519,363
1938	2,604	2,929	505,422	464,445	578,846	492,863

SOURCE: *Statistics Canada, Manufacturing Statistics.*

of being a transport centre. Between 1851 and 1901, as may be seen from Table 6, Montreal was close to the market for final products in the sense of being near the centre of population. In 1851, and indeed up to 1881, the "centre of gravity" of the Canadian population was still a few miles to the east of Montreal. In 1881, it was at Valleyfield, barely to the west of Montreal. As for raw materials, no one could deny the richness of Quebec's forests, and the mining sector expanded throughout this period more rapidly in Quebec than in Ontario. When it comes to energy, the rapids which were such a nuisance for water transport were a source first of simple water power, and then, as electricity became the major form of energy for industrial purposes, of hydro-electric capacity.

And so we find Montreal, between the two world wars, the industrial capital of Canada. As may be seen from Table 7, Toronto had more industrial establishments throughout this period, but Montreal had more capital invested and a higher value added, suggesting, at least, that Montreal's industries were not only more capital-intensive but more technologically advanced than Toronto's.

But it is apparent that Montreal's advantages as an industrial centre could be undermined by decisions and actions taken by people who not only did not live in Montreal, but who did not have Montreal in mind when the decisions and actions were taken. The tens of thousands of people who decided to establish themselves in Ontario, or in the prairies, and later in British Columbia, were not thinking of the impact of their decisions, in the aggregate, on Montreal's position as an industrial city. But the certain impact of these decisions taken together was that the centre of population continued to move west, and by the beginning of World War II was much closer to Toronto than to Montreal. Montreal's advantage in terms of "proximity to the market" — if "the market" is the Canadian one — was gone. Moreover, the same sort of movement was taking place, somewhat in advance, in the United States. As we shall see in more detail below, one of the elements in growth of a city is its interactions with other cities. So long as the United States centre of population remained east of the Alleghanies, and so long as the major industrial centres of the United States were on the Atlantic coast, Montreal had some advantage over Canadian cities further west in terms of proximity to the American cities on the Atlantic seaboard. But once the centre of population moved west of the Appalachian range and the industrial heartland moved to the Great Lakes, all the advantages of "proximity" lay with Toronto, Hamilton, and other cities of "the Golden Triangle." With the construction of the St. Lawrence Seaway, Montreal also lost much of its advantage in terms of "closeness" to Europe by ocean shipping.

Table 8 tells the story from 1870 to 1940. In 1870 the value of Montreal's manufacturing production was more than double that of Toronto, although Ontario as a whole was already well ahead of Quebec as a whole. By 1890, Montreal's output was only 50 percent above that of Toronto. By the end of World War I (1920), Montreal's lead was no longer significant, although it was still there; and by the eve of World War II, the gap was narrower still.

Table 2 above continues the story up to 1971. In 1961 Montreal still had more manufacturing establishments than Toronto, and these enterprises still employed more people than those of Toronto. Already, however, Toronto had a clear advantage in terms of value of output, and a more clearcut advantage in terms of value added per employee. By 1971 Montreal was lagging all across the board, particularly in value added and salaries paid.

Commerce

Montreal was a commercial centre before it was an industrial city, and its commercial activities continued to grow with the growth of the population of the city, the province, and the country. Its wholesale and retail activities were related mainly to the growth of population of the metropolitan area itself, although for specialized goods and services the city served a wider zone of influence. Providing groceries to residents of Montreal is not something that retail grocers situated in Toronto can easily take over. More interesting as an index of Montreal's position as a commercial centre, therefore, is the volume of exports from and imports into the city.

Retailing is not confined to big cities. By 1930 Montreal had 13,000 retailers, but these were only 37.3 percent of the total number in Quebec. However, Montreal's retailers were relatively large and their employees were relatively well paid. Montreal accounted for 60.3 percent of total retail sales in the province, 66.88 percent of the personnel, 71.1 percent of the salaries. Wholesaling is more clearly a metropolitan activity. By 1930 Montreal had nearly 2,000 wholesalers; 63.4 percent of the Quebec total, with 83.1 percent of the total personnel, 86.4 percent

TABLE 8

Chronological statistics of the number of employees and of the raw value of products from manufacturing industries for the cities of Montreal and Toronto, and for the provinces of Quebec and Ontario, 1870–1940

Years	Montreal		Quebec		Toronto		Ontario	
	Number of employees	Raw value of products (thousands of dollars)	Number of employees	Raw value of products (thousands of dollars)	Number of employees	Raw value of products (thousands of dollars)	Number of employees	Raw value of products (thousands of dollars)
1870	22,955[4]	35,935	66,714	77,205	9,400[7]	13,686	87,281	114,707
1880[1]	33,355[5]	52,510	85,673	104,662	13,245[8]	19,563	118,277	158,045
1890[2]	38,135[6]	67,654	116,753	147,460	26,242	44,964	166,322	239,241
1900[3]	44,633	71,100	110,329	158,288	42,515	58,415	166,619	241,533
1910	67,811	166,297	158,207	350,902	65,274	154,307	238,817	579,810
1915	85,226	237,162	148,329	381,204	72,798	219,144	243,905	715,532
1920	113,078	593,882	205,431	1,121,228	106,630	588,970	333,992	2,013,186
1925	91,624	467,055	168,245	820,564	82,728	447,099	262,483	1,527,155
1930	98,905	532,405	204,802	1,022,281	94,745	521,540	307,477	1,713,025
1935	94,612	383,548	189,671	821,021	86,226	385,883	281,438	1,423,562
1940	118,774	604,806	252,492	1,357,376	112,136	595,913	372,643	2,302,015

TABLE 8 (con't.)

1. SOURCE: from 1870 to 1920 inclusively, the decennial census of industry in Canada; from 1920 to 1940: manufacturing statistics of the manufactures' service of the Federal Statistics Office for the provinces of Quebec and Ontario. These statistics do not compare very well from year to year for the same territory, since they reflect the influence of prices on value of products or the rationalization of the fabrication process on the number of employees, because from one census to the next the definition of what is known as "manufacturing industry" changed, and because, finally, the territory of towns was frequently modified during this long period. Therefore, they should only be interpreted in a very broad sense. However, these statistics having been taken everywhere in the same manner, by the same central organization, and, the prices having changed basically in the same fashion in both provinces, their interpretation takes on a much more precise meaning if, analysing relations of town to town, towns to provinces or province to province, we compare changes that have occurred on a year to year basis.

2. "La colonne des employés contient toutes personnes appartenant aux forces administratives et industrielles," vol. III of the 1901 census, page 319.

3. Data for the years 1880, 1890 and 1900 were corrected according to the revised data published in vol. III of the 1901 census.

4. Montreal, centre, west and east.

5. With Hochelaga and Jacques Cartier.

6. The town itself, according to statistics of that period, excluding Hochelaga, whose production is calculated at four million dollars.

7. Toronto, west and east.

8. Production of the suburbs (York and Simcoe) reaches approximately 4 million dollars.

of the salaries, and 85.5 percent of the net sales. There were also 4,102 service establishments, representing only 37.6 percent of the number in Quebec, but 76.5 percent of the personnel, 82.4 percent of salaries, and 75.4 percent of value added.

However, as pointed out above, what has distinguished Montreal from the beginning is the city's role on the international scene. Up to World War II, Montreal's role in international trade is reflected in figures of port activity. Indeed, up to World War I, at least, the activity of the Port of Montreal was almost an index of the level of economic activity of Canada as a whole. As early as 1832, 117 ocean vessels reached Montreal, loading 300,000 bushels of wheat and 91,000 barrels of flour. Fifteen years later, the traffic had swelled to 628,000 bushels of wheat and 651,000 barrels of flour. But then came one of those faraway events of the sort that have so often determined the fate of Montreal: Great Britain repealed the Corn Laws, and Canada's favoured position in the British market was lost. In 1848, the exports of flour were little more than half of what they had been in the previous year, and the exports of wheat considerably less than half. The result was a flurry of business failures.

Charts of tonnage passing through the Port of Montreal between 1840 and 1940 show sharp fluctuations for both ocean-going and lake vessels, but they also show trends along a growth curve with an inflection point around 1900 (that is, the rate of growth in traffic tapered off after that date). Inland traffic reached a peak in 1914 which had not been regained on the eve of World War II. Ocean traffic did not reach its peak until 1937. The total value of trade passing through the Port of Montreal also follows a growth curve, with an inflection point around 1910, and a sharp peak for exports in 1917 and for imports in 1920.

It was the opening up of the west and the expansion of the "wheat economy" that brought the highest figures of tonnage handled by Montreal. In 1929 Montreal was the most important port for export of grains in the whole of North America. One reason was that Montreal served at the time for the export of even more American-grown grain than Canadian (Table 9). But then two things happened at once. Shipment of American cereals through Montreal fell off drastically, and Vancouver became for a time a more important port for export of Canadian grains than Montreal. The combined effect of these two new trends was to cut total exports of grains from Montreal nearly in half. Since these events coincided with the onslaught of the Great Depression, the

TABLE 9

Volume of exportation of cereals by the ports of Montreal and Toronto
(millions of bushels)

Year	Montreal			Vancouver
	Canadian cereals	American cereals	Total	Canadian cereals
1920	41.6	12.3	53.9	
1921	52.0	38.2	90.2	
1922	46.8	81.5	128.3	8.0
1923	71.7	52.4	124.1	18.2
1924	78.2	27.5	105.7	55.8
1925	82.6	82.1	164.7	31.7
1926	75.2	44.2	119.4	44.3
1927	63.8	47.7	111.5	40.8
1928	95.3	76.3	171.6	96.4
1929	41.5	65.1	106.6	77.1
1930	37.3	19.1	56.4	64.2
1931	64.7	9.8	74.5	66.4
1932	84.2	5.8	90.0	105.7
1933	50.8	4.2	55.0	70.9
1934	37.7	0.4	38.1	52.5
1935	31.5	—	31.5	51.6
1936	55.9	2.9	58.8	56.7
1937	52.0	0.5	52.5	33.6
1938	48.9	32.7	81.6	12.9
1939	55.5	8.9	64.4	41.0
1940	42.3	9.9	52.2	10.0

SOURCE: Statistics Canada.

impact on the Montreal economy was little short of disastrous. Vancouver shipments of grains subsequently fell off again, but on the eve of World War II shipments from Montreal were still less than half their 1928 peak.

Montreal also suffered from competition with American ports on the Atlantic seaboard. Even during the best years of traffic at Montreal, nearly half the Canadian grain shipped overseas went through New York, Albany, Philadelphia, Boston, and Portland.

Montreal became a railway centre by mid-nineteenth century. By 1851 there was a direct service to Boston and a year later there was direct service to New York. In 1899 the Grand Trunk had lines to Boston, New York, and Washington. The northern settlements of Quebec were opened to railway traffic towards the turn of the century.

Communications

Montreal was from the beginning a centre of communications in Canada. It was inevitable that it should be so, since before the telegraph and the telephone, "good communications" was the same thing as "good transport facilities." Up to 1850, in Canada, transport meant water transport, and as we have seen, Montreal owes its very existence to its position with regard to water transport. Even in the early nineteenth century Montreal was linked by courier, providing incredibly fast service between the city and Quebec, Kingston, the more remote settlements of the west, Albany, and New York. Hugh Maclennan reports that a letter survives which was sent by *express canoe* from Montreal on 6 May 1817 and received at Rainy Lake, west of Fort William, on 3 June. How much better might one hope to do today? Certainly one might be envious of merchants in Montreal who, once steam vessels started service between the city and Quebec, could obtain replies to letters addressed to Quebec City within twenty-four hours.

Today, of course, communications as such can be separated from transportation, although the two remain related. The telegraph, the telephone, radio, satellite telex — today it is telecommunications that count.[21] So far, Montreal has managed not to fall too far behind the advance of communications.

48

Finance

In some respects, "finance" is the most "footloose" of all industries. Money, or capital, is easily moved from city to city. Proximity to raw materials or sources of energy is of little importance. To be sure, appropriate premises must be found or built; but if need be banks or insurance companies can adapt existing office space to their needs without too much difficulty. There are, nonetheless, locational factors even for financial institutions. To begin with, the city chosen must be of a sort that top managers and professional staff find attractive. Secondly, good communications with the rest of the country and with the world today (telecommunications and computer networks), are extremely important to such institutions, which must be able to make decisions quickly on the basis of good information about financial development in all their areas of interest. Finally, financiers like to be close to their clients. Great financial institutions are seldom found very far from centres of commerce and industry. At the same time, large-scale industries and commercial enterprises like to be near the major financial institutions — commercial banks, investment banks, stock exchanges, insurance companies. There is a natural symbiosis among commerce, communications, industry, and finance. Small wonder, then, that Montreal, as well as being the commercial, industrial, and communications centre of Canada until recent years, was the financial centre as well.

The Bank of Montreal ("the First Canadian Bank," as we are constantly reminded on television) was founded in 1792, one year after the first bank was established in the United States, although it took two decades after that for it to obtain a charter. The half century that followed brought an explosion of financial institutions, clustered together, as in the City of London itself, along a narrow band running from Place d'Armes to Dominion Square. In 1867, the year of confederation, there were eight banks. Three of these (City Bank, People's Bank, and Mechanics Bank) have since failed. Three others (Molson's, Merchant's, and British North America) have been bought out by other banks. The Bank of Montreal and the Banque Jacques-Cartier, reincorporated in 1900 as the Provincial Bank, survived. Six others were established between confederation and World War II. The Royal Bank appeared on the scene and soon rivalled the Bank of Montreal in importance. The Bank of Hochelaga was founded in 1874 and in 1924 became the Canadian National Bank, after its amalgamation with the Banque Nationale de Québec. Barclays Bank came on the scene in 1929. Three other banks established in this period failed after a short existence.

In the early years of the war the picture appeared like this:

TABLE 10

Banks in Montreal and Toronto
31 December 1942

	No. of Branches
Banks with Head Offices in Montreal	
Canadian National Bank	65
Bank of Montreal	45
Royal Bank	38
Provincial Bank	31
Barclay's Bank	0
	179
Banks with Head Offices in Toronto	
Bank of Toronto	13
Canadian Bank of Commerce	9
Dominion Bank	7
Bank of Nova Scotia	6
Imperial Bank	2
Total	37

SOURCE: Statistics Canada.

Between confederation and the end of 1942 the number of head offices and branches of banks in Montreal had grown from 13 to 179, including the 37 branches of chartered banks with head offices in Toronto. Montreal's share in the total capital of Canada's chartered banks had grown to 60 percent and her share of savings deposits, to 55.3 percent. Montreal's banks had significantly more demand deposits, savings deposits, and federal government deposits than Toronto banks; only for provincial government deposits did the Toronto banks show a slight superiority. Montreal's banks were also making more than half the total volume of loans for the country as a whole. Montreal banks held 60.8 percent of the federal and provincial obligations held by all Canadian banks, 68.8 percent of the municipal bonds, two-thirds of the mortgages. On the eve of World War II, Montreal was clearly Canada's leading banking centre. Reflecting on Montreal's role as Canada's most important *international* city, the supremacy of her banks was even more marked in the international sphere: Montreal banks held 73.5 percent of the foreign assets of all Canadian banks.

Montreal dominance in life assurance was less apparent: on 31 December 1941 Montreal companies accounted for about 40 percent of total premiums, about the same proportion of investments, and a somewhat smaller share of the total value of policies in force. Once again, however, Montreal's pre-eminence in the international sphere was clear: 68.3 percent of the cash held abroad and 66.3 percent of loans to foreign clients. Moreover, of the dozen British life insurance companies operating in Canada, ten had their head offices in Montreal.

Summary and Conclusions

The history of Montreal, like the case history of any biological organism, follows a growth curve. Whether growth is measured by population, income, industrial production, commercial activity, financial operations, cultural and intellectual activity, or a composite index of all of these, the curve does not rise far above the base axis for two centuries after the arrival of Jacques Cartier. The two cataclysmic events of the late eighteenth century — the conquest of Quebec by the British and the American War of Independence — together with the industrial revolution in Europe and the expansion of world trade, provided the injection of hormones that accelerated Montreal's growth. Unfortunately, these hormones had serious side effects. Montreal became a British city, and Ontario was settled by United Empire Loyalists and immigrants from Great Britain who brought with them relatively high levels of education, relatively high levels of "need-achievement" (to use Harvard psychologist David Maclelland's well-known term for high self-imposed standards of performance) and capital, or means of getting capital. Within two generations these settlers in Upper Canada were challenging the supremacy of Lower Canada and of Montreal, despite the fact that the Montreal economy itself was by that time dominated by the same sort of anglophone settlers. A vicious circle had set in, in which the French Canadians withdrew from competition with the British, retreating into their traditions and their culture.

The nineteenth century brought the industrial revolution to Canada, to Quebec, and to Montreal. Most of the people who moved to Montreal to take over the new jobs in industry, and the related jobs in commerce and finance, were francophone, and Montreal became once again a francophone city, but one whose economy was still dominated by anglophones, an inherently unhealthy situation which was to produce unpleasant symptoms. The nineteenth century also brought the shift of the industrial heartland of the United States from the Atlantic coast to the Great Lakes region, and the movement of the Canadian centre of population from just east of Montreal to Toronto. Basic changes were taking place in the Canadian and in the North American economy which were to have serious repercussions on the health of the Montreal economy. The city was finding itself increasingly isolated in the northeast corner of the continent while the centres of economic progress were moving ever farther away.

CHAPTER 3

THE DECLINE OF MONTREAL

We saw in Chapter 1 that even when Montreal reached the height of its splendour during Expo '67, there were already signs of decay beneath the surface. By the time of the 1976 Olympics these signs were all too apparent. The atmosphere was not the same in Montreal during the Olympics as it was during Expo. The city acquitted itself well in the end, but the Olympics were far from being a specifically *Canadian* celebration and did not bring the same sense of national unity that Expo had done. On the contrary, the continuing economic deterioration of Montreal was causing financial difficulties for the city, which led to unpleasant bickering amongst the municipal, provincial, and federal governments as to who should bear the Olympics' staggering deficit. Then in November that year came the provincial elections and the Parti Québécois victory; the independence issue, which had been left quietly in the wings during the election campaign, was suddenly front stage centre, and the unfavourable trends which had been scarcely noticeable to the untrained eye in 1967 were unmasked for all to see. And just to prove that calamities never come singly, the period after 1972 has been one of world recession in which Canada, Quebec, and Montreal have all shared.

Population

Between 1971 and 1976 Montreal was one of the slowest growing metropolitan regions in the country. By the first quarter of 1976 the metropolitan region of Toronto (as defined by the census) was already bigger than that of Montreal, which meant that Toronto's urban system had a population substantially bigger than that of Montreal's. Toronto's metropolitan region alone grew three times as fast as Montreal's during the 1971–76 period. After 1976 the growth of Toronto accelerated while that of Montreal decelerated. From the first quarter of 1976 to the first quarter of 1977 the active population (15 years and over) of Toronto (metropolitan region) grew by 5 percent, while Montreal's was stagnant. From the third quarter of 1976 to the third quarter of 1977 Toronto's active population grew by 3.2 percent, while Montreal's fell slightly. Some of the small cities in Montreal's "couronne" and some of the other satellite cities grew faster than Montreal itself, as the decentralization process proceeded. Others, however, stagnated or even declined. On balance, the economic region of Montreal grew slightly faster than the metropolitan region. Nonetheless, the Montreal region's share of the Quebec total was slightly lower at the end of 1978 than it had been in 1971. Within the Montreal urban system the island of Montreal suffered a sharp decline in its share of total population, the city of Montreal an even sharper decline. The "couronne" cities experienced a substantial increase in share of the total, while the satellite towns and intermediate centres both declined slightly in relative importance within the system. But whether we look at the city proper, the metropolitan region, the economic or administrative region, or the entire urban system, the picture is one of stagnation in Montreal and vigorous growth in Toronto. By 1978, Montreal had clearly become a second-class citizen in Canada's urban structure.

Employment and unemployment

Nothing indicates more strikingly Montreal's increasing weakness than figures of employment and unemployment. For a while the growth of the labour force (active population) tapered off, becoming negative for the metropolitan region in the second half of 1978; but employment grew still more slowly and consequently unemployment increased. In 1977-78 total employment in the metropolitan region actually fell, and unemployment rose above

11 percent at the beginning of 1978. Even in the economic region as a whole, total employment was stagnant between 1975 and 1978. Because population was growing somewhat faster in other urban centres of the region than in Montreal itself, unemployment was even higher for the economic region than for the metropolitan region. Moreover, Montreal had ceased to be an effective escape valve for unemployment in other parts of the province. In the past, unemployment in Montreal had been significantly lower than in other Quebec cities. In 1977 and 1978 Montreal unemployment was close to the provincial average, and higher than in the Quebec economic region or even the Cantons de l'Est. It is no surprise that unemployment in Montreal was significantly higher than in Ottawa-Hull and Toronto, although even in these cities the record was nothing to be proud of.

The Quebec Regional Office of the Department of Manpower and Immigration notes that the performance of the Montreal metropolitan district during 1977-78 was considerably worse (with respect to employment and unemployment) than that of Quebec as a whole. The province registered a modest increase in total employment, while the city suffered a decline. The report adds:

> Il est évident que l'économie de la région métropolitaine n'exerce plus le même rôle moteur qu'on lui reconnaissait, vis-à-vis celle de la province, ce qui peut entraîner des répercussions très sérieuses au cours des prochaines années si des mesures gouvernementales ne sont pas prises pour contrecarrer ce phénomène.[1]

Nearly all industrial sectors shared in the decline of employment in 1977-78 by comparison with the previous year.

When we look at individual industries within the manufacturing sector, we see that virtually all of them registered declines. Hardest hit were the already weakened traditional industries, such as textiles, leather goods, clothing and furniture, all of which suffered losses of more than 10 percent. Printing, metal products, hosiery, paper and paper products, electrical products, and chemicals all declined by between 5 and 10 percent; food and drink, tobacco, rubber, wood products, non-metallic minerals and petroleum products declined somewhat less, but declined nonetheless. Thanks to increased exports to the United States, primary metal products and machinery showed modest gains; and as a consequence of renewed activity by Canadair, manufacture of transport equipment also registered an increase in employment.

The year 1978-79 was somewhat less dismal. The Montreal administrative region managed a small gain in total employment, 1.6 percent, slightly more than the growth of the labour force. All sectors but agriculture made small gains. However, the growth of the public administration sector dropped to 2.2 percent and that of the finance and insurance sector to 3.0 percent. In the various industries in the manufacturing sector there was little change one way or another. The really significant fact is that the only industry with more than 5 percent of total manufacturing employment in 1976-77 which had more employment in 1978-79 than in the previous year was transport equipment, due in large measure to the pickup of activity by Canadair.

Over the whole period from 1976, the picture of Montreal's industrial activity is one of relative decline giving way to absolute stagnation. A major lesson of economic history is that economic stagnation is more often than not a harbinger of absolute decline to come.

Commerce

In commerce, too, Montreal has lost its pre-eminence, slipping further and further behind Toronto. The growing gap is all the more significant because Montreal accounted for so much larger a share of Quebec's total retail trade than Toronto did of Ontario's. In the late 1970s Montreal accounted for nearly half of Quebec's retail trade, while Toronto's trade was just over a third of the Ontario total. Ontario's total retail trade was nearly 50 percent above Quebec's in both years.

If we look at the administrative regions of Quebec, we see a slight decline in the relative importance of the Montreal region with respect to retail sales at the end of the decade. The Trois Rivières and Cantons de l'Est regions also showed relative losses, while Saguenay–Lac St. Jean and the Nord-Ouest remained unchanged and the other regions made slight gains (Table 11).

Ontario had a larger number of commercial failures than Quebec in these years, but the total liabilities involved were larger in Quebec. Because of the Montreal region's predominance in Quebec commercial activity, it seems obvious that a large share of these losses occurred to Montreal firms.

Nowhere does the decline of Montreal as a commercial centre appear more strikingly than in the statistics of activity of the port. In 1977 the port of Montreal loaded and unloaded less than half

TABLE 11

Retail Sales and Per Capita Income, Administrative Regions of the Province of Quebec

| | Retail Sales | | | | Personal Disposable Income Per Capita | | | |
| | 1976 | | 1977 | | 1976 | | 1977 | |
	('000)	Percentage of Quebec	('000)	Percentage of Quebec		Index Quebec		Index Quebec
Gaspésie/Bas St-Laurent	423,600	2.2	496,500	3.2	3,348	69.3	3,647	68.7
Saguenay/Lac St-Jean	566,500	3.9	600,700	3.9	4,430	91.7	4,860	91.6
Quebec (region)	2,277,000	15.6	2,476,800	16.1	4,397	91.0	4,800	90.5
Trois-Rivières	894,800	6.1	912,600	5.9	4,103	84.9	4,419	83.3
Cantons de l'Est	573,400	3.9	577,700	3.7	4,066	84.2	4,443	63.7
Montreal	8,642,900	59.5	9,027,200	58.8	5,242	108.5	5,777	108.9
Outaouais	513,700	3.5	552,000	3.6	4,579	94.8	5,055	95.3
Nord-Ouest	362,500	2.5	382,600	2.5	4,250	88.0	4,660	87.8
Côte-Nord, Nouveau-Québec	274,600	1.9	330,400	2.1	5,390	111.6	5,980	112.7
Quebec (province)	14,529,000	100.0	15,356,800	100.0	4,830	100.0	5,306	100.0

SOURCE: Compiled from *Financial Post, Survey of Markets*, redefined according to administrative regions of M.I.C. (1966).

the tonnage handled at Vancouver. Even Thunder Bay handled more cargo than Montreal (Table 12). Only 18 percent of the total traffic handled by all Canadian ports was loaded or unloaded at Montreal. The port of Montreal was even less important for international arrivals and departures (Table 13) where it accounted for some 10 percent of the total; Montreal's share of domestic arrivals and departures was about 3 percent, although its share of total domestic tonnage was higher. Montreal's importance as a trans-shipment point was gone. Table 14 gives another picture of the decline of the port of Montreal.

TABLE 12

Short Tons of Cargo Loaded and Unloaded in
Selected Ports in International and Domestic Shipping
(000 Tons)

	1977	1975
Montreal	18,044	18,526
Quebec	15,078	11,885
Toronto	5,509	4,757
Thunder Bay	21,935	20,036
Vancouver	39,031	33,630

SOURCE: Statistics Canada, Cat. No. 54-002.

Finance

Figures for the financial sector tell the same tale. In terms of total employment, Montreal held up fairly well until the 1970s. Indeed, during the first half of the 1960s Montreal made slight gains over Toronto in the finance, insurance, and real estate sector as a whole. In 1960 Quebec had 26.4 percent of Canada's total employment in this sector, while Montreal had just under 75 percent of Quebec employment or not quite 20 percent of Canada's total. Toronto had nearly 55 percent of Ontario's employment in the sector and Ontario 45 percent of the Canadian total; Toronto had nearly 25 percent of the Canadian total. By 1970 Montreal's share of financial employment was below the 1960 level while Toronto's

TABLE 13

Number & Tonnage of Vessels Arrived at & Departed from Selected Ports in International & Domestic Shipping

	Arrivals 1977		Departures 1977		Arrivals 1975		Departures 1975	
	No. QV.	Gr. Tonnage (000)	NO. V.	Gr. Tonnage (000)	NO.A.V.	Gr. Tonnage (000)	NO.V.	Gr. Tonnage (000)
International:								
Canada	23,079	197,901	23,173	197,907	20,027	174,855	20,086	175,341
Montreal	2,016	20,505	1,992	20,317	1,785	17,222	1,779	17,379
Toronto	428	4,505	389	3,977	401	3,907	391	3,904
Quebec	4,222	63,174	4,821	71,707	3,978	56,664	4,403	63,018
Ontario	5,261	38,137	4,698	30,286	4,684	35,800	4,272	30,425
Domestic:								
Canada	40,232	125,088	40,068	124,309	46,630	125,539	46,676	125,587
Montreal	1,359	7,441	1,336	7,444	1,570	7,916	1,579	7,808
Toronto	283	1,403	309	1,858	312	1,630	321	1,597
Quebec	6,386	39,462	5,762	30,841	7,285	35,852	6,874	29,512
Ontario	4,181	31,532	4,737	39,406	4,324	30,457	4,662	35,701

SOURCE: *Statistics Canada Catalogue*, Number 54-002.

TABLE 14

Relative Importance of the Port of Montreal
Amongst Canadian Ports
(in percentage)

	Total traffic	International traffic	Bulk Merchandise	General Merchandise
1961	38.2	37.5	38.7	36.2
1962	36.8	36.2	36.9	35.3
1963	34.9	33.2	35.1	33.0
1964	32.8	31.1	32.3	34.5
1965	32.5	31.4	32.3	33.5
1966	33.1	30.5	33.8	30.4
1967	29.4	28.0	28.8	31.7
1968	28.5	25.9	28.0	30.0
1969	28.5	24.5	27.6	32.2
1970	29.6	23.0	28.9	32.7
1971	24.9	20.3	24.0	29.0
1972	21.6	17.1	21.5	21.8
1973	16.2	12.1	15.4	22.0

SOURCES: Government of Canada. Annual Report. Council of National Harbours-Cargo Tonnage. Handled at Selected National Harbours, 1961–1970. Council of National Harbours, 1971.

60

was above it. During the 1970s the gap grew more rapidly. By July 1978 employment in the financial sector in Montreal was less than two-thirds that of Toronto. Average weekly earnings in the sector were also lower in Montreal than in Toronto. Had there been any doubt before that date, it was by then abundantly clear that Canada's financial centre had shifted from Montreal to Toronto.

If one looks at financial activity rather than at employment it is clear that the shift had taken place a good deal earlier. For example, the total value of cheques cleared in Montreal had fallen from 95 percent of the Toronto figure in 1946 to 55 percent in 1971. In that same year, according to estimates made by Professor André Ryba of the University of Montreal, the velocity of circulation of all deposits in Montreal — a good measure of intensity of financial activity — was only 59.5 percent of that in Toronto.[2]

More serious for the Montreal and Quebec economies, however, is the fact that the financial activities where the shift to Toronto is most marked are those which are most closely related to the financing of enterprises, and particularly of new enterprises: the stock exchange, the head offices and trading desks of the banks, the investment dealers, the "money market" and the bond market. Nowhere does Montreal's decline as a financial centre appear more sharply than in the figures of activity of the stock exchanges. Until 1973 there were six stock exchanges in Canada: two at Montreal, the Montreal Stock Exchange and the Canadienne, since merged into one: the Toronto Stock Exchange; and much smaller exchanges at Winnipeg, Calgary, and Vancouver (the Toronto and Montreal exchanges together account for over 90 percent of total transactions in Canada). By 1971 the value of transactions on the Toronto exchange was already 3.0 times that of Montreal. Since the average value of each transaction fell in Montreal and rose in Toronto, the picture in terms of volume of transactions is different for these years. In 1976 the volume of shares traded on the Montreal exchange was not much more than one-fifth of the Toronto volume, the total value just over one-third of the Toronto figure. By 1977 Montreal's volume of trading was less than one-sixth that of Toronto's, its value just over one-fifth. In the following year Montreal had less than one-seventh of the Toronto volume of transactions.

The import of these figures goes far beyond the impact of the stock exchanges on income and employment generated directly as financial institutions. They reflect the scale of activity of the entire economies of the two cities and the two provinces. It is worth noting that by 1976 both the value and volume of trading on the Montreal exchange were not only far below Toronto's, but were well below the 1974 level on the Montreal exchange itself.

Professor Ryba puts particular emphasis on Montreal's loss of head offices and trading desks of financial institutions:

> De plus, le siège social a un rôle vital en soi. (Here Prof. Ryba adds in a footnote: Nous nous référons ici au siège social "véritable" et non à celui dénoué de sa pleine signification économique à la suite d'un déplacement du bureau exécutif, du "trading desk", ou du centre de recherches...) C'est le centre de décision de la compagnie, les prêts d'importance sont entérinés sinon directement autorisés par le bureau-chef et l'on ne saurait assez souligner l'importance des contacts personnels dans le domaine financier; le siège social abrite le "trading desk" et une concentration de "trading desk" dans une ville est un indice de marché financier actif; il véhicule une information sophistiquée par son centre de recherche et les experts qu'il réunit.[3]

He maintains that there is a two-way reaction between financial operation at the highest level and economic activity in general, and that financial institutions play a primary role in regional economic development. He then goes on to point out, what since has become well known, that in effect the Bank of Montreal, the Royal Bank of Canada, and other major Montreal banks have transferred their real headquarters to Toronto, including the Trading Desk, which undertakes all transactions of importance in the money market. In effect, he adds, of all the chartered banks in Montreal, only the two Quebec banks, la Banque Canadien National and la Banque Provinciale have kept (when he was writing in early 1974) their Trading Desk in Montreal. The ratio of the number of head offices of financial institutions in general, for Montreal in comparison with Toronto, dropped from 1.20 to 1.0 in 1952 to 0.64 to 1.0 in 1972. This trend has accelerated since, and especially after the Quebec elections of 1976.

Ryba underlines the point that the transfer of decision-making centres of financial institutions is not something to be undertaken lightly. To move the Trading Desk of a chartered bank or a brokerage office is a large-scale operation which cannot be mounted every few years in response to the business cycle; it is a major undertaking in response to interpretations of long-run trends. Relocating the head office of a financial enterprise encompasses large costs which must be put side by side with the expected benefits of the move before the decision is taken to make it. Since the institutions in question are enterprises whose operations are national in scope with branches in several provinces, it takes more than a simple cyclical downturn to justify the transfer of their main office. In short, once having left Montreal, it will not be easy to lure them back.[4]

The heart of any true financial centre is "the money market," a somewhat loose term used to describe an amalgam of institutions dealing in short to medium term obligations: treasury bills and other federal government obligations with a maturity of less than three years; short term obligations of provincial and municipal governments; similar obligations of Crown Corporations like Hydro-Quebec and Ontario Hydro; commercial paper, bankers acceptances, short term bills of sales, finance companies, and the like. The "money market" serves not only as a source of short term finance for a wide range of governmental bodies and private enterprises but also as an investment outlet for temporary excess funds. It was the money market, centred on Lombard Street, which made London the world's financial centre during the eighteenth and nineteenth centuries and which keeps London a major financial centre even today. In Canada, the money market is almost entirely in Toronto, as is the bond market and especially the market for industrial bonds.

In Canada the money market is largely a postwar affair. In the 1950s Montreal shared in its growth. By the 1970s, the money market was clearly concentrated in Toronto, to such a degree that even Quebec firms were frequently compelled to go to Toronto for financing. Ryba reports that in 1971, of 131 members of the Investment Dealers' Association, 43 had their head offices in Quebec, of which 36 were in Montreal. There were 67 with their head offices in Ontario, of which 64 were in Toronto. There were 68 branch offices in Quebec (31 in Montreal) and 183 in Ontario, 27 in Toronto. Moreover, of the 31 branch offices in Montreal, 25 were branches of Toronto firms; and of the 68 in Quebec, 37 were of Toronto firms and only 25 of Montreal firms. Of the 183 branches in Ontario, 135 represented Toronto head offices and only 25 Montreal head offices. The three brokerage houses in Montreal accredited by the Bank of Canada as agents in the money market do most of their business in Toronto. The brokerage houses divided on linguistic lines; the anglophone firms had 12 branches in Toronto and 24 in Ontario and only five branches in Quebec. The francophone firms had 20 branches in Quebec, 6 in

Ontario and only 3 in Toronto. In addition, the Toronto brokerage houses had 85 branches in the other eight Canadian provinces; the anglophone houses in Montreal had 29 branch offices in these provinces; but the francophone firms of Quebec had only one branch in these provinces, in Moncton, a nearly 50 percent francophone city.

Even these figures do not properly reflect the degree of concentration of the money market in Toronto, since most of the large-scale operators are in Ontario and especially in Toronto. The Bouchard Report pointed out that 14 percent of the brokerage houses control 61 percent of all the places of business in Canada and abroad, and that 76 percent of the most important houses had head offices in Ontario.[5] A study of 90 firms in Ontario and Quebec showed that the Ontario houses had 63 percent of the total capital, earned 93.7 percent of the profits before tax, earned 68.8 percent of total commissions, undertook 66.1 percent of research expenses, had nearly two-thirds of total employees and handled 79.9 percent of new issues of enterprises. Of the sixteen brokers accredited by the Bank of Canada and which can obtain direct loans from the Bank to finance their inventories of short-term obligations, thirteen have their headquarters in Ontario, only three are in Montreal, and these three are anglophone firms doing most of their business in Toronto. Needless to say, the tendency towards concentration of the money market in Toronto has accelerated in recent years.

In 1971 Quebec's Mutual Funds had 62 percent of the assets of Ontario's Mutual Funds, and Quebec's investment houses (providing long term venture capital) had 54 percent of Ontario's assets. Quebec's mortgage companies had assets only 27 percent of the assets of Ontario's mortgage companies. The assets of Quebec's finance companies were a miniscule 1 percent of the assets of Ontario finance companies. Not one of the ten biggest finance companies was in Quebec; eight had their head offices in Ontario (six in Toronto) and the two others were in Vancouver. As for small loan companies, there were simply none in Quebec, and 96 percent of the assets of small loan companies in all of Canada were in Ontario.

As headquarters of the Sun Life Assurance Company, and with 11 other Canadian and 8 foreign companies, Montreal had long been regarded as a major centre for life insurance. Yet already in 1970 Toronto had more than three times as many companies in this field as Montreal, 21 Canadian and 45 foreign.

Moreover, Quebec's life insurance business was much more concentrated in its major city than was Ontario's. Montreal had 92 percent of the life insurance assets of the province (including all of the foreign companies) while Toronto had only 50 percent of the total assets of foreign life insurance companies in Ontario and 64 percent of the total assets of all companies. Thus Quebec companies had total assets only 42.7 percent of the total for all Ontario companies.

With the transfer of the Sun Life Assurance Company head office from Montreal to Toronto, Montreal becomes virtually unimportant as a life insurance centre in comparison with Toronto. The Sun Life was by far the most important life insurance company with headquarters in Montreal, and its move to Toronto tips the scales heavily against Montreal. The Sun Life, of course, is far from being alone in making the decision to move out of Montreal since 1976. The Royal Trust, much the biggest of Montreal's trust companies, has also decided to move, along with a good many other major financial and manufacturing firms.

Heading for Toronto

When the HMR Report was written, the relative decline of Montreal seemed to be more a matter of enterprises deciding to locate or expand in Toronto rather than in Montreal, than of individual enterprises pulling up stakes in Montreal and moving to Toronto. By the end of December 1978 that could no longer be said. It had become all too clear that a major exodus of large, sophisticated, rapid growth and high productivity enterprises was taking place. In its December 1978 issue the London *Economist* published a table, reproduced here as Table 15, listing companies which have moved from Quebec or made a decision to do so since 1976. The table is taken from a report prepared by a Liberal member of the Quebec Parliament, Mr. Reed Scowen, former director of the federal price control program.

Mr. Scowen estimates that these moves will cost Montreal 5,480 jobs. However, a glance at the list will show that the true loss to the Montreal economy cannot be measured in terms of new jobs created directly in other cities; the loss is far greater than that. In the first place, almost all of the companies on the list are engaged either in sophisticated services or in advanced-technology manufacturing. In the second place, where the entire operation is not moved out of Montreal, the divisions that are transferred are

TABLE 15

List of Enterprises which Relocated, or which Decided to Transfer Administrative Activities out of Quebec Since 1976

Company	Department	Moved to	Number of persons relocated	Number of lost jobs
Allis Chalmers Canada	Manufacturing	Guelph	80	80
Aluminium Co. of Canada	Research group	Kingston	85	85
Amalgamated Power Equipment	Registered office	Toronto	22	22
Atco Industries	Manufacturing	Calgary	60	115
**Bank of Montreal*	-S.S. Banking Services group in Canada -S.S. Banking Services group to Enterprises -S.S. Master Charge Group -S.S. Interna. Opera. Banking Group Canada Division -S.S. Funds Administration Group	Toronto	?	*950*
*Bell Canada	Engineering and Technical Division	Ottawa	46	66

Company	Function	Location		
Boeringer Corp.	Registered office	Burlington, Ont.	25	40
Brinco Limited	Registered office	Toronto	40	47
Bristol Myers Canada	Pharmaceutical division	Ottawa	25	55
British Airways	Registered office	Toronto	53	53
Cadbury Schweppes Powell	Manufacturing	Whitby, Ont.	—	200
Canadian Pacific	Treasurer and investments group	Toronto	98	106
*C.A.E. Industries	Registered office	Toronto	7	14
Canadian Industries	Engineers	Toronto	246	246
Combustion Engineering	Registered office	Ottawa	300	323
Commerce Capital Corp.	Registered office	Toronto	8	8
Domglas	Registered office	Toronto	60	60
Dupont of Canada	Plastics Group	Toronto	106	110
Electrolux (Canada)	Registered office	Toronto	85	110
Flakt Canada	Registered office	Ottawa	75	75
*Johnson Wire Indus.	Registered office	Ottawa	40	55
Joy Manufacturing	Engineers, Accounting	Toronto	48	55
MacDonald Tobacco	Registered office, Marketing	Toronto	100	190
Monenco	Registered office	St. Catharines	47	47
*Monsanto	Registered office	Toronto	35	45
Northern Telecom	Miscellaneous	Toronto	200	200
Perkins Paper	Registered office	Toronto	18	18
Price Company	Computer Group	Toronto	40	40
Prudential Assurance	Miscellaneous / Computer Group	Kitchener	25	50
Redpath Industries	Registered office	Toronto	14	21

TABLE 15 (con't.)

List of Enterprises which Relocated, or which Decided to Transfer Administrative Activities out of Quebec Since 1976

Company	Department	Moved to	Number of persons relocated	Number of lost jobs
Robin Hood Multifoods	Marketing	Toronto	40	60
Royal Bank	Miscellaneous	Toronto	113	130
Royal Trust	Registered office,			
	Miscellaneous	Toronto/Ottawa	290	580
*Simmons Mattress	Registered office	Toronto	50	50
Smith, Kline & French	Registered office	Toronto	150	150
Solo Products	Registered office	Toronto	5	105
Standards Brands	Sales, Marketing,			
	Miscellaneous	Toronto	200	200
Sun Life	Registered office	Toronto	?	575
United Corporations	Registered office	Toronto	10	17
Herbert A. Watts	Registered office	Toronto	80	80
Warnock Hersey Int.	Registered office	Ottawa	10	10
Westmount Life Ins.	Registered office	Calgary	37	37

TOTAL: 42 Enterprises   TOTAL: 5,480 jobs

(a) The "number of lost jobs" represents the number of persons who are now working in the new location where the groupings were relocated.

(b) The Bank of Montreal has told us that it was impossible to supply us with the information relative to the movement of its personnel or departments outside of the province of Quebec. The data provided in this list were therefore obtained through independent but trustworthy sources.

(c) Bell Canada has also relocated nearly 250 of its employees from Montreal to Hull since 1977. The number of relocated jobs has now reached 450. We estimate that at least 50% of this group is now residing in Ontario.

(d) The number of persons dismissed in Montreal by Cadbury reaches nearly 500. We estimate that approximately 200 new jobs only will be created in Whitby.

   * These companies have moved at least part of their installations in 1976. We estimate the number of lost jobs at approximately 550 for the year.

SOURCE: Reproduced by R. Scowen, *La réalité du transfert des entreprises en dehors du Québec*, Montréal, November 1978.

those requiring the highest levels of training, skills, technology, and sophistication: head offices, research branch, computer groups, international divisions, engineering and technical divisions. In short the *people* who are being moved out of Montreal are precisely those who are needed in Montreal to make it a centre of innovation and a diffuser of ever more advanced technology to the other cities of Quebec — and of Canada. As we have seen above, it is primarily in this fashion that Montreal has the potential of becoming a "development pole" for the province as a whole. But it cannot hope to play this role if all the propulsive industries move out one by one, taking their ablest and most highly trained personnel along with them.

The migration of the Sun Life Assurance Company to Toronto seems particularly sad. The Sun Life was a particularly "Montreal" institution, its building for many decades a feature of the Montreal skyline, the city's first real skyscraper. A truly distinguished enterprise with a fine world wide reputation, it played a role in the city as a whole, and not just in anglophone Montreal. Because of the global range of acquaintanceship with distinguished people of the Company's senior officers, the Sun Life was frequently the official host of such people during their visits to Montreal. I remember personally how privileged I used to feel when invited to lunch with such people in a private room of the University Club, by the late Raleigh Parkin, then Treasurer of the Sun Life. That sort of company, and that sort of person, are precisely the kind that Montreal cannot afford to lose.

Education

Montreal's need to keep its educated people is borne out by the fact that its educational levels remain low when compared to Toronto. As may be seen from Table 16, in 1976 the labour force (population of fifteen years of age and over) was virtually identical in Montreal and Toronto. But Montreal had more people in its labour force who had left school with less than a Grade 5 education that did Toronto, and also more who left between Grades 5 and 10. At the secondary school level the picture looks a little better: Toronto had substantially more people who had gone to secondary school than did Montreal, but Montreal had some-what more who had finished secondary school and Toronto's advantage was clearcut. Toronto had more people in its labour force who had gone to university, virtually the same number as

TABLE 16

Population 15 years & over not attending school full-time, by age-groups & sex, showing level of schooling for CMA, (1976)

	popula-tion 15 years & over	Education (Number in '000) Elementary and Secondary only		Grades 11-13		Post-Secondary Non-University only		University only			University and Post-Secondary Non-university			
		less than Grade 5	Grade 5 to 10	without sec. sch. certificate	with sec. school certificate	without certificate or diploma	with certificate or diploma	without certificate, diploma or degree	with certificate or diploma	with degree	without Post. Sec. certificate diploma or degree	with Univ. certificate or diploma	with Univ. certificate or diploma	with degree
Canada	15,402.0	856.1	6,456.0	1,910.0	1,696.0	987.0	1,251.2	558.0	124.0	632.0	164.1	326.0	117.4	326.0
Urban Canada	11,752.0	599.5	4,607.0	1,495.0	1,379.4	799.0	991.0	470.4	102.0	560.2	140.0	270.0	97.4	283.0
Quebec	4,191.2	312.8	1,970.4	275.0	507.0	256.0	279.1	153.1	33.0	140.0	51.0	94.4	36.0	85.0
Montreal	1,944.0	127.4	834.0	140.0	251.0	123.0	119.3	94.4	20.1	89.3	30.0	49.0	19.3	49.0
Quebec City	364.3	18.2	153.0	24.0	56.0	23.0	31.2	13.0	4.0	17.0	4.2	10.0	4.0	9.0
Ontario	5,550.3	247.0	2,212.0	789.2	650.0	351.0	458.2	196.0	40.0	247.0	55.0	118.4	42.0	147.0
Toronto	1,921.0	102.0	662.4	280.2	219.4	138.3	156.4	83.0	19.3	116.0	24.0	44.4	18.0	59.0

SOURCE: Statistics Canada, Cat. No. 92-829.

Basic Table 6: Population, Land Area & Population Density for CMA & Census Agglomerations
B. Population. Source: Statistics Canada, Cat. No. 92-806.

	Population 1971	1976	Percentage Change	Land (Sq. km.)	Density, 1976 (pop./sq.km.)
Montreal City	2,729,211	2,802,485	2.6	2,811.1	996.9
Urban Core	2,589,267	2,630,889	1.6	1,097.4	2,397.4
Quebec City	501,365	542,158	8.1	2,817.8	192.4
Urban Core	476,337	507,911	6.6	513.2	989.7
Toronto City	2,602,098	2,803,101	7.7	3,742.8	748.9
Urban Core	2,512,992	2,678,961	6.6	1,151.6	2,326.3

Montreal who left with a certificate or diploma, but substantially more who had obtained degrees and substantially fewer who left university with no piece of paper to show for it.

Income

One consequence of the progressive weakening of the Montreal economy was that in 1976 and 1977 the Montreal administrative region was no longer the most prosperous in Quebec. By 1976 the per capita disposable income of Côte Nord/Nouveau Quebec had risen to 111.6 percent of the Quebec average, while Montreal's had fallen to 108.5 percent of the provincial average. A year later Montreal's per capita income remained virtually unchanged as a percentage of the provincial average, while that of Côte Nord/ Nouveau Quebec had climbed to 112.7 percent of the average. All other regions except Trois Rivières and the Cantons de l'Est had made gains on Montreal since 1970 and 1961. Had this convergence been due entirely to strengthening of the other regional economies it could have been regarded as cause for rejoicing; unfortunately, it reflected as well the relative stagnation of the economy of the Montreal region.

Montreal in the Early 1980s

During the 1980s Montreal was still an expanding city in most respects, but there were no signs of its recapturing its position of primacy with regard to population, industry, commerce and finance. Indeed, in most of these fields the gap was still widening.

Population

The population of the province of Quebec as a whole grew only slowly during the late seventies and early eighties. The 1976 census figure for Quebec population was 6.2 million, the April 1984 estimate was 6.5 million, an increase of less than 5 percent in eight years. In that period Quebec was a region of modest net emigration. Between 1976 and 1981, 102,252 people migrated to Quebec from abroad, but 103,624 emigrated from Quebec to foreign countries, and over 100,000 people to other provinces. Quebec also had the lowest natural rate of population growth of all provinces; "le revanche de berceau" seemed to be over. Net

TABLE 17

Migratory Balance of Canada and Its Provinces, 1976-1984

	Canada	Newf.	P.E.I.	N.S.	N.B.	Que.	Ont.	Man.	Sask.	Alta.	B.C.
Population											
1976	22,992,604	557,725	118,229	828,571	677,250	6,234,445	8,264,465	1,021,506	921,323	1,838,037	2,466,608
1981	24,343,180	567,680	118,230	847,445	696,405	6,438,400	8,625,110	1,026,245	968,310	2,237,725	2,744,470
1984 (April)	25,082,000	578,990	125,000	868,100	712,300	6,540,100	8,916,800	1,054,400	1,003,300	2,349,100	2,863,200
International migration (1976-1981)											
Emigrants	371,655	4,557	970	6,739	5,510	103,624	163,880	8,416	7,604	17,790	51,691
Immigrants	598,389	2,753	1,020	7,397	5,673	102,252	278,806	26,807	12,622	70,447	89,623
Migratory balance	226,734	-1,804	50	658	163	-1,372	114,926	18,391	5,018	52,657	37,932
The provinces' internal migratory balance											
1981	-18,983	-3,552	-1,251	-2,836	-4,989	-22,841	-33,247	-9,403	-3,808	44,250	37,864
1976-1981		-829	-7,140	-10,351	-156,496	-74,846	-42,218	-9,716	186,364	122,625	

SOURCE: Statistics Canada Cat. 91-208, Cat. CS 11-202.

immigration into Ontario also dwindled during this period and population increased only from 8.3 million to 8.9 million between 1976 and April 1984. Meanwhile the Atlantic provinces were virtually stagnant in total population. The western provinces all had substantial net immigration, especially Alberta and British Columbia, and there was a renewed westward shift of the Canadian centre of population (see Table 17).

These demographic trends in the Canadian economy had their impact on Montreal. The population of the metropolitan region grew only from 2.80 million to 2.83 million between 1976 and 1981, a mere 1 percent in five years. Toronto's metropolitan region grew from 2.8 to 3.0 million, and as we have seen the "metropolitan region" as defined is less of a statistical anomaly for Montreal than for Toronto; contiguous Hamilton already had half a million people in 1976 and added another 12,000 in the five years following. The really fast growing cities were those in the west, Calgary, Edmonton, and Vancouver, in that order. Montreal retains its position as Canada's second biggest city, but shows no sign of climbing back to the top of the totem pole.

Manufacturing

During the decade 1971-81 as a whole, Montreal's manufacturing sector continued to grow and to improve in quality. In terms of employment, however, the growth was far from being spectacular: 7.5 percent, or from 284,000 to 305,300, in ten years.[6] The growth rate of manufacturing employment was almost twice as high in both Toronto and Vancouver (see Table 18). However, the growth in Montreal was about as high as in the rest of Quebec, and Montreal held its position as the locale of slightly more than half of total manufacturing employment in the province. Montreal's growth was, moreover, quite impressive in comparison to the 6.6 percent loss of manufacturing employment between 1967 and 1977 in the fifty major metropolitan regions of the United States. If Montreal grew more slowly than the dozen biggest metropolitan centres in the American west, it did better than the southern, north central, and northeast regions. Indeed, there is a world-wide tendency in the industrialized market economies for manufacturing to play a smaller role in the employment of big cities. The more urbanized regions of the European Economic Community lost 6 percent of their manufacturing employment between 1973 and 1979; the larger Japanese cities have also experienced

TABLE 18

Structure of Manufacturing Employment in Metropolitan Regions of Montreal, Toronto and Vancouver, 1971 & 1980

Major groups or reassemblies	Montreal		Toronto		Vancouver	
	1971 %	1980 %	1971 %	1980 %	1971 %	1980 %
Food, drink and tobacco	11.3	11.4	10.0[b]	10.2[b]	16.9	16.6
Leather	3.0	2.6	1.7	1.2	n.d.[c]	n.d.[c]
Textile	5.6	4.2	2.3	2.5	n.d.[c]	1.3
Hosiery	3.9	3.1	n.d.[c]	1.0	n.d.[c]	n.d.[c]
Garment	19.6	16.3	4.9	4.3	n.d.[c]	3.6
Wood	1.7	1.9	1.0	1.1	23.7	19.4
Furniture	3.2	3.4	3.5	4.5	2.6	2.3
Paper	3.2	3.7	5.5	4.8	5.0	4.6
Printing	5.0	6.1	8.9	9.5	6.9	7.6
1. Metal transformation	2.8	3.6	1.8	n.d.[c]	n.d.[c]	n.d.[c]
Metal products	9.2	8.6	11.8	11.2	12.8	12.6
Machinery	3.8	5.9	6.2	5.9	4.3	7.1
Transport equipment	5.1	7.9	9.0	10.2	5.8	6.8
Electrical products	6.4	5.5	10.9	10.1	3.6	3.8
Non-metallic min. products	3.3	3.0	3.1	2.5	2.9	3.0
Chemical, rubber, petroleum coal products	8.5	8.5	9.9[d]	11.2[d]	4.3	5.4
Miscellaneous	4.4	4.3	7.6	7.8	2.6	5.9
Other groups	—	—	1.9	2.0	8.6	
Total, in %	100.0	100.0	100.0	100.0	100.0	100.0
Total, in (000) jobs	(284,0)	(305,3)	(309,1)	(349,5)	(64,9)	(74,6)

Sources: Montreal: Data bank of I.N.R.S.-Urbanisation; Toronto and Vancouver: Statistics Canada, cat. 31-209.
a) See appendix 1, cover of the data bank of the I.N.R.S.-Urbanisation.
b) Excludes tobacco, included in "Other groups."
c) Included in "Other groups," in 1971 and/or 1980.
d) If we exclude petroleum-coal, included in "Other groups" in 1971, the percentage is of 10.8% in 1980.

TABLE 19

Exterior Shipping by Manufacturing Exporters for the Rest of Quebec in % of Their Total Shipping

Destination	Rest of Canada		Outside Canada		Total, Exports	
	1976 %	1980 %	1976 %	1980 %	1976 %	1980 %
Major groups						
Food, drink	25.2	17.7	6.5	14.6	31.7	32.4
Tobacco	n.d.	n.d.	n.d.	n.d.	n.d.	n.d.
Rubber	44.3	36.9	12.2	10.4	56.5	47.3
Leather	53.8	54.1	3.1	2.6	56.9	56.7
Textile	39.3	36.3	6.2	9.0	45.5	45.4
Hosiery	55.8	50.8	n.d.	n.d.	55.7	56.7
Garment	54.8	52.9	0.9	3.7	54.9c	51.9
Wood	25.9	20.1	28.9a	31.9	52.8	57.3
Furniture	50.2	51.3	2.7	6.0	77.2	80.1
Paper	19.6	19.6	58.0	60.5	23.0c	36.5
Printing	21.6	34.6	1.4a	1.9	70.5	72.7
1. Metal transformation	37.1	20.6	33.4	52.1	59.1	n.d.
Metal products	45.4	22.4	13.7	n.d.	59.8	61.0
Machinery	41.4	45.6	18.4	15.5	54.1	37.7c
Transport equipment	20.7	17.6	33.4	20.1b	67.4	58.7
Electrical products	59.3	38.0	8.0	20.7	63.1c	62.8
Non-metallic min. products	21.3	16.4	41.9a	46.4	n.d.	n.d.
Petroleum, coal	n.d.	n.d.	n.d.	n.d.	46.7	49.9
Chemical products	29.7	26.9	17.0	22.9	64.3	60.2
Miscellaneous	49.6	46.1	14.7	14.1		
Total, 20 groups	30.9	25.0	29.2	34.3	60.2	59.3
Total, excl. pulp and paper and non-met. min. products	36.9	27.2	15.1	24.2	52.0	51.4

SOURCES: B.S.Q., 1983.

a) In 1977.
b) In 1979.
c) Estimation (see notes a and b).

declining manufacturing employment since 1965; and the metropolitan region of London lost 38 percent of its manufacturing employment between 1971 and 1981.

The more important message of Table 18, however, is that Montreal's manufacturing sector has undergone further structural change within it of a highly favourable nature. There has been a sharp decline in relative importance of such low-productivity industries as leather goods, textiles, clothing, woodwork, and furniture, and a corresponding increase in the relative importance of high-productivity groups, such as foods, beverages and tobacco, printing, machinery, and transportation equipment. In this respect, Toronto has not done so well. The share of low-productivity industries in total manufacturing employment has remained more or less unchanged, and some of the industries whose productivity is farthest below the average have actually increased their shares of the total.

This favourable structural change has also improved the quality of Montreal's exports of manufactures. As a consequence, the share of the international market in Montreal's exports increased from 13.8 percent to 16.8 percent between 1976 and 1980, while for the rest of Canada this share fell from 36.4 percent to 33.9 percent (see Table 19).

The rest of the province of Quebec sends a much higher proportion of its exports abroad, and has also increased the share of such exports in the total. The importance of the world market for such exports as pulp and paper and mineral products helps to explain the greater importance of exports abroad in the rest of Quebec than in Montreal.

Montreal also shares with other large metropolitan centres of the western world the tendency for manufacturing enterprises to desert the central city in favour of suburbs and satellite towns. There is a strong tendency towards dispersion of manufacturing activities and disindustrialization of the central city.

In the race with Toronto, however, Montreal falls further and further behind. In 1977 manufacturing firms with headquarters in Montreal earned 24 percent of the total Canadian gross receipts from manufacturing, Toronto 47.8 percent.[7] As may be seen from Table 20, Montreal continued to lose out in the competition for head offices of industrial companies after 1977, and not so much to Toronto as to Vancouver and Calgary. It is interesting to note that among the top ten companies (in terms of sales) there was no change between 1976-77 and 1983: three in Montreal and four in

TABLE 20

The top 200 industrials: Head Office

Rank by sales	Montreal			Toronto			Vancouver			Calgary		
	76-77	79-80	83	76-77	79-80	83	76-77	79-80	83	76-77	79-80	83
Top 10	3	3	3	4	4	4	0	0	0	0	0	0
Top 50	15	13	10	22	23	21	3	3	3	2	4	6
Top 100	28	24	19	44	40	36	6	9	13	6	9	12
Top 200	47	39	32	85	72	72	13	18	23	9	16	24

SOURCE: The Financial Post 500, 1984, 1980.
The Financial Post 300, 1977.

Toronto, none in Vancouver or Calgary. In all the other size categories, Montreal had substantial *absolute* losses, Toronto more modest losses, and both Vancouver and Calgary substantial absolute gains.

Services

As in other large North American metropolitan centres, employment in Montreal is becoming ever more concentrated in the tertiary sector. Between 1971 and 1981 employment in services grew by 48.3 percent, to reach 66.8 percent of the total active population. This figure is almost identical to Toronto's (66.8 percent) and somewhat below Vancouver's, (72.0 percent). Even this last figure is below that of some of the more dynamic American cities. In 1981 San Francisco, for example, had more than 80 percent of its total employment in the tertiary sector.

A breakdown of tertiary employment by sub-sector, for Montreal, Toronto, and Vancouver, is given in Table 21. It can be seen at a glance that the structure is roughly the same. Toronto lagged a bit in medical and social services, Montreal in services to enterprises, in financial insurance, and real estate services. Montreal, although not a provincial capital, nonetheless had a somewhat higher share of its services employment in government. On the whole, however, the differences are not very significant.

When it comes to the rate of growth between 1971 and 1981, however, substantial differences do appear, both among the subsectors for the three cities combined, and from one city to another (see Table 22). Of the three main groups it was services to production that grew most rapidly, and within that group services to enterprises grew much faster than the others, while transport and communications grew significantly more slowly. Within the "services to consumption" category, it was restaurants and lodging that grew fastest. Montreal led the way in growth of services to consumption, especially in entertainment and leisure pursuits, but Toronto was out in front for restaurants and lodging. Toronto was also well ahead in growth of services to enterprises and finance, insurance, and real estate services. It would be hard to say, however, that any one of the three cities "performed" better than the others, in terms of improvement of quality of services, during this decade.

Lamonde and Polese explain the greater relative importance of the "para-public" sector in Montreal (universities, hospitals,

TABLE 21

The Structure of Tertiary Manpower, 1981, Montreal, Toronto, Vancouver

Sectors	Montreal Number	%	Toronto Number	%	Vancouver Number	%
Total number						
Consumer services						
Commerce	239,500	24.9	298,000	26.2	126,500	25.5
Recreation	17,600	1.8	25,900	2.3	8,500	1.7
Personal services	22,600	2.4	25,800	2.3	9,600	1.9
Lodging and catering	70,700	7.4	84,400	7.4	42,600	8.6
Miscellaneous services	41,200	4.3	45,800	4.0	20,600	4.1
	391,600	40.8	479,900	42.2	207,800	41.8
Production services						
Transport, communications and other public services	133,900	13.9	130,600	11.5	69,600	14.0
Financial, insurance and real estate businesses	87,600	9.1	139,200	12.2	47,300	9.5
Services to enterprises	70,300	7.3	115,400	10.1	42,000	8.4
	291,800	30.3	385,200	33.8	158,900	31.9
Governmental and parapublic services						
Teaching and related services	91,700	9.5	93,600	8.2	41,000	8.3
Medical and social services	108,400	11.3	95,500	8.4	52,300	10.5
Public administration	77,400	8.1	84,400	7.4	37,900	7.6
	277,500	28.9	273,500	24.0	131,200	26.4
TOTAL	960,900	100.0	1,139,900	100.0	497,100	100.0

Source: Statistics Canada, special compilation for the I.N.R.S.-Urbanisation.

TABLE 22

The Increase in Tertiary Manpower, 1971-1981 by Sector for Montreal, Toronto, Vancouver

Sector (Change 1971–1981)	Montreal Number	Montreal Indication* of structural change i.s.	Toronto Number	Toronto i.s.	Vancouver Number	Vancouver i.s.	Growth rate 1971–1981 for the 3 metropolises
CONSUMER SERVICES							
Commerce	77,900	1.00	90,200	0.83	40,800	0.83	45.7
Recreation	8,100	1.73	11,500	1.58	2,700	0.79	74.5
Personal services	500	0.03	600	0.03	-1,000	0.00	1.7
Lodging and catering	31,300	1.64	44,400	2.11	20,000	1.53	92.2
Miscellaneous services	18,600	1.73	20,200	1.53	8,100	1.11	73.4
	136,400	1.10	166,900	1.02	70,600	0.83	53.1
PRODUCTION SERVICES							
Transport, communications and other public services	31,000	0.61	37,100	0.77	19,700	0.67	35.8
Financial, insurance and real estate businesses	26,100	0.87	54,700	1.23	19,100	1.12	57.5
Services to enterprises	33,100	1.86	63,100	2.35	23,200	2.10	101.9
	90,200	0.93	154,900	1.30	62,000	1.09	58.3
GOVERNMENTAL AND PARAPUBLIC SERVICES							
Teaching and related services	21,100	0.61	19,800	0.52	13,500	0.82	36.1
Medical and social services	43,400	1.39	30,000	0.89	22,000	1.23	59.1
Public administration	21,400	0.79	67,400	0.64	51,000	1.07	37.2
	85,900	0.93	67,400	0.64	51,000	1.07	44.5
TOTAL	312,600		389,500		183,600		51.7

* The structural change index, i.s., is calculated as follows: $\text{i.s.}^i = \dfrac{A^{71-81}/A^{v71-81}}{M^i71/M^n71}$ or i.s. = the indication for sector 1

a71-81 = manpower growth between 1971-81 in sector 1
A^{v}71-61 = manpower growth between 1971-81 in all sectors
M^i71 = manpower in sector 1 in 1971
M^n71 = manpower in all sectors in 1971

etc.) by the greater dominance of Montreal in its peripheral region. Ontario has several university and hospital complexes in other cities, most of them quite close to Toronto, such as London, Kingston, Waterloo, Guelph, etc. Montreal is comparatively isolated in this respect, and has to serve a much bigger area.

Lamonde and Polese also point out that in contrast to Toronto and Vancouver, the relative importance within the tertiary sector of Montreal of services to enterprises suggests that the services sector is becoming less export-oriented than is the case with her two rivals. In 1971 the opposite was the case. If that is true, it may reflect the fact that Montreal is becoming less of a national and international centre and more of a regional centre, as a good many observers of the Canadian scene have argued. They also underline the much lower proportion of total growth of the tertiary sector, which is accounted for by finance and services to enterprises in Montreal: 18.9 percent compared to 22.6 percent in Vancouver and 30.2 percent in Montreal. They conclude that the manufacturing sector and the services sector in Montreal have moved in opposite directions: industry has become more export oriented, services less so. In the tertiary sector, Montreal is becoming less a Canadian centre and more a Quebec centre. It is providing support to manufacturing and other activities within Montreal and other parts of Quebec rather than selling services abroad or to the rest of Canada.

While this argument is certainly to some extent correct, it should not be exaggerated. In engineering consulting services, for example, Montreal retains its leadership, and some of those services are certainly exported. A survey conducted by the Centre for Studies in International Administration of the University of Montreal found that 90 percent of the engineering consulting firms in their sample had their head offices in Montreal. Of these, 15 percent had annual turnovers (fees plus reimbursed expenses) of $750 million or more, 15 percent had $15-$50 million in revenues, the others were smaller. More than 60 percent of them were operating in the international market.[8]

Bonin states that Montreal clearly dominates the services sector in Quebec, and despite playing second fiddle to Toronto at the national level, does not face serious competition from firms situated in Toronto within its own province. To the contrary, of the twenty categories of services distinguished in the census, Montreal captures 90 percent of the Quebec market. Bonin also insists that this fact does not mean that Montreal is squeezing out

TABLE 23

Manpower in Financial Services and Services to Enterprises,
Montreal and Vancouver as Compared to Toronto 1971-1981 (Toronto = 1.00)

	Montreal		Vancouver	
	1971	1981	1971	1981
FINANCE, INSURANCE AND REAL ESTATE (TOGETHER)	0.72	0.63	0.33	0.34
Banks and other deposit institutions	0.84	0.76	0.36	0.37
Brokers in real estate (& stock exchange)	0.54	0.30	0.27	0.31
Trusts & "holdings"	0.83	0.45	0.39	0.31
Insurance agents	0.60	0.53	0.17	0.17
Insurance and real estate agencies	0.73	0.62	0.38	0.34
Real estate holder	0.58	0.54	0.54	0.54
SERVICES TO ENTERPRISES (TOGETHER)	0.71	0.61	0.36	0.37
Placement offices	0.60	0.32	0.28	0.20
Data processing services	0.72	0.33	0.29	0.22
Security and investigation	1.15	1.09	0.38	0.29
Accounting (offices)	0.89	0.77	0.43	0.41
Publicity	0.61	0.47	0.19	0.20
Architects (offices)	0.61	0.54	0.31	0.58
Scientific studies and services (engineering-consultant)	0.86	0.87	0.58	0.61
Lawyers & solicitors	0.62	0.53	0.34	0.38
Management — consultant	0.58	0.58	0.29	0.42
Miscellaneous	0.55	0.57	0.30	0.29
MANUFACTURING SECTOR	0.88	0.83	0.25	0.25
OVERALL ACTIVITIES	0.88	0.85	0.39	0.41

service enterprises in the smaller Quebec cities; if they were not in Montreal they would not be in Quebec at all. The relationship is one of complementarity rather than competition.[9]

Finance

Table 23 provides figures of employment in the financial and "services to enterprises" sectors in somewhat more detail. It provides further evidence of the increasing importance of Toronto and the declining importance of Montreal in financial services. Vancouver is holding its own against Toronto, but that is about all. Montreal shows significant decline in share of employment in every sub-sector of the financial sector.

Services to enterprises

The same picture emerges for services to enterprises. Vancouver has made some relative gains on Toronto, especially in architects and management consultants, has suffered some relative losses (information services, security and investigation) but overall has held its own. Montreal has suffered an overall decline in its share of employment in the sector, a loss which is particularly pronounced in employment bureaus, information services, advertising, and architecture. Only in engineering consulting has it made a slight relative gain.

The Port

The Port of Montreal remains a major Canadian port. The tonnage-handled in 1980 was less than that of Sept-Iles, in part because of the concentration of the latter port on exports of minerals, but it was nearly double that of Halifax:

The picture with respect to growth, however, is a bit mixed: Montreal did better than Sept-Iles and Halifax, but worse than St. John and Quebec. Moreover, considering the fact that the Atlantic provinces now present a more stubborn problem of regional lag than Quebec, and that Quebec's problems lie mainly in the eastern portion of the province, such growth as there has been in traffic through the Port of Montreal is a mixed blessing from a national point of view. A significant part of it represents the success of Montreal in competing with Quebec City and Halifax for

TABLE 24

Total Tonnage of Certain Ports in the East of Canada
(000 metric tonnes)

	1980
Halifax	13,594
St-John	16,282
Sept-Iles	27,819
Quebec	17,027
Montreal	24,898

SOURCE: National Ports Commission, *Annual Report*, 1980.

container traffic. Professor Fernand Martin explains the relative success of Montreal in expanding its container traffic by the extension of Montreal's "hinterland" to the American midwest. Professor Martin points out that this success is not due to Montreal's geographic location, which is on balance a disadvantage, and asks:

> How could this happen since in terms of physical land distances, the difficulties of winter navigation, etc. Montreal has no great advantage over Baltimore for the U.S. Midwest traffic and over New York for other U.S. traffic? The answer is that... transport rates can vary in a discriminating fashion as far as the competing ports are concerned, thereby redesigning each port's hinterland. Transport costs can vary (vis-à-vis the ports concerned), because of changes in the technology of transport, changes in fuel costs or because of institutional factors that modify (in a discriminating way) the pricing behaviours of

TABLE 25

Tonnage handled, 1975 and 1980, East Canadian Ports
(metric tonnes)

	Montreal	**Quebec**	**Sept-Iles**	**St. John**	**Halifax**	**Total**
1975	20,561	11,517	27,315	4,894	11,331	75,618
1980	24,898	17,027	27,819	16,282	13,594	99,620
% increase	21.09	47.84	01.84	232.61	19.97	31.74

SOURCE: National Ports Commission, Special Documentation. Cited by Fernand Martin, May 1982, p. 58.

shipping and railway companies. The first two factors (technology and fuel costs) are unlikely to have affected in a substantially different way the competing ports during the period studied. We are thus left with the so-called institutional factors.[10]

The institutional factors that Martin considers important in the case of Montreal's container traffic are two:

1. The changing behaviour patterns of the shipping companies, which are organized into cartels called "conferences," together with the financial or equity participation of Canadian railway companies in shipping firms and shipping consortia. There is an interaction between the marketing objectives of the shipping companies and those of the railways which alters the pricing methods of the railways.
2. Canadian government regulation of railways influences their rate-setting and their participation in joint ventures. The United States government, in turn, has a "peculiar" regulation of foreign transport companies operating within the U.S.

Martin states that intermodal transportation (ship, railroad, truck, air) is better coordinated in Canada and has a definite advantage over the American system. One cannot help but think,

TABLE 26

*Number of Containers Handled
in 1979 in Different Ports
in American Tons*

New York	1,800,000
Rotterdam	1,733,463
Bremen	692,210
Antwerp	666,647
Hamburg	637,402
Le Havre	450,809
Hampton-Roads	416,634
London	401,467
Montreal	266,203
Halifax	233,510
Philadelphia	167,742

SOURCE: C.I. December 1980. Does not comprise containers handled in domestic transport.

however, that if indeed such institutional factors play such a strategic role, the situation could change again, almost overnight, and the port of Montreal might lose its comparative advantage for container traffic to and from the American midwest. In any case, whatever advantage it may have over some other ports in the North American east, Montreal hardly ranks as a container port among the giants of the world:

Fernand Martin provides a "shift-and-share" analysis of the evolution of *international* container traffic for Montreal and three other eastern Canada ports. The figures for absolute tonnage are these:

TABLE 27

International Container Traffic, 1971, 1974, 1980
(metric tonnes)

	Halifax	St. John	Quebec	Montreal	Total
1971	452,041	88,758	527,141	1,023,423	2,091,266
1974	1,477,203	367,768	657,409	1,289,745	3,789,125
1980	1,935,371	965,320	0	3,058,238	5,958,974

SOURCE: *Stat. Can.*, Cat. no. 54 003.

Martin then calculated what the tonnage of each individual port would have been if all of them had expanded their container traffic at the same rate as the growth for all four combined, which he calls the "theoretical" tonnage, and compares that figure with the actual one:

He concludes that Montreal has gained at the expense of Quebec City and to a certain extent at the expense of Halifax, and has captured some of the transit traffic to the United States. St. John has also gained at the expense of Halifax.[11]

As for exports of cereals, historically such an important factor in the life of the port, the period 1971-81 saw more recovery of Montreal's share of the total for Quebec ports, but the 1981 figure remained far below the figure for 1960, and was below that of both Quebec City and Baie Comeau:

TABLE 28

Relative Gains and Losses of Eastern Canada Ports
1974-1980 (metric tonnes)

	Halifax	St. John	Quebec	Montreal
Actual Tonnage 1980	1,935,371	965,320	0	3,058,283
Theoretical tonnage 1980	2,323,126	573,653	1,033,876	2,028,320
Improvement relative (+) during the period (or deterioration) (-)	-387,755	+391,667	-1,033,876	+1,029,963

SOURCE: Calculated from the previous table.

TABLE 29

Distribution of Traffic in Cereals in Quebec Ports (in %)

	1960	1970	1977	1981
Montreal	59.9	27.9	17.6	21.6
Sorel	10.4	9.8	7.6	9.0
Trois-Rivières	8.2	11.8	7.0	5.2
Québec	7.3	8.8	15.6	24.4
Baie Comeau	14.2	19.9	21.2	23.4
Port Cartier	—	21.8	31.0	16.6
Total	100.0	100.0	100.0	100.0

SOURCE: Bulletin économique, Banque provinciale du Canada, Jan. Fev. 1979 and *Journal de Finances*, 15 mars, 1982 (Montréal).

G. Norcliffe notes that the stagnation of port activity of large cities and especially in bulk freight, is at least partly a product of the industrial decentralisation that we have already noted above.

Where there is water transportation, necessarily there are ports. And in these ports, historically, there were gathered along the waterfront various industries associated with the port. It is very apparent however, that this traditional conception of a port bristling with port-related industries along the central waterfront now needs revising. Even a cursory glance at such Canadian ports as Vancouver, Toronto, and Montreal shows that their central waterfronts, once dominated by warehouses, cranes and port industries are now populated by luxury hotels, high-rise apartment buildings, office blocks, marinas and restaurants. Most of the industries connected with the port have moved to other parts of the waterfront — in the case of Montreal, downriver, while in Vancouver they have dispersed around the shores of Burrard inlet, and to the banks of the Fraser river.[12]

In sum, the port of Montreal is serving its natural hinterland well with water transportation services, and is even succeeding, for the moment at least, in extending the geographic borders of that hinterland. The activities of the port, however, cannot be depended upon to make a major contribution to the enlargement and strengthening of the Montreal economy as a whole. The causal connection runs mainly in the inverse direction.

Montreal and Quebec

Those who fear that growth of Montreal may "stifle" economic expansion in the rest of the province might be expected to rejoice at the recent decline of Quebec's metropolis. They would be foolish to do so. Does the faltering of Montreal's commerce, industry and finance create opportunities in these fields elsewhere in the province ? Obviously not. To be sure, some — not all — of the cities in the "couronne" of Montreal and some of Montreal's satellite cities have profited by deconcentration of certain of the city's industrial activities ; but these smaller towns are still part of the Montreal urban system. The cities which have gained at Montreal's expense are outside the province of Quebec altogether, particularly in Ontario and above all in the Toronto system. If Quebec has slipped somewhat less than Montreal, it is because the activities that have suffered most are sophisticated services and high-technology industries, and within Quebec these are heavily concentrated in Montreal. Indeed, the enterprises that are leaving Quebec for Ontario are mainly of a sort that only Montreal could attract to the province; for them, "leaving Montreal" means "leaving Quebec" altogether. The decline of Montreal injures Quebec, less because Montreal provides a market for the goods and services produced elsewhere in the province (although this factor plays some role) than because to so high a degree the Montreal economy *is* the Quebec economy.

CHAPTER 4

MONTREAL IN THE QUEBEC ECONOMY

For residents of Quebec it is easy to think of Quebec as a "region" and of Montreal as the metropolitan centre of that region. From there it is an easy step to one or another of two images of Montreal's role in Quebec. The great vogue of the "growth pole" or "development pole" concept among economists, and later among politicians, led many of these to think of Montreal as the development pole *par excellence* of the "region of Quebec." In this view, growth of Montreal would generate "spread effects" to the rest of the province, creating income and employment in the city's natural "peripheral region." This view naturally appealed to the denizens of Montreal, and particularly to the dominant anglophone minority of that city. But impoverished farmers and fishermen in the east of Quebec, unemployed textile workers in the Cantons de l'Est, many politicians in Quebec City, and even some economists, took a very different view: Montreal was seen as a monstrous mollusc, whose growth was stifling the development of other potential industrial centres of the province.

Neither of these views is strictly correct. The truth is that Montreal operates in an "economic space" that is ultimately world-wide. A variety of raw materials, of scientific and technical knowledge, of capital, or entrepreneurial and managerial skills come from the United States, from western Europe, from Japan, from elsewhere in Asia, from Latin America, from Africa. Imports into Montreal of finished products come from all over the world. And Montreal exports her own goods and services to the entire world. The growth of such a city can have only a limited impact on income and employment elsewhere in the province, and particularly in the more retarded subregions, such as Gaspésie and the east of Quebec. At the same time, the quality of economic activities in Montreal, both in manufacturing and in the services sector, is superior to those which cities like Rimouski or Rivière du Loup, or even Sherbrooke and Quebec City, can hope to attract. If development of Montreal is not assuring high levels of income and employment throughout the province, neither is it luring to the city enterprises that might have gone elsewhere in Quebec if Montreal had not been there.

The team of three economists from the University of Montreal who in 1970 were asked by the Department of Regional Expansion and the Office of Planning of Quebec to assist in the design of a strategy for the regional development of Quebec, were asked to include in their studies the consideration of three cities to the east of Montreal as potential alternative "development poles," with the idea that policies to encourage their growth would help to pull industrialization and urbanization away from Montreal, towards the disadvantaged subregions in the eastern part of the province. The three cities were Trois-Rivières, Québec, and Sept Iles. The team quickly reached the conclusion that none of these cities were, ever had been, or would soon become true development poles, whose expansion would generate prosperity for a larger region of Quebec. Trois Rivières was a moribund industrial town; Québec was a capital city, a services city, with a rather dilapidated industrial structure. Sept Iles was indeed a vigorously expanding city, but it was clearly a "central place" responding to the development of the mining region to the north, rather than an urban centre generating "spread effects" to its own or any other peripheral region. However, in the course of looking at these cities as potential development poles some interesting things were learned about the relationship of Montreal to other urban centres of the province and thus (since most Québécois live in cities) to the province as a whole.

Trois-Rivières

In opening its section on Trois-Rivières, in what became known as the HMR Report, the team wrote:

> Il serait difficile de trouver une ville plus éloignée du concept du "pôle de croissance" tel que nous l'avons défini au chapitre 4, que Trois-Rivières. La structure industrielle de la ville, à l'opposé d'une agrégation d'entreprises dynamiques et innovatrices, générant des effets d'entraînement, est un centre d'industries traditionnelles et en difficulté.[1]

However, the city was showing signs of life. After a decline in manufacturing employment between 1951 and 1961, it had increased in 1965. There was a heavy concentration in industry (33.6 percent of the labour force) and more interesting, 46.2 percent of the industry was producing for export. In this respect the city compared favourably with Montreal. Pulp and paper were the principal industrial products, followed by textiles, clothing, furniture, and chemical products. The pulp and paper industry was in difficulties because the forest reserves of its own region were depleted, requiring imports from Gaspésie and the Atlantic provinces. To that extent Trois-Rivières was a "development pole," generating income and employment in the forest of Gaspésie and the Atlantic provinces; but unfortunately the industry was stagnant. The textiles industry too was stagnant.

An interesting point is that Trois-Rivières had built grain elevators and had become a trans-shipment point of some importance, from lakers to ocean going vessels. It was importing wheat from Port-Arthur/Fort William (Lakehead), Duluth, and Superior and exporting it to the USSR, Algeria, Yugoslavia, Bulgaria, India, Pakistan and China. It was importing corn and soya beans from Chicago and Toledo and shipping them to Italy, Spain, Holland and Japan. In short, Trois-Rivières was beating Montreal at its traditional game. The growth of Montreal was not doing much for Trois-Rivières, but neither was it "stifling" Trois-Rivières.

Sept Iles

The frontier mining town of Sept Iles, with a population of about 20,000 was even less closely tied to Montreal than Trois-Rivières. It was the major port for shipping iron ore in the whole province. Moreover, like Trois-Rivières, it had begun to rival Montreal as a trans-shipment point for grain.[2] Thanks to the expansion of mining to the north, Sept Iles grew at the staggering rate of 13 percent per year between 1956 and 1966. It was a prosperous little town; its hinterland region was the only one, apart from the economic region of Montreal, to have a per capita income above the provincial average. The level of unemployment was high, but this was partly because the city's very prosperity drew jobseekers from nearby Gaspésie and Bas Saint-Laurent. The city was a typical "central place," providing services to its hinterland region. Including construction, 78 percent of the labour force was engaged in the tertiary (services) sector.

Small as the city was, it was operating in a very wide economic space. Its most important connections were with the United States and western Europe. In 1966 some 14.5 million tons of cargo were loaded for American ports, 60 percent of the total: 3.7 million to Baltimore, 2.7 million to Cleveland, 1.2 million to Detroit, 1.1 million to Philadelphia. Another 2.2 million tons were loaded for Great Britain and 0.6 million for Italy. About 0.5 million went to Ontario and Nova Scotia ports, and an insignificant 9,200 tons to Montreal.

It is interesting to note, however, that Montreal was one of the major destinations of airline flights from Sept Iles, along with Quebec City, Rimouski and Wabush, Newfoundland. Since Montreal was not an important trading partner for the city, one can guess that the trips to Montreal were connected with finance, recreation, specialized and sophisticated shopping, visits to friends and families, and transfers to international airlines.

Quebec City

As the capital city, Quebec City clearly has a special relationship with the province's metropolitan centre. To begin with, many government departments have branch offices in Montreal, which in itself involves movement in both directions between the two cities. The government has connections with Montreal's financial centre, although these are probably less important than its connections with the financial centres of New York and Boston. Finally, since Montreal accounts for more than half of the provincial economy, a buoyant Montreal means increasing tax revenues for Quebec, and a consequent tendency for the provincial government to spend more on buildings and personnel. Indeed, an unpublished study made at the University of Montreal after the

HMR Report indicated that there is a certain threshold of growth of economic activity in Montreal below which Quebec City grows more slowly, and above which Quebec City grows more rapidly, than Montreal itself. The government also purchases a significant proportion of its consulting services from firms in Montreal.

In terms of purchases and sales of other services, or of goods, however, Quebec City is little more closely tied to Montreal than are other cities of the province. It had been a slow-growing metropolitan region in 1966. The city proper grew at an average rate of only 0.2 percent in the previous decade, and actually lost population between 1961 and 1966. This stagnation was partly due, however, to a movement into suburbs; the three peripheral counties had growth rates above the provincial average. On balance, nonetheless, population growth of the administrative region of Quebec was well below the provincial average. Average income was a bit above the provincial average and personal income per worker slightly below the average (the dependency ratio was well below the provincial average).

Unlike the other two cities in the 1970 study, Quebec City had little to do with the outside world, especially where manufacturing was concerned. There was little industry in any case, and what did exist was traditional, low-growth, and low-productivity (tobacco, leather, wool). Most of the manufactured goods purchased by its residents were imported. Nearly three-quarters of Quebec's labour force was engaged in the services sector.

In terms of airline traffic, Quebec City's most important connection was with Montreal, for much the same reasons as applied to Sept Iles, with movements of civil servants added. Toronto-Hamilton was the second most important connection. Almost no one flew between Quebec City and Ottawa — fewer than between Quebec City and Sept Iles and about the same as between Quebec City and New York.

The importance of Montreal

Thus we see that Montreal's role in the economic life of *other* parts of the province is very limited. To be sure, its large population provides a market for some of the province's farmers; but there are few of these left and Quebec's future does not depend on the fate of its agriculture. As for Quebec's other cities, each has its own life, its own connections with the outside world and, except to some degree in the case of Montreal's own satellites, income, employment, and population growth depend rather little on what happens in Montreal. The precise relationship to Montreal varies from case to case, and only case studies could reveal exactly what it is. But for all of them events occurring or trends unwinding outside Montreal, and indeed outside of the province or even outside the country, can be more important for their prosperity than anything happening in Montreal itself.

But if Montreal is neither a goose laying golden eggs around the province, nor a voracious beast gobbling up the economic activities of other Quebec cities, just what is its roles in the Quebec economy? There are three parts to the answer to this question, presented here in ascending order of complexity and uncertainty:

1. Since Montreal accounts for more than half of the Quebec economy, what happens to Montreal obviously affects the prosperity of the province as a whole.

2. Because of the relationship of the structure of economic activity to city size, and the tendency for certain sophisticated services and high-technology manufacturing to concentrate in the largest cities, some high-productivity activities would not exist in Quebec at all if Montreal did not exist or were in another province.

3. Large metropolitan centres serve as centres of diffusion of innovations, or of scientific and technological progress, and a region without any such centre is likely to lag economically, socially, and culturally.

The first point requires little elaboration. In 1971 metropolitan Montreal had nearly half the total population, more than half the total value of output, and considerably more than half the manufacturing production or services of the entire province. If we look at the administrative region of Montreal among the ten administrative regions of the province, the concentration of economic activity is still more striking (Table 30). In 1961, the Montreal region had 53.5 percent of the total population, in 1971 56.8 percent. Its share of manufacturing employment remained essentially unchanged, at 70 percent, during this decade; but its share of gross domestic product rose from 59.1 percent to 65.0 percent. No other region came close to comparing with Montreal in any of these respects. Moreover, during the whole postwar period no region except Côte-Nord/Nouveau Québec compared with Montreal in rate of growth of gross domestic

TABLE 30

The Importance and Evolution of the Regions of Quebec
(in Percentage of the total for Quebec)

Regions	Population		Manufacturing Employment		Gross Domestic Product	
	1961	1971	1960	1971	1951	1966
Gaspésie/Bas St-Laurent	4.7	3.9	1.0	1.2	2.5	2.3
Saguenay/Lac St-Jean	5.2	4.6	3.3	3.3	4.9	4.2
Quebec	16.3	15.6	9.1	9.3	12.7	11.9
Trois-Rivières	7.9	7.0	8.1	8.7	8.3	6.1
Cantons de l'est	4.0	3.7	4.4	4.1	4.5	3.4
Montreal	53.5	56.8	70.7	70.0	59.1	65.0
Outaouais	3.9	4.0	2.0	1.9	3.4	3.1
Nord-Ouest	2.9	2.5	0.8	1.1	3.7	1.9
Côte-Nord, Nouveau-Québec	1.6	1.9	0.6	0.6	0.9	2.1
Quebec (total)	100.0	100.0	100.0	100.0	100.0	100.0
Quebec (basic)	85.6	87.1	94.3	93.8	88.0	89.5
Quebec (resources)	14.4	12.9	5.7	6.2	12.0	10.5

SOURCES: Gouvernement du Québec, l'Aménagement du territoire et le développement économique, Office de planification et développement du Québec, 1973 — R. Jouandet-Bernadat, Les Comptes régionaux québécois, Office de planification et développement du Québec, 1969 — Statistics Canada, Manufacturing Industries of Canada, Geographical Distribution, 1971, Ottawa, May 1975.

CHART 1

Raw Value of Manufacturing Production, Quebec and Ontario

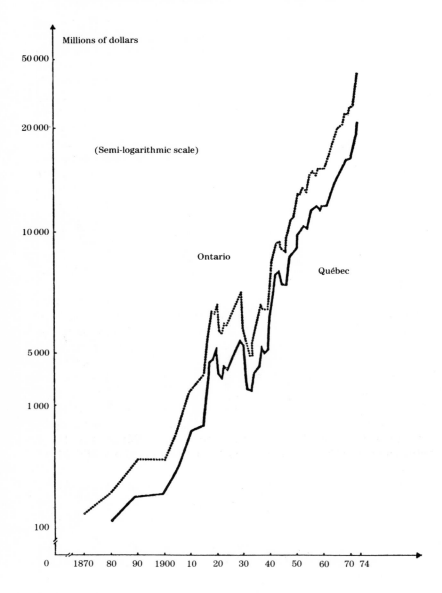

SOURCE: Statistics Canada. Canada Yearbook, 1932. Manufacturing industries of Canada's general review. Manufacturing industries of Canada: Quebec. Manufacturing industries of Canada: Ontario.

product (Chart 1). Montreal had a lower average rate of unemployment than the other regions, (Table 31) and, taking proportion of the labour force in industry and services together, the most advanced structure of employment (Table 32). It is thus not surprising that Montreal was the region with the highest per capita income (Table 33), although its advantage in this respect is diminishing. In 1951 Montreal's per capita income was more than double that of Gaspesie/Bas Saint Laurent, in 1970 significantly less than double; all regions made some gain on Montreal during this period, except the Nord-Ouest; but Côte Nord/Nouveau Quebec was the only region other than Montreal to have a per capita income above the provincial average. In short, Quebec owes much of such prosperity as it has to Montreal in terms of simple arithmetic; Montreal comprises the major portion of the Quebec economy and it is at the same time a relatively prosperous portion.

Income and Size of City

The second argument is more subtle. It states in effect that Montreal is relatively prosperous among regions (or cities) of Quebec because it is the only really large city in the province. Table 34 is taken from the 1977 study by the Economic Council of Canada, *Living Together: a Study of Regional Disparities*.[3] It shows very clearly that per capita incomes tend to rise with size of city, although in the prairies, Winnipeg, the one city with a population above 500,000, had a slightly lower per capita income than prairie cities between 200,000 and 500,000, which in that year included Edmonton and Calgary, benefiting from the oil boom. It also shows, incidentally, that Montreal's per capita income was below that of both Toronto and Vancouver, these being the three Canadian cities with populations above 500,000 in 1970.

Why should productivity be higher in large cities than in small ones? The main reason is that the more sophisticated services (what has come to be called, following the lead of French economists, the "quarternary sector") and the more scientifically oriented industries prefer to locate in the larger cities. It is a well established law of urban and regional economics that in any country there are thresholds of city size below which one does not ordinarily find certain types of economic activity, and that by and large the types of activity that appear as one moves up the scale to

TABLE 31

The Rate of Unemployment by Region

Regions	Average Annual Rate	1955-1964 Monthly Rate		1973 Annual Rate	1973 Monthly Rate	
		Minimum	Maximum		Minimum	Maximum
Gaspésie/Bas St-Laurent	15.2	3.8	30.3	13.8	7.4	20.7
Saguenay/Lac St-Jean	13.7	7.7	22.9	7.6 (with Côte-Nord)	5.9	9.7
Quebec	9.0	4.0	15.4			
Trois-Rivières	11.0	6.0	17.3			
Cantons de l'est	9.0	4.3	14.6	8.4	7.4	10.5
Montreal	7.5	4.5	11.2	6.3	5.3	8.6
Outaouais	8.5	3.3	16.4	9.1	5.4	12.8
Nord-Ouest	9.1	5.4	18.0			
Côte-Nord, Nouveau-Québec	12.7	4.0	23.3	—	—	—
Quebec (total)	8.6	4.5	14.0	7.5	6.0	10.2

Sources: Conseil d'orientation économique du Québec, Rapport du Comité sur le chômage saisonnier, Québec 1966 — Gouvernement du Québec, l'Aménagement du territoire et le développement économique, Office de planification et de développement du Québec, 1973 — Statistics Canada, Survey on the Labour Force, unpublished data.

TABLE 32

Sectoral Distribution of Gross Domestic Product — 1966
Regions of Quebec
(in Percentage of Regional Total)

Regions	Primary Sector	Secondary Sector	Tertiary Sector
Gaspésie/Bas St-Laurent	15.0	9.4	75.6
Saguenay/Lac St-Jean	10.4	37.2	52.4
Quebec	8.9	19.5	71.6
Trois-Rivières	8.0	42.8	49.2
Cantons de l'est	12.7	36.8	50.5
Montreal	1.5	30.3	68.2
Outaouais	8.4	24.1	67.5
Nord-Ouest	31.8	12.2	56.0
Côte-Nord, Nouveau-Québec	38.4	13.5	48.1
Quebec (total)	5.4	28.9	65.7
Quebec (basic)	3.7	29.8	66.5
Quebec (resources)	21.0	21.9	57.1

SOURCES: R. Jouandet-Bernadat, Les Comptes régionaux québécois, Office de planification et de développement du Québec, 1969 — Gouvernement du Québec, l'Aménagement du territoire et le développement économique, Office de planification et développement du Québec, 1973.

TABLE 33

Per Capita Disposable Income by Region
Regions of Quebec
(in Percentage of the Quebec Average)

Regions	1951	1961	1970
Gaspésie/Bas St-Laurent	57.4	60.1	62.2
Saguenay/Lac St-Jean	79.4	78.6	79.8
Quebec	82.1	84.3	90.3
Trois-Rivières	85.6	84.5	87.4
Cantons de l'est	85.6	86.1	89.6
Montreal	118.6	116.2	110.1
Outaouais	89.1	81.5	90.9
Nord-Ouest	83.6	78.9	80.0
Côte-Nord, Nouveau-Québec	101.0	81.4	102.2
Quebec (total)	100.0	100.0	100.0
Quebec minus Montreal	81.1	80.8	86.0

SOURCES: Gouvernement du Québec, l'Aménagement du territoire et le développement économique, Office de planification et développement du Québec, 1973 — R. Jouandet-Bernadat, Les Comptes régionaux québécois, Office de planification et développement du Québec, 1969.

TABLE 34

Income [1] Per Capita, by Size of Urban Centre and by Region, 1970

| | Rural and Semi-urban | Size of urban centre (in thousands) | | | | | | | Regional average |
		5-10	10-25	25-50	50-100 (Dollars)	100-200	200-500	500 and over	
Atlantic region	1,575	2,096	2,314	2,391	2,199	2,226	2,896	—	1,948
Quebec	1,461	2,063	2,224	2,377	2,409	2,805	2,701	2,970	2,489
Ontario	2,599	2,591	2,934	2,749	3,048	3,002	3,171	3,579	3,097
Prairie region	1,763	2,574	2,661	2,652	—	2,760	3,099	2,961	2,453
British Columbia	2,523	2,845	2,875	2,801	—	3,117	—	3,280	3,000
Canada	1,900	2,391	2,606	2,560	2,709	2,805	3,074	3,244	2,700

— Not applicable.

1. The sum of wages and salaries; interest and dividends; government transfer payments; and farm, business, or professional incomes.

SOURCE: Estimates by the Economic Council of Canada, based on the 1971 Census.

larger and larger cities are those with the higher value of output per manyear. (The law doesn't even seem to be culture-bound; the Canadian team that prepared the regional development plan for Pahang Tenggara in Malaysia found precisely the same phenomenon in that country). The Economic Council study provides further support for this law, reproduced here as Table 35. Some activities such as retail trade, public utilities, education, and health and welfare show little difference by city size. Food and lodging actually declines somewhat with city size. All the others, however, show a marked tendency to increase in importance with size of city. Moreover, as these sectors are broken down, the comparative advantage of the big cities becomes more apparent. For example, as the Economic Council points out, "education services are found in every urban centre, but specialized institutions such as universities, which serve a much smaller fraction of the populace and which require a higher minimum level of operation, tend to locate close to the majority of their clientele, thus choosing the larger agglomerations."[4] The Council also points out that within each industry there is a tendency for the head office, where the more highly paid employees are engaged, to be located in a large centre. The relative importance of managers in the occupational structure rises with size of city. It can also be shown that technologically advanced industries tend to prefer large cities.

Another reason why incomes are higher in large cities is that participation rates (proportion of the population in the labour force) are higher, especially among women. The Council also maintains that there are economies of agglomeration, at least up to a level of population of 1.4 million. To measure this factor separately they corrected for differences in industrial structure, in an effort to isolate the effect of size *apart from* the correlation between size and industrial structure. They found an increase in value added per worker of $200 in moving from 25,000 to 100,000 and another $200 in moving from 500,000 to one million. "Soon thereafter, the gains begin to fall off, and they become negative when larger city sizes are reached."[5] This statement applies, of course, only to economies of agglomeration as measured, not to actual per capita income, which continues to rise *despite* the conversion of economies into diseconomies of agglomeration above the 1.4 million mark. The estimated value added per worker in manufacturing alone was $18,113 and seven urban centres attained higher figures than Toronto. The Council reports that a

TABLE 35

Number of Workers per Thousand Inhabitants in the Median City,
Five Hierarchical Levels, Service Industries, 1971

	Hierarchical Level				
	1	2	3	4	5
Transportation and warehousing	22.1	16.3	13.6	15.7	13.6
Communications	10.0	6.9	6.4	6.9	5.7
Public utilities	4.2	3.9	4.5	3.8	3.7
Wholesale trade	21.0	15.0	11.9	13.0	10.9
Retail trade	49.5	48.0	48.3	46.4	48.4
Finance, insurance, and real estate	22.0	14.8	13.1	12.1	10.7
Education	29.9	29.3	27.9	24.2	24.7
Health and welfare	27.4	28.7	27.1	27.1	27.8
Personal services	9.0	9.1	8.8	8.6	9.4
Food and lodging	15.5	15.7	17.1	16.8	17.0
Other service industries	26.5	21.0	17.2	16.0	14.7
Public administration	32.5	26.0	22.9	16.8	22.0
Total	269.6	234.7	218.8	207.4	208.6

1. The hierarchical level of a city is determined by its approximate population: Level 1) 250,000 and over; Level 2) 80,000–250,000; Level 3) 35,000–80,000; Level 4) 15,000–35,000 and Level 5) 5,000–15,000

SOURCE: Estimates by the Economic Council of Canada, based on 1971 Census data.

more detailed study of American experience corroborates the existence of agglomeration economies, but does not examine the possibility of diseconomies in the largest centres.

The higher incomes of the larger cities have a cumulative effect; they tend to lead to more rapid growth of the large cities (Table 36). The Council states:

> If service industries that increase the fastest prove to be those which for the sake of efficiency settle in the large centres, then one would naturally expect the large centres to grow the fastest. That seems to be what happens. The fast-growth service sectors most likely to locate in large centres include, among others, communication; finance; insurance and real estate; and public administration. A more detailed industrial classification would provide other examples.[6]

But why do the high-growth, high-productivity enterprises prefer large cities? The reasons are imperfectly understood, but have to do with the concentration in larger cities of research institutions and universities, the superiority of communication, being close to "the action," access to cultural activities, and the like. We shall return to this question below.

The third argument might be regarded as more controversial. It was one of the major arguments presented in the HMR Report, to support the authors' recommendation that urban and regional development policy should be directed towards strengthening the Montreal economy, rather than towards pushing and pulling industrialization and urbanization away from Montreal towards centres farther east. The authors repeat the arguments of the well-known American urban and regional economist, John Friedmann:

1. Innovations are a function of the number and intensity of problems which traditional approaches cannot solve (poverty, pollution, crime).
2. Innovations coincide in large measure with the points of highest interaction potential in a communications field. A diversity of mentalities helps. Exchange of new information is basic.
3. Innovations are more effective in a social system which is capable of assimilating them without self destruction. Elements in such a system are multiplicity of decision centres, vertical mobility, popular participation, and mechanisms for conflict resolution.
4. Innovations depend on individual mental attitudes of people confronted with them. Certain societies or certain populations produce or attract innovative personalities, others don't. Immigrants and other social groups that are deviationist or oppressed form the reservoir of entrepreneurs.

TABLE 36

Population Growth Rate, by Size of Urban Centre and by Region, 1961-71[1]

	Rural	Semi-urban[2]	Size of urban centre (in thousands), 1961 (Percent)							Regional average
			5-10	10-25	25-50	50-100	100-200	200-500	500 and over	
Atlantic region	5.9	11.5	11.2	0.3	11.7	5.7	18.3	—	—	8.4
Quebec	0.2	-2.0	9.3	14.2	12.0	7.6	17.6	26.8	23.8	14.6
Ontario	13.5	11.5	9.3	9.6	16.6	21.5	29.0	24.3	37.0	23.5
Prairie region	-9.7	33.9	13.6	14.4	4.3	32.3	23.7	28.7	—	11.4
British Columbia	41.1	30.8	27.9	44.6	39.3	—	26.7	—	31.0	34.1
Canada[3]	4.6	11.5	11.5	16.4	14.9	15.3	23.2	26.4	30.0	18.3

— Not applicable.

1. After corrections required by changes in the boundaries of urban centres to ensure comparability between 1961 and 1971.

2. Estimates based on the set of municipalities whose boundaries remained unchanged.

3. Including the Yukon and Northwest Territories.

SOURCE: Estimates by the Economic Council of Canada, based on the 1961 and 1971 Census.

For purposes of comparison, it is interesting to note that, in the United States, total population between 1960 and 1970 grew by 13.3 percent, whereas metropolitan population grew by 16.6 percent. It is true, however, that the three largest metropolises showed weaker performance, especially New York City, which had a rate of 7.8 percent.

5. Human and financial resources of a very diversified sort are needed to realise the various stages of innovation, from the original ideas to putting it into effect and its diffusion throughout the entire system.
6. Innovation occurs only where it leads to social approval and financial success for the entrepreneurs who undertake it. The gains must correspond to the high risks entailed. The power inherent in innovation must be legalized and institutionalized.

The authors go on to argue that these conditions are met only in the large urban centres:

> En effet, nous pourrions reprendre une à une les conditions de l'innovation mentionnée plus haut et faire ressortir la supériorité remarquable des grandes agglomérations sur les petites à cet égard...
>
> ... L'ensemble urbain est un champ d'information (communications field) et le siège par excellence d'économies externes à l'entreprise.
> ... Il est admis aujourd'hui que la présence des (activités quaternaires) dans le milieu environnant est plus déterminant pour la localisation des entreprises que les coûts de transport ou même les salaires, deux variables-clefs des modèles traditionnels. Ce sont ces effets positifs d'agglomération qui expliquent l'urbanisation elle-même, phénomène universel dont l'ampleur ne cesse d'étonner.[7]

This thesis has not gone unchallenged. In a study prepared for the Department of Urban Affairs as part of their preparation for HABITAT, André Trudeau undertook a critical review of the HMR report and particularly of its thesis concerning the importance of innovations and the concentration of innovation in large cities. He begins by challenging the proposition that innovation is the major source of development, while admitting that the theory of entrepreneurship and innovation, as conceived by Joseph Schumpeter and François Perroux, is generally accepted by specialists in economic development. In these theories, innovations are regarded as new techniques, new commodities, new forms of organization which bring fundamental changes in the way things are done, leading to "clusters of followers" and related changes in sectors other than the one in which the change is first introduced. Examples would be the power loom, steam, the railway, the automobile, electricity, the airplane, the high speed computer, etc. Trudeau argues that such innovations are rare. The majority of innovations, he says, take place within existing structures without transforming them. He suggests a distinction between "development innovations" which really do transform an economy and a society, and "growth innovations" which increase the dimensions of existing structures without changing the inter-relations within them. He goes on to point out that today most research and development is institutionalized, taking place in the research departments of existing organizations. The large corporations, he says, are not interested in upsetting any applecarts, and tend to introduce innovations with as little transformation as possible.

Trudeau next maintains — somewhat inconsistently — that there is a good deal of evidence that the majority of important innovations during the twentieth century came from isolated inventors and from small and middle-sized firms. Trudeau also repeats the often made accusation that the large firms buy up patents only to prevent their being used.

However, it would appear that Trudeau misunderstands the theory of innovations. In the first place, he fails to make the basic distinction, so much stressed by Schumpeter and Perroux, between *innovation* and *invention*. Schumpeter in particular had little regard for mere inventors, the people who come up with new gadgets. His admiration was reserved for the true innovators, the men who see and seize the opportunity for "doing things differently," who set up an organization and assemble the capital, the management, the scientific and technical skills, and the labour force to turn the gadget into a new industry. It does not matter much where the gadgets are invented; it is where the true entrepreneurs choose to set up their establishments that counts. It is, of course, not unknown for inventors to serve as innovators as well; and it is interesting to note that M. Bombardier, who invented the snowmobile in a village of the eastern Townships, when choosing a site for the head office of the large enterprise set up to manufacture his invention, rejected Sherbrooke and chose Montreal.

In the second place, the distinction being made is not between large firms and small firms; it is between technologically advanced and traditional firms. There are many large-scale but relatively traditional enterprises in small towns: pulp and paper, textiles, furniture, boots and shoes. And there are many sophisticated but small-scale enterprises in big cities: consulting firms, electronics, optics, scientific instruments, etc. Also, the HMR Report recognized that sophisticated enterprises can be attracted to small towns if these are satellites of metropolitan centres, and the main thrust of their policy recommendations was not to encourage new enterprises to settle in the city, but to strengthen Montreal's satellite towns by encouraging dynamic, rapid-growth, high-productivity enterprises to establish themselves there.

Finally, the distinction between "growth" and "development" is less significant in industrialized countries than it is in developing countries. Development economists have learned to their sorrow that quite high rates of growth of national income can take place without much structural change and with little improvement in the welfare of the masses of poor people. But in a country like Canada or a region like Quebec there are few farmers left to move into industry or services, and even the shift to services cannot go very much further. Moreover, the welfare state is so highly evolved that growth brings some improvement to nearly all social groups. Many Québécois would be happy to see Quebec grow more rapidly than Ontario and the rest of Canada, even if the "growth" was not accompanied by "development" in the sense of structural change, social transformation, or increased equality of income distribution; and if growth of the Montreal economy could assure expansion of the entire Quebec regional economy, they would be happy to see the Montreal economy grow.

After challenging the theory of development through innovation, M. Trudeau turns to the question, "What kinds of innovations are born in big cities"? He suggests that with continuing improvement in communications, the researcher or creative genius might find it more advantageous to settle in a smaller city where there is less congestion and pollution. Here again, Trudeau is confusing the innovator with the inventor. And as for improvement in communications, holding a meeting from one's Caribbean island home by picture-telephone is still not the same thing as inviting the director of research of a rival firm for lunch, in hopes that over cocktails he will disclose some secrets about his recent work. For the true entrepreneur, a major consideration in location decisions, is ready access to a wide range of other entrepreneurs, scientists and engineers, — in short, to people like himself. Both multiplicity and continuity of contact are important. The renaissance of the Boston and New England economies during World War II and after, replacing the traditional textile, pulp and paper, and boot and shoe industries which had migrated south and west, with much more productive scientifically-oriented industries, was based mainly on the concentration of educational, scientific, and research institutions in the Boston area, plus the fact that — as Dean Burchard pointed out — people who have once lived in "the Cambridge community" don't like to leave it. Montreal, we have maintained, is another such community; and the fact that scientists, engineers and managers trained at the Université de Montréal, McGill, Concordia and Université de Québec à Montréal want to go on living in Montreal gives scientifically-oriented firms a locational advantage in that city.

Trudeau also suggests that the quality of invention is more important than the number. On this point I would tend to agree. The *number* of patents, or even the number of inventions, is not a good measure of the importance of the innovations introduced in a particular locality. The problem here is — and it is a problem that has plagued economists interested in development for generations — that one cannot judge the "significance" of an innovation apart from its impact, and consequently one is very quickly trapped into circular reasoning: growth of output and income comes from innovations: and we know that there is more innovation in big cities than in small ones because output and income grow faster in big cities than in small ones. For this reason it seems safer to rely for proof of the greater dynamism of big cities on statistics regarding the quality of enterprises in large and small towns, value of output per manyear, rate of growth in value of output, proportion of the labour force engaged in R & D, numbers of persons with advanced degrees in science, engineering, management economics, etc. On these grounds the case seems clear.

At the end of his discussion, Trudeau himself comes round to something very close to this point of view. "La grande ville," he says, "apparaît alors comme un foyer majeur de modernisme, d'innovation et d'information, susceptibles de rayonner sur sa zone d'influence régionale ou nationale." The big city plays a major role in the national and international *diffusion* of innovation because (1) it is part of a network of exchange of technological and economic information and (2) the large city can more easily receive innovations because its socio-economic framework is more flexible and its infrastructure more complete. Trudeau also recognizes that innovations have more impact if they lead to a whole complex of industrial activity, as in the case of petro-chemicals (witness Houston, Texas) or iron and steel (witness Pittsburgh) than if they are in the vanguard of scientific advance, but narrow in scope. For industrial *complexes* the larger cities offer many economies of scale. Big international airports, a stock exchange, container ports, conference centres — any region and indeed any country can support only so many of them, and they tend to seek the facilities of the larger cities.

On balance, however, Trudeau remains unconvinced, particularly by the suggestion that Montreal, if its economy were strengthened, could serve as a development pole generating spread effects to the entire province. He quotes the distinguished French economist, Jacques Boudeville, who knew Montreal and Quebec well and whose death at mid-career a few years ago deprived the field of urban and regional economics of one of its most creative thinkers:

> Le rapport HMR n'avait émis qu'une hypothèse de recherche; il n'avait à peu près rien mesuré. Les seules mesures fournies dans ce rapport indiquaient que Montréal n'était pas tellement un concurrent des autres espaces urbains québécois de sorte que lorsqu'il y avait migration de l'industrie, c'était surtout au profit des autres provinces canadiennes... L'essence du rapport consistait à dire qu'à partir de la prémisse que l'innovation n'est possible que dans les grands ensembles urbains, Montréal est le seul candidat à la fonction du pôle de développement au Québec. Le rapport recommandait justement, entre autres choses, de faire des recherches pour que Montréal en vienne à irradier des effets de croissance.[8]

Boudeville spent much of his career seeking policies that would stem the growth of Paris and spread industrialization, urbanization, and employment to other French cities. He tended to identify, to my mind wrongly, the relationship of Paris with France with that of Montreal with Quebec. Wrongly, because in the first place Montreal is not a "Quebec" city to the same degree that Paris is a "France" city; Montreal is not even the capital, and is perhaps more linked to the rest of Canada than to Quebec. But even more important, Quebec does not have cities like Lyons, Marseilles, Toulouse, Lille, which are major industrial centres in their own right, to which industries can be dispersed. But Boudeville, in tackling the problem of agglomeration in Paris, was one of the first regional economists to understand that a city does not necessarily generate spread effects to the rest of the country — or even to its own peripheral region — just because it is big. The HMR report was not so naive as to think that all problems of retarded subregions of Quebec could be solved by encouraging the expansion of the economic region of Montreal. It did recognize the need for specific policies and projects in these retarded regions, and for policies directed towards strengthening Montreal's capacity to diffuse innovation, technological progress, and thus rising employment and incomes. Nonetheless, it is fair to say that the report left the very strong impression that the authors regarded Montreal as a true development pole for the region of Quebec. Indeed one of the authors, André Raynauld, who became Chairman of the Economic Council of Canada after publication of the HMR Report, seemed still to hold that view in 1976:

> In a large degree, the greater autonomy of the Canadian economy is the result of the economic and cultural output (essor) of certain large cities like Toronto, Montreal, and Vancouver. It flows also from numerous connections which are focussed in these cities, but also between each of them and its periphery. Such a fabric of relations has given birth to an autonomous structure of institutions and complementary activities of which the connections with such American cities as New York, Chicago, and San Francisco are progressively extended.[9]

On this score I now find myself closer to Boudeville than to Raynauld. Expansion of the Montreal economy may not "stifle" development elsewhere in Quebec, as Boudeville once insisted; but neither does it do much for the *rest* of Quebec. No doubt, it could be used as the basis for policies to promote development elsewhere in the province, but such promotion would require active policy intervention. It will not occur automatically. At the time of his death Boudeville was working on a very promising approach, in which urban and regional policy was to be defined in terms of a whole system of cities, and designed to fill in gaps in their inter-relationships in such a way as to maximize the positive interactions of growth in one city on growth in others, in all directions. I am convinced that it is in this direction that we must go.

A more recent study, prepared for the Economic Council of Canada with Fernand Martin (the "M" of "HMR,") as principal author, argues that seeping down from top to bottom of the urban structure is only one of four possible modes of diffusion of innovation.[10]

The others are diffusion "by epidemic," diffusion controlled by the economic and institutional environment, and diffusion determined by the particular characteristics of the enterprises involved. The analysis has the "on the one hand this, but on the other hand that" flavour all too common in contemporary economic analysis, and no very clear conclusions emerge. In the "epidemiology" model the spread innovations is likened to a "contagion." The shorter the distances involved, the better the network of communications, and the higher the populations densities, the more rapidly the contagion spreads. The authors suggest that this model has some application to minor, routine innovations of small enterprises, but not to the major innovations that account for fundamental technological change. The message of the "environment" model is, "it depends." In scientifically-oriented industry especially, the speed and direction of the spread of technology depend upon the economic and institutional environment, as in the Schumpeter theory of fluctuations and growth. The "particular characteristics" model takes another form of "it depends," but this time diffusion depends upon various attributes of the enterprises themselves. Distance, urban structure, and market structure may all be similar, and still the rate of diffusion may vary with the country, the region, or the industry. The authors believe that the two "it depends" models are not mutually exclusive.

In the "urban hierarchy" model innovations seep down from big cities to ever smaller ones, but particular innovations may stop their downward journey at some threshold of size. The authors find this model appropriate in the case of TV stations, telephone exchanges, and some services, but maintain that it fails to take account of distance and lacks sufficient empirical support to warrant general application. The authors also attempt to isolate a purely "regional" factor which is present when there is a systematic difference in the diffusion process among regions.

The models are tested against Canadian experience with computers, electric furnaces (for steel), trusses, containers for international marine transport, special presses for newsprint, and shopping centres. The final conclusions are well buttressed with cautions to the reader regarding their limitations and uncertainties; but the authors find that Ontario was the leader and the Atlantic provinces the laggard in most cases, with British Columbia second and Quebec and the prairies tied for third (or second last). Assuming that technological progress raises productivity by 1.25 percent per year and that the lags in introducing innovations found in the case studies are typical of each regional economy as a whole, the lags would cause a retardation of growth of 6.9 percent in the Atlantic provinces (behind Ontario) and of 3.1 percent in Quebec, which could explain a large proportion of the actual differences in productivity.

To the extent that it is possible to generalize from this study, it appears to confirm the suspicion that Quebec is lacking in entrepreneurship in comparison to Ontario, which comes as no surprise. It does not, however, tell us much about the relationship of this deficiency to the urban structure. It casts relatively little

114

light upon the question we are specifically raising: would the rate of technological progress be more rapid in Quebec if a substantial proportion of Montreal's population and economic activity were transferred to other urban centres within the province? There is nothing in the study to suggest that it would. To answer the question we would need to determine the impact of dispersion on the volume and nature of innovations as well as on the rate of diffusion. But we need not insist upon the "seeping down" theory in order to state that to achieve a high rate of technological progress, any urban system needs at least one large and dynamic metropolitan centre within it; and that for the province of Quebec, it is better if that centre is located within the province rather than outside it.

Montreal: Neo-Colonial Enclave?

We turn now to a still more serious question: would not a policy of encouraging the economic expansion of the Montreal region, willy-nilly, merely aggravate its status as a neo-colonial enclave within the North American economy and society? Of what use is Montreal to Quebec, or even to Canada, if it is merely an appendage to the American, West European, and Middle East economies, with the basic decisions regarding investment, employment, and output being taken in New York, Chicago, Los Angeles, Toronto, Tokyo, London, Paris, Milan, and Abu Dhabi?

This concern has been forcibly expressed by N.L. Gill, and he attacks the HMR Report on those grounds.[11] He first accuses the authors of the report of counselling the retarded regions of Quebec to wait passively for improvement in their situation for the diffusion of "spread effects" from Montreal; meanwhile they should integrate themselves with economic activity of which Montreal is the centre, or empty themselves to the benefit of other urban centres, of which Montreal is the most important. This statement is, to be sure, a caricature of the recommendations of the HMR Report, but sometimes caricatures can be useful in focussing attention on real problems. Gill continues in pointing out that "imperialist domination" of the Montreal economy by foreigners would intensify the tendency towards neo-colonial domination of the entire Quebec economy; the mines and forests of Abitibi, Mauricie, Côte-Nord and Gaspésie are already, in his view, excessively subject to exploitation by foreign capitalists, and if Montreal goes the same way, what is left for the indigenous

115

Québécois ? By accepting foreign domination, "l'économie québécoise demeurera une économie désarticulée, qui n'existe qu'en fonction de l'économie dominatrice dont l'orientation du développement échappe aux décisions de la collectivité québécoise, et dont 'l'équilibre' est toujours menacé par les fluctuations mondiales." [12]

Gill's choice of terminology and of vehicle for publication of his views might be grounds for classifying him among the "radical political economists." But a very similar view has been expressed by Gilles Paquet, Dean of the Faculty of Administration of the University of Ottawa, who is not usually so classified. "Il peut sembler fort dangereux de parier sur Montréal s'il pouvait s'ensuivre un pattern de développement violemment dualiste et des formes de colonialisme intérieur..." [13]

It must be admitted that there is a large element of truth in these arguments. The position of "second-class cities" in any urban hierarchy is always a difficult one; and as we have seen, rather than being the "Queen City" of an independent economic system — whether we speak of Quebec or of all of Canada — Montreal is part of an urban system that extends throughout North America, and beyond, to Europe, Japan, and the Middle East. In that structure Montreal is far from being the Queen. Today Montreal is second to Toronto even within Canada, in terms of investment, output, income, industry, commerce, and finance. Montreal may be a "primate city" within Quebec as a geographically and politically defined entity; but Montreal is not linked primarily to the Quebec economy. The city operates in a worldwide "economic space." Such a city really has only three policy options: to accept whatever level of output, income, standard of living, and cultural life is consistent with rejection of all foreign enterprise (and in this context, "foreign" should probably include anglophone Canadian enterprises); to accept a degree of "foreign" domination for a certain period, until the city has reached a size and a quality of economic, social and cultural activity where it becomes one of the dominant rather than a dependent city in the structure; or quickly to develop indigenous entrepreneurship in a quantity and of a quality which will permit the city to become dominant without going through a prolonged period of transition during which domination remains in the hands of foreigners.

Obviously the third solution is the ideal. The argument for it has been well put by Gerald Fortin:

Il ne suffit pas qu'au point de vue du management nous soyons reliés à l'extérieur, il faut aussi pouvoir agir sur l'extérieur; ... À première vue la situation de Québec et de Montréal apparaît comme celle d'une économie dominée semblable à celle de la plupart de l'Amérique latine. ... Peut-on vraiment parler de développement si la croissance est basée sur l'exploitation des matières premières et le développement sur une production innovatrice que nous devons à Montréal ou ailleurs que si nous réunissons (seul ou avec d'autres), non seulement pour nous, mais surtout pour les autres, c'est-à-dire si notre industrie est présente sur le marché international.[14]

Unfortunately, however, it is not possible to breed a race of indigenous entrepreneurs overnight (although Harvard psychologist David McClelland thinks it can be done rather quickly if there is a massive and appropriate effort at training indigenous entrepreneurs).[15] It was for this reason that the HMR Report proposed a combination of options two and three, rather than relying on three alone. For Montreal and Quebec to reject all foreign enterprise — by nationalizing what there is and refusing entry to any new ones, let us say — might create such a dearth of capital, entrepreneurship, and scientific and engineering skills that indigenous Québécois entrepreneurship could not recover fast enough to put the Montreal (and Quebec) economy in a position to compete on a world scale. Better to complete the build-up of indigenous capacities first, and gradually reduce or eliminate foreign "dominance" later, from a position of strength rather than a position of weakness. (Orthodox Marxist theory would lead to the same conclusion.)

It should be emphasized that Montreal is far from being alone in its position of dependence, despite a position of comparative dominance *within* the national economy. Toronto, despite its current greater strength than Montreal's, is still essentially dependent too. Moreover, a good many national capitals throughout the world are in the same position. Professor François Perroux has contended in one of his more recent publications that no Latin American city has yet become a "development pole" in its own right, and that all of them remain dependent upon European capitals (and, perhaps, Japan and the Middle East).[16] Yet São Paulo, Rio de Janeiro, Buenos Aires, Caracas, and Mexico City are all considerably bigger cities than Montreal. Sydney and Melbourne in Australia also remain dependent, and they too are bigger than Montreal.

Nor is the dilemma posed by the idea that the major metropolitan centre has become "too big" and is "stifling" growth of other cities in the hierarchy of the national or regional economy, while at the same time the city remains "too small" to become dominant or even independent in the larger international hierarchy of which it is a part, unique to Montreal. For instance, some years ago I assisted the Malaysian government in designing a strategy for urban growth and regional development. The government felt at the time that the capital city, Kuala Lumpur, then a city of about 750,000 inhabitants, had become "too big" and was stifling industrialization elsewhere in the country, and particularly in the retarded regions to the east and northeast. The policy was to restrain industrial growth in Kuala Lumpur and encourage it on the east coast, especially in Kuantan, a small town with less than 100,000 population, selected as a growth pole for the east. (The analogy with Quebec is strengthened by the fact that the industry, commerce, and finance of the cities are controlled by the minority group of Chinese, while the majority Malay group is on the land and controls the government; also, the poorest regions were those with the heaviest concentration of Malays). Two things were learned from this experiment. First, by a combination of incentives, investment in infrastructure, and very heavy capital investment in resource development in a rich region to the south, it was indeed possible to convert Kuantan into a dynamic industrial city; but the growth of Kuantan did little or nothing for the poor people in the poor states (Trengganu and Kelantan) to the north of Kuantan. Second, since the Kuala Lumpur economy was still heavily dependent on foreign capital, technology, entrepreneurship and management, and had not nearly arrived at the point of being able to stand on its own feet, efforts to deflect enterprises away from Kuala Lumpur were likely to deflect them out of the country altogether. While being the national capital and much the largest city in the country, Kuala Lumpur was a minor city in an international hierarchy which included Singapore, Hong Kong, and Tokyo, as well as Bangkok, Sydney, and London. In short, developing a city and its peripheral region on the basis of indigenous entrepreneurship is a very hard thing to do if the indigenous entrepreneurship does not exist.

One more point should be stressed. The problem is not very different whether the solution is sought within a capitalist or a socialist framework. The insistence on entrepreneurship and innovation as a basis for development is too often taken as a recommendation for domination by *private* enterprise. Not so. As I have argued elsewhere, the crucial role of entrepreneurship and innovation in economic development is not tied to the capitalist system. Socialist countries too have need of new techniques, new products, new resources, and new organizational systems; and the men who see and seize the opportunity to introduce these "ways of doing things differently," who bring together the factors of production to do all that, and organize them into effective enterprises, play a significant role in economic progress and tend to be rewarded for this role in one way or another. Moreover, even socialist countries have not found it easy to eliminate regional gaps, despite their greater degree of direct control over industrial location. As for the classic efforts to reduce regional gaps within non-socialist frameworks — the Italian south and the Brazilian northeast — the result of a massive effort has been essentially to raise the *rate* of growth in the retarded region to that of the advanced region; so that, given the wide disparities in levels of per capita output and income at the beginning of the planned intervention, absolute disparities continue to increase. It should never be imagined that eliminating regional gaps is an easy task. I do not believe that strengthening Montreal will solve the problems of Gaspésie/Bas Saint-Laurent; but I firmly believe that weakening Montreal will weaken not merely Quebec, but Canada as a whole.

CHAPTER 5

GROWTH AND CHANGE: CANADA, QUEBEC, MONTREAL

Montreal, we have seen, is a Canadian metropolis, not just the major city of Quebec. It is affected by events and trends in all of Canada, in North America, in Europe, in the world. Yet no city is completely detached from its hinterland. For Montreal the hinterland is first of all the plain of Montreal, roughly contiguous with the administrative region of Montreal; and beyond that, the province of Quebec and, to a lesser degree, eastern Ontario. Moreover, Montreal comprises more than half the Quebec economy; and as "the second biggest French-speaking city in the world," it is linguistically and culturally a *French*-Canadian city. The fate of Montreal cannot be divorced from the fate of Quebec. The reverse is also true; there are fundamental interactions and feedbacks in both directions. Why has the province containing Canada's leading metropolitan centre lagged continuously behind the Canadian average, and still further behind neighbouring Ontario, in terms of per capita income? How does the fact that Montreal is situated in a lagging province, and next to a lagging region of another province, affect the development of the city itself? In this chapter, we look at growth and structural changes in Canada, in Quebec, and in Montreal, and the feedbacks among them, in order to understand Montreal's present problems better.

A myth

Among the most frequently repeated explanations for the relative economic and social retardation of Quebec is a myth : that Quebec has lagged because it remained for a long time after Confederation a traditional, agricultural society, typified by the *habitant* in his village. Thus Professor Everett C. Hughes, eminent sociologist, then at McGill and a specialist on French-Canadian society, wrote in 1943 :

> The people who have undergone such industrial invasions (Industrial Revolution brought in from outside) are of many kinds. Some have been completely outside the sway of European culture. Others are of the European culture but have stabilized their life about the earlier and simpler institutions of the capitalistic system of production and exchange. The French Canadians are of the latter sort... The French Canadian province of Canada is, indeed the seat of North America's most stable and archaic rural society.[1]

Philippe Garigue, professor of Anthropology and later dean of the Faculty of Social Sciences at the University of Montreal, destroyed this legend in no uncertain terms :

> "The argument that French Canada is essentially rural in character has been so extensively repeated that it has become 'myth' supporting numberless assertations."[2]

> "Traditional French-Canadian culture has had traits which allow individual French Canadians to adapt themselves without too great an effort to the industrial changes. French-Canadian culture is a variation of the total North American culture, not something completely different from it."[3]

The truth is that Quebec has never been significantly less industrialized than Ontario. At the beginning of the nineteenth century Lower Canada (Quebec) was more advanced than Upper Canada (Ontario) because the latter was still essentially empty. As Prof. O.J. Firestone puts it :

> At the turn of the 19th century, Lower Canada was the key dynamic region of British North America, with Quebec the gateway to the east across the Atlantic and Montreal the gateway to the west, the interior of a vast continent. Commerce using the St. Lawrence and

the ocean route was expanding rapidly. The fur trade was still flourishing. Wheat production had become a significant source of income for the habitant population, with demand expanding both for local use and for exports. And a beginning was made to develop forest resources leading to the establishment of a thriving industry building wooden sailing vessels that plied the Atlantic both for sale abroad and for operation by residents of the territory. At the turn of the 19th century, Lower Canada had an estimated population of about 210,000.

By comparison, Upper Canada was largely a wilderness, with the first significant impetus to settlement coming from the influx of some 11,000 United Empire Loyalists who moved from the United States northward in the 1780's and the 1790's. By 1800 Upper Canada's population still only numbered an estimated 40,000 spread thinly around Lake Ontario and along some of the rivers coming from the interior like the Ottawa.[4]

For 1851 Firestone estimates that for Canada as a whole 32.0 percent of value added was generated in agriculture, 13.6 percent in forest operations, 18.3 percent in manufacturing, 18.9 percent in the tertiary sector, plus 4.2 percent in construction, and 1.2 percent in fishing and mining. In that year the populations of the two provinces were much the same; 952,000 in Upper Canada and 890,000 in Lower Canada. The structure of output and employment was much the same too.

By 1870, we have seen, Montreal had established itself as Canada's leading industrial centre, a position it did not lose until the 1950s. Montreal already dominated Quebec manufacturing by 1870, with over one-third of the total employees and nearly half the value added. Ontario manufacturing activities were (and remained) much more dispersed. Toronto accounted for less than 10 percent of either employment or value added, and total manufacturing production in Ontario already exceeded that of Quebec.

From 1911 on we have census data of employment by major sector, which permits a more accurate comparison of structure and of structural change. Figures are presented for all provinces (except Newfoundland) in Table 37 from 1911 to 1981. The picture that emerges is clear. Throughout this whole period Quebec has been more industrialized, in terms of employment, than Canada as a whole, and only slightly less industrialized than Ontario. Moreover, the rate of structural change has been virtually the same in Quebec as in Ontario.

TABLE 37

Distribution in Percentage of the Work Force Aged 15 years and over, by Occupation and Sex, Canada and Provinces, 1911-1981

		P.E.I.		N.S.		N.B.		Quebec		Ontario		Manitoba		Saskatchewan		Alberta		B.C.		Canada	
		M.	F.	M.	F.	M.	F.	M.	F.	M.	F.	M.	F.	M.	F.	M.	F.	M.	F.	M.	F.
1911																					
Agr.		68.54	14.82	31.76	6.44	43.51	5.55	36.67	3.06	36.02	3.74	44.32	4.14	67.31	12.41	53.01	10.65	12.69	2.46	38.97	4.44
Others	1	5.07	0.43	23.19	0.13	7.77	0.04	3.81	0.01	3.60	0.06	1.02	0.01	1.48	0.25	4.42	0.03	16.48	0.46	4.83	0.07
	2	14.28	25.25	26.51	26.07	31.24	31.89	36.85	40.81	38.43	42.28	28.88	27.79	16.63	17.01	23.22	22.39	41.86	34.16	33.57	37.30
	3	12.12	59.50	18.53	67.36	17.48	62.51	22.67	56.10	21.95	53.92	25.77	68.06	14.57	70.33	19.35	66.93	28.96	62.93	21.63	58.17
1921																					
Agr.		66.61	11.46	30.38	5.17	40.47	5.09	32.99	2.64	31.22	2.77	46.12	4.03	70.95	9.08	56.63	8.10	17.67	2.92	37.90	3.68
Others	1	4.66	0.05	18.42	0.05	6.91	0.03	2.84	0.01	1.97	0.00	0.52	0.01	0.48	0.00	4.78	0.01	13.75	0.02	4.21	0.01
	2	17.02	21.58	30.16	25.28	34.02	30.73	39.75	41.70	41.47	44.79	28.55	33.02	14.66	20.79	19.26	27.09	38.17	32.71	34.65	38.62
	3	11.67	66.77	20.90	69.32	18.51	63.98	24.04	54.93	25.15	52.24	24.65	62.76	13.85	70.06	18.20	64.70	30.19	64.23	23.03	57.36
1931																					
Agr.		63.84	13.00	2.78	4.66	38.09	4.50	26.82	2.28	27.08	2.67	40.36	4.14	66.58	9.58	56.41	9.03	16.05	3.25	33.73	3.61
Others	1	5.25	0.00	18.58	0.09	6.96	0.14	3.32	0.02	2.67	0.08	2.63	0.12	0.98	0.26	4.52	0.02	12.12	0.11	4.52	0.07
	2	16.98	21.43	30.27	22.55	35.00	24.16	41.07	37.59	41.14	39.18	31.28	28.46	16.78	16.25	19.96	21.03	38.72	29.31	35.40	33.83
	3	13.88	65.52	23.32	72.68	19.90	71.15	28.75	60.19	29.05	57.99	25.68	67.20	15.64	73.91	19.08	69.92	33.07	67.31	26.31	62.46
1941																					
Agr.		62.58	6.10	23.94	1.73	34.25	2.36	26.72	1.34	23.11	1.68	41.96	3.01	67.43	7.42	56.04	5.91	15.49	2.55	31.50	2.26
Others	1	6.81	0.06	19.65	0.01	14.82	0.04	5.18	0.03	3.88	0.03	4.08	0.10	1.60	0.12	4.64	0.04	13.16	0.06	5.97	0.04
	2	14.56	14.51	29.02	23.53	26.59	24.07	37.70	41.03	42.98	43.90	27.61	30.05	14.54	17.47	19.17	22.33	36.98	29.64	34.57	37.08
	3	15.95	79.20	27.17	74.65	24.14	73.33	29.99	57.34	29.73	54.16	26.20	66.75	16.27	74.90	20.00	71.61	34.04	67.60	27.68	60.41
1951																					
Agr.		45.05	4.20	12.88	1.17	19.37	1.19	16.47	2.16	13.42	2.14	30.28	5.09	56.43	11.35	38.36	5.31	7.76	1.59	19.30	2.77
Others	1	7.82	0.07	15.18	0.04	14.94	0.04	4.60	0.01	2.78	0.02	2.16	0.02	2.16	0.02	1.12	0.01	8.83	0.09	5.33	0.02
	2	20.62	29.42	34.31	33.63	33.62	36.53	43.23	49.81	47.98	52.93	34.66	43.76	19.61	27.17	26.90	35.50	41.78	42.31	40.55	46.89
	3	25.67	65.20	36.12	63.82	30.49	60.56	33.82	46.68	34.84	43.84	32.16	50.33	22.35	60.72	30.82	58.39	40.17	54.81	33.58	49.18
1961																					
Agr.		32.76	8.02	6.69	0.83	9.16	1.28	9.09	3.20	8.78	3.30	21.32	7.70	43.18	15.94	25.16	10.25	5.07	1.97	12.21	4.30
Others	1	8.52	0.27	10.21	0.03	10.41	0.09	3.75	0.02	2.41	0.02	2.08	0.01	1.70	0.03	2.33	0.02	5.49	0.06	3.85	0.03
	2	24.96	29.03	36.01	34.31	37.49	35.04	44.03	45.28	46.19	46.59	36.23	39.13	23.84	26.54	31.92	34.48	42.56	40.91	41.54	42.56
	3	31.65	59.90	45.07	62.81	40.64	61.01	40.12	48.27	40.09	48.29	37.91	50.97	29.01	54.65	38.26	52.74	43.87	54.02	39.75	50.64

SOURCE: B.F.S., 1961 Census.
Note: Agr.: Agriculture; Others 1: other primary activities; 2: industry; 3: services.

1971

Agr.	22.5	2.7	—	3.7	—	4.7	2.1	4.8	2.1	14.1	6.7	33.0	14.2	15.1	8.9	4.0	2.3	7.1	3.4
Others 1	6.5	6.5	—	5.7	—	2.2	—	1.4	—	1.3	—	1.4	—	1.2	—	4.1	—	2.5	—
2	23.3	39.1	17.0	42.7	34.7	41.5	42.9	43.2	45.0	35.4	32.3	26.5	27.9	33.6	33.6	40.7	39.8	40.3	40.3
3	20.5	44.4	64.9	39.6	50.0	43.0	40.9	43.4	43.6	41.8	50.3	32.3	44.7	41.6	47.0	43.1	47.0	42.4	44.7

1: other primary activities; 2: industry; 3: services.
SOURCE: (1971) STAT CAN, Cat. 94-716.

1981

Agr.	13.2	3.7	3.1	1.1	3.2	1.1	3.3	1.1	4.2	2.1	11.4	3.7	24.3	8.3	8.6	3.7	2.8	1.8	5.3	2.2
Others 1	9.2	1.5	7.1	0.4	7.2	1.0	2.1	0.1	1.2	0.1	1.8	0.1	2.3	0.2	3.1	0.1	4.5	0.4	2.7	0.2
2	20.1	36.5	27.1	40.0	28.5	42.5	33.2	47.0	34.1	46.9	27.8	41.6	18.4	34.6	22.9	42.0	30.0	42.1	30.8	44.8
3	54.4[a]	55.7	59.3	55.5	57.0	51.8	58.1	47.7	57.7	48.6	56.3	53.1	52.7	55.2	63.3	53.1	60.3	53.9	58.4	50.2

1: other primary activities; 2: industry; 3: services.
SOURCE: (1981) STAT CAN, Cat. 92-927.
a) Because not stated workers are not included, the sum may not total 100.

Classification 1961

Agricultural
(1) Fishing, hunting and trapping; Logging; Mining and quarrying
(2) Proprietary and managerial; Clerical; Manufacturing and mechanical; Labourers
(3) Professional; Construction, Transportation; Commercial; Financial; Service

Classification 1971

Agriculture: Farmers and farm workers
(1) Loggers and related workers; Fishermen, trappers and hunters; Miners, quarrymen and related workers
(2) Craftsmen, production process and related workers; Labourers; Clerical
(3) Sales; Service and recreation occupations; Transport and communication occupations; Managerial; Professional and Technical

Classification 1981

Agriculture: Farming, horticultural and animal husbandry occupations
(1) Fishing, trapping and related occupations; Forestry and logging occupations; Mining and quarrying including oil and gas field occupations
(2) Clerical and related occupations; Processing occupations; Machining and related occupations; Product fabricating, assembling and repairing occupations; Material handling and related occupations; Other crafts and equipment operating occupations
(3) Managerial, administrative and related occupations; Occupations in natural sciences, engineering and mathematics; Occupations in social sciences and related fields; Occupations in Religion; Teaching and related occupations; Occupations in medicine and health; Artistic, literary, recreational and related occupations; Sales occupations; Services occupations; Construction trades occupations; Transport equipment operating occupations

Note: We have maintained for 1971 and 1981 the *clerical* occupation in the industry sector in order to respect uniformity with the period 1911-1961. Thus, the percentages in the services sector do not necessarily correspond to existing figures.

If there are anomalies in the structure and structural change among regions, they are not in Quebec. Saskatchewan, for example, had an extraordinarily high proportion of its labour force still in agriculture, and an unusually low proportion in industry and services, for so prosperous a region ; but this fact obviously reflects the province's comparative advantage in agriculture. The Atlantic provinces had a remarkably high proportion in services, reflecting in part the importance of shipping, government, and the armed forces, and in "other primary" reflecting the continuing importance of fishing and forestry. But if we wish to explain the retardation of Quebec's economic development, we must look elsewhere than at the relative importance of industry, services, and agriculture. And if Montreal has problems, they are not due to the failure of Quebec to industrialize.

Table 38 presents some corroborative evidence in a different form. Here we see that the structure of income sources in Quebec is virtually the same as the Canadian average, except that Quebec derives considerably *less* of its income from agriculture than does Canada as a whole.

Charts 2 and 3 provide still further evidence. Quebec lags persistently behind Ontario in manufacturing production, but the growth rates are virtually identical and the gap does not increase. Much the same is true of farm production. Mining production also remains lower in Quebec than in Ontario, but throughout much of the period 1870 to 1967, Quebec mineral output increased faster than that of Ontario.

Urbanization

Urbanization came slowly to Canada and was confined to a narrow strip close to the American border. As late as 1901 there were only two cities (Montreal and Toronto) with more than 200,000 people. The capital city, Ottawa, had a population of 60,000, Quebec City also had 60,000, and Hamilton, Ontario 52,000. No other city approached 50,000 population. On the eve of World War I this situation had changed relatively little, except that Vancouver had enjoyed an expansion of nearly 400 percent in the decade from 1901 to 1911, reaching a population of 100,000, and the development of the wheat economy brought a more than 300 percent growth to Winnipeg, making it a city of 136,000 people. In terms of absolute numbers, this growth was small in comparison to that of the established centres, especially

TABLE 38

Categories of Personal Income in Quebec and in Canada
(in Percentage of Total Income)

Categories		1946	1951	1956	1961	1966	1971	1976	1981
Workers' renumeration	Quebec	63	69	70	70	73	71	70	66
	Canada	56	63	67	68		70	70	67
Farmers' net income	Quebec	6	6	3	2	2	1	1	1
	Canada	10	11	5	3		2	2	2
Net income of individual	Quebec	13	10	11	10	8	8	5	4
non-agricultural contractors	Canada	13	12	12	11		8	5	4
Interests and dividends	Quebec	6	7	6	7	8	8	8	12
	Canada	6	7	6	7		8	9	14
Transfers	Quebec	11	7	9	10	9	12	16	16
	Canada	12	6	8	9		12	13	13
Personal income total	Quebec	100	100	100	100	100	100	100	99
	Canada	100	100	100	100		100	99	99

SOURCE: Statistics Canada, National income and expenditure accounts.
Statistics Canada, National income and expenditure accounts, 1969-1983, Cat. 13-201.
Comptes économiques des revenus et des dépenses : Québec 1961-1981.
Bureau de la statistique du Québec.

127

CHART 2

Growth Indicators

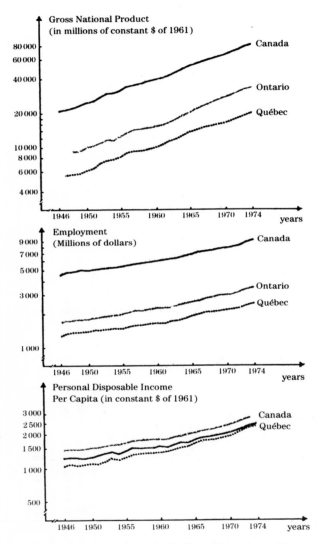

Gross National Product
(in millions of constant $ of 1961)

Canada

Ontario

Québec

80 000
60 000
40 000
20 000
10 000
8 000
6 000
4 000

1946 1950 1955 1960 1965 1970 1974   years

Employment
(Millions of dollars)

Canada

Ontario

Québec

9 000
7 000
5 000
3 000
1 000

1946 1950 1955 1960 1965 1970 1974   years

Personal Disposable Income
Per Capita (in constant $ of 1961)

Canada
Québec

3 000
2 500
2 000
1 500
1 000
500

1946 1950 1955 1960 1965 1970 1974   years

SOURCE : Gouvernement du Québec. Comptes nationaux du Québec. Ministère de l'Industrie et du Commerce — Government of Ontario,
Ontario Statistical Review, Toronto, — Statistics Canada, National
Income and Expenditure Accounts, The Labour Force, Prices
and Price Indexes, Canadian Statistical Review.

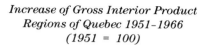

CHART 3

Increase of Gross Interior Product
Regions of Quebec 1951–1966
(1951 = 100)

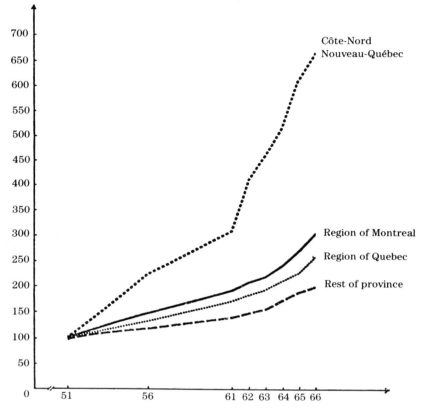

Source: R. Jouandet-Bernadat. Une expérience de comptabilité régionale et ses enseignements. L'Actualité économique, January–March, 1971, pp. 19–38.

Montreal, which was a city of about half a million when the war began.

Vancouver has continued to be a high-growth city ever since. Winnipeg's fortunes, however, have been very different. The collapse of the wheat boom after World War I retarded the growth of the wheat economy's "capital city"; between 1911 and 1931

Winnipeg grew less rapidly than the total population — or more slowly than Toronto and Montreal — even in percentage terms. During the 1930s and 40s, Winnipeg hardly grew at all; the impact of the great depression was particularly severe in the prairie provinces, and when World War II brought employment opportunities elsewhere, there was a large-scale movement out of the region and a long-delayed change in both the geographic and occupational structure. During World War II, the war industries were concentrated in the Montreal and Toronto areas, and there was net emigration from the prairies to seize job opportunities in those areas. As a consequence, the centre of population moved east.

The smaller mid-western centres, such as Calgary, Edmonton, Regina, and Saskatoon, grew rapidly between 1911 and 1931, but their growth too was retarded by the great depression and the war. The smaller industrial centres of Ontario, such as London, Oshawa, Windsor, and Hamilton had fairly high growth rates between 1911 and 1931. It slowed during the depression, and accelerated again during and after World War II. Least dynamic were the older centres of the Atlantic provinces.

The fifties brought a new spurt of urban growth to Canada, without affecting very much the distribution of population among major regions. Total population grew 30 percent in the decade, "urban" population (people living in centres of more than 1,000 persons) grew 47 percent and population in cities of more than 100,000 (in 1961) grew by 59 percent.

Montreal increased its relative importance in the Canadian economy with a growth in its metropolitan region (area of 1961) of 43.3 percent. Toronto's metropolitan region grew by 50.7 percent, much faster than the total population and somewhat faster than the urban population. Ottawa and Vancouver (metropolitan regions) expanded at rates comparable to the growth of the total urban population, while Winnipeg and Quebec City grew at about the same rate as the total population. The most spectacular growth took place in the four leading cities of Saskatchewan and Alberta — Edmonton, Calgary, Saskatoon, and Regina. Oil and nickle contributed to this growth, although the direct on-site employment provided by the petroleum discoveries was limited. Perhaps more important was the fact that these cities together had become large enough to constitute a significant market in their own right, attracting market-oriented and some footloose industries. The newer industrial cities of Ontario (London,

Hamilton) had growth rates of around 50 percent, above that of the total population, but somewhat below that of the aggregate urban population. Halifax enjoyed a modest resurgence of growth, while St. John, New Brunswick remained virtually stagnant. In most cities the growth was faster in 1951-56 than in 1956-61, but Montreal, Vancouver, and Ottawa enjoyed slight acceleration of growth in the last half of the decade.

Thus up to 1961 the pattern of urban growth in Canada did not remove the differences in economic characteristics among major regions, which remain much sharper than they are in other large, resource-rich, industrialized countries of recent settlement, such as the United States or Australia. If anything, the industrial heartland was more concentrated in the Montreal-to-Windsor area than ever before. Canada had yet to achieve the wide geographic spread of urbanization and industrialization that characterized the American or Australian economy. In 1961, the ratio of rural to total population was 23 percent in Ontario, 26 percent in Quebec, and 27.4 percent in British Columbia; but it was 36 percent in Manitoba, 36.7 percent in Alberta, and 57 percent in Saskatchewan. In that year there were still only three cities with populations above half a million, and of these three, Toronto and Montreal, the only real metropolitan centres, were still growing faster than Vancouver.

There were several reasons for the slow rate of urbanization in Canada. One of these was that total population remained low and population density very thin. As we have seen, the settlement of Ontario scarcely began until the beginning of the nineteenth century and the opening up of the prairies and British Columbia came at least a half century later. Natural increase of the population was not high, for while birth rates were fairly high (36.2 per thousand in 1851 and 27.2 in 1900) death rates were high too (18.4 in 1851 and still 16.2 in 1900), mainly because of a very high infant mortality rate. During the period 1851-1870 there was enough net immigration to bring overall growth rates to just over 2.0 percent per year on the average, raising total population from 2.5 million to 3.7 million. But then a curious thing happened, for so young a nation and so empty a land: the net immigration turned into net emigration. Partly because of the great depression of the 1870s and 1880s, emigration from Canada, mainly to the United States, exceeded immigration into Canada. During the peak years of the outflow, 1882-85, 350,000 immigrants arrived and 370,000 emigrants departed. Over the whole second half of the nineteenth century, some 2.1 million people came to Canada, while 2.2 million left.

Second, the financial crashes in New York and Vienna in 1873, which marked the beginning of one of the worst "long wave" world recessions in history, led to tight money and dried up the flow of capital to Canada — and to Montreal. Once again we see how faraway events can affect the life of Canada's metropolis. Both industrialization projects and investment in the infrastructure (transport, energy, housing) needed for industrialization had to be postponed. Neither the French nor the British governments had encouraged in their colonies industrialization of a sort that might lead to competition with enterprises at home; and when Canada finally became an independent nation the economic conditions were not favourable for industrialization and urbanization.

Third, Canada throughout her economic history has been in a way "cursed" with abundant land, rich natural resources, cheap water transport and energy. So long as people could do reasonably well by tilling the soil and exploiting natural resources there seemed little reason to process these resources very much. Particularly in her pattern of foreign trade, Canada stayed close to her natural resource base. We moved from lumber to pulp and paper and then to newsprint, from wheat to flour, from cattle to beef. This kind of natural-resource-based development brings relatively slow industrialization and urbanization. Indeed, when the long-wave recession turned into a long-wave upswing about 1896, it was the prairies that boomed, responding to a high world price of wheat which made high costs of transport to the lakehead bearable. The wheat boom brought intense activity to the Port of Montreal. As Kenneth Buckley points out:

> The prairie frontier finally passed the critical margin separating potential from actual resources when the opportunity it afforded became definitely superior to alternative opportunities open to migrants. This shift in character of the frontier occurred quite suddenly in the mid-nineties. ... Two factors were fundamental. The interior of the continent is a single, continuous plain and the movement into western Canada was a natural extension of the American frontier after the occupation of more accessible free land in the United States. This natural movement of population was accelerated by a sharp upturn in the price of wheat in the mid-nineties.[5]

Railroad construction facilitated the westward movement, and the westward movement made more railway construction necessary. Mary Innis writes:

> After 1896 people poured into the West as they had poured into Upper Canada sixty years earlier. The railroad had provided them with easy access to the prairies, but settlement pushed rapidly into the back country and railroad lines followed population as well as preceded it.[6]

Montreal of course shared in the opening of the prairies, serving as the major port for the export of wheat and cattle, building grain elevators, becoming the major Canadian centre for financing the railways, producing rails and railroad equipment, and sharing in the output of agricultural implements. Yet it is hard to say whether the net impact of development on the basis of natural resources pulled population away from the east, shifted the centre of gravity of population towards Toronto, led to increased concentration of heavy industry in Toronto and Hamilton, and delayed the development of the more sophisticated and "urban" manufacturing and service activities which are the only solid foundation for a strong urban economy of the mid to late twentieth century.

Harold Innis, with his usual perspicacity, has pointed out that development on the basis of a series of "staples" plus "cheap" water transport that in the long run turns out to be very expensive in capital investment has marked disadvantages. "It is difficult to summarize the importance of transportation as a factor in Canadian economic history," Professor Innis writes, but he has no doubt of

> "the overwhelming significance of the waterways and especially of the St. Lawrence. Cheap water transportation favoured the rapid exportation of staples and dependence on more highly industrialized countries for finishing products. It favoured the position of Canada as an exporter of staples to more highly industrialized areas in terms of fur, lumber and finally wheat, pulp and paper, and minerals... We cannot in this paper describe the economic effects of dependence on these staple products other than to indicate the drain which they made in transportation costs on the energy of the community. ... We can suggest the changes in technique, improvements in the waterways and the types of boats which are responsible for rather sharp fluctuations in economic development through the dependence on staple raw materials. It is scarcely necessary to describe the effects of dependence on water transportation on problems of finance involved

in the heavy expenditures which led ultimately to subsidies and government ownership."[7]

But of course, industrialization and urbanization did come to Canada, with profound effects on Montreal. Obviously, the industrial expansion and urban growth, accompanied by a continuous decline in the relative importance of farming, fishing, and forestry, which characterized the development of the country as a whole, converted Montreal into a large industrial city. Commerce and finance expanded along with the growth of base industries in the city. Less obviously, this same process sowed the seeds of Montreal's current problems.

One of the byproducts of the overall process was reduced population density on the plain of Montreal. Montreal's growth and industrial expansion, combined with the stagnation of agriculture in Quebec and the earlier and more rapid industrialization in the United States, encouraged emigration of farmers in the Montreal region. Some went to Montreal, some went to the United States. The population of the plain had grown rapidly up to 1851, from 10,500 inhabitants in 1765 to more than 41,000 in 1790, 160,000 in 1831 and 240,000 in 1851. But then the rate of growth tapered off. During the decade following, the population of the plain grew by only 27,000. Then came the decline: 245,000 in 1871, the same in 1881, 236,000 in 1891, and 232,000 in 1901. The early decades of the twentieth century brought a temporary reversal of trend. In 1931 the population was back up to 260,000. Nonetheless, the population in that year was 7,000 less then it had been in 1861. After 1931 the situation changed again; there was a modest increase in population, but not because people were returning to the land but because the industrialization of Montreal was starting to spill out onto the plain. Thus the counties with industrial satellite towns of Montreal grew, while others continued to lose population. On the eve of World War II, the *countryside* of the region of Montreal had lost close to one-third of its population. It is not known precisely how the emigration was divided between Montreal and the United States; but Professor Blanchard believes that up to 1900 it was about the same and that after that the majority of migrants went to Montreal. And of course, farmers from other parts of Quebec, especially those most disadvantaged, also flocked to Montreal.

This kind of interaction between urban growth and regional development is by no means unknown elsewhere. Something of the kind happened in New England with the growth of Boston, and in New York and Pennsylvania with the growth of New York City and Philadelphia. The same phenomenon occurred again, much later, in the Houston area of Texas. Between 1920 and 1940 the growth of Houston brought increased population density to its peripheral region. Between 1940 and 1960 the accelerated development of Houston brought depopulation in the nearby counties of east Texas. Migration from farm to factory, reducing population pressure on the land and permitting industrial expansion, is one of the ways in which economic development takes place. But this traditional pattern of structural change proved to be a mixed blessing for Montreal. The farmers who swarmed into Montreal were mainly francophone. The reconversion of Montreal into a predominantly French-speaking city was directly linked to the process of industrialization and urbanization. Most of the peasants who went to Montreal to seek their fortune, or merely to escape misfortune on their ever-smaller holdings (so long as population grew and land was divided amongst the children) were for the most part poor, ill educated and unskilled. They provided Montreal with a "reserve army" of cheap unskilled labour. They could not afford much by way of housing, and crowded into the tenements of East Montreal, making East Montreal between the wars the site of some of the world's most spectacular and depressing slums.

The industrialization of Montreal and the related immigration into the city from other parts of the province also led to the "partition" of Montreal, the division of the city into two sharply demarcated sections. Hugh MacLennan describes the prewar situation in his usual pungent language, reflecting thirty-three years afterwards on his famous novel *Two Solitudes*:

> Here the two cultures of Canada, without even planning it, had evidently decided that the best way to coexist was to ignore the existence of one another... The absurdity of the situation was visible to everyone except the natives. It was visible even geographically. The "British Empire" extended west and northwest from Guy Street to the rich farmland of Montreal Island... The "French Fact" began at Bleury Street and extended indefinitely east and northeast, embracing in the process one of the most gifted Jewish communities in North America. Between these two distinct territories, for that is what they were, was a common ground, a kind of miniature Belgium, along the two-mile stretch of St. Catherine Street, where the two so-called founding races of Canada encountered each other in small shops owned by French Canadians and Jews and in four large

department stores owned by Anglophone companies, two of them based in Toronto.[8]

MacLennan goes on to describe the famous "square mile" from Sherbrooke to Pine Avenue and from University to Côte des Neiges where, it used to be said at the time, lived families owning among them one-third of Canada's total wealth:

> On the steep streets that ran up the slope of Mount Royal between University Street and Côte des Neiges were the massive mansions, each one with its conservatory, owned by the descendents of the railway builders, the bankers, the brewers, and the merchants of the nineteenth century, who still controlled more money power than could be found in any other part of Canada. Most, though not all of them, were anglophones... This was the Montreal of only yesterday, and one quickly learned to accept that its loyalties were totally divided.[9]

As we have seen above, the second wave of industrialization in Canada saw the beginnings of the shift of the industrial heartland to western Ontario and coincided with the wheat boom in the prairies. In this period, then, the immigrants from abroad who had some capital, some education, or some ambition did not stop at Montreal but went further west. Few immigrants to Montreal in this period, whether from the countryside or from abroad, had the qualities that would enable them to dislodge from their seats the English-speaking barons of commerce, industry, and finance. The abundance of cheap unskilled labour was very convenient at the time for the kind of industries then growing up in Montreal, which were not technologically advanced and did not require much by way of labour skills. Cheap unskilled labour can be an advantage in the short run but a disadvantage in the long run, just because it inclines investment decisions towards that type of industry which does not rely on advanced technology and high-level skills. In this way the beginnings of the income gap can also be attributed to the peculiar pattern of industrialization, urbanization, and growth that took place in Canada, in Quebec, and in Montreal between 1850 and World War II.

This pattern of urbanization also started the long process by which Montreal became stranded in an industrial desert, while Toronto became the centre of a vigorously expanding industrial region. This process had two aspects: the failure of the satellite cities in the "couronne" of Montreal to develop into dynamic industrial towns; and the decline of eastern Ontario as the industrial heartland of Ontario.

The "couronne" of Montreal

As early as 1938, if not before, the difference in quality of the smaller industrial cities in Ontario and in Quebec had become apparent. The manufacturing census of that year revealed that there were 99 urban centres in Ontario producing more than a million dollars' worth of industrial products, compared to fifty in Quebec; 23 producing more than $10 million, but only 12 in Quebec; and 3 Ontario cities producing more than $100 million worth of manufactured goods, whereas Quebec had only Montreal in that category. In 1938 Toronto accounted for only 28.8 percent of the value of industrial production of its province, Montreal for 60 percent in its province. Adding nearby Hamilton and Windsor to Toronto, the complex produced together $775 million of industrial output; Montreal plus Trois-Rivières, $636 million. Clearly, the industrial supremacy of Montreal was already being challenged, largely because Montreal remained virtually alone in its region as an industrial city with any strength and dynamism.

Jean Delage, writing in 1943, showed a great deal of perspicacity in his predictions of the outcome of the race between Toronto and Montreal.

> En somme, on s'en rend compte, cela fait boule de neige et l'on reste surpris de voir combien nos petites villes semblent, dans l'ensemble, avoir déployé peu d'efforts vraiment efficaces en matière de prospection industrielle. À Montréal, un phénomène même aussi important se perd dans la masse d'une activité économique considérable. Mais nous ne saurions, ici plus qu'ailleurs, rester indifférents. Il faut pour le bien général de la Province que Montréal, par la prospection industrielle, supplée à l'apathie, à l'indifférence ou à l'incompétence des centres moins importants. N'allons pas imprudemment nous en remettre trop exclusivement aux avantages de notre beau fleuve et des rapides de Lachine.[10]

Delage was not very hopeful that his advice would, or even could be taken. He pointed out that the tendency for British capital to be replaced by American in Canada, a tendency increasingly apparent since World War I, acted against Montreal because American management showed a strong preference for Toronto, especially where branch plants were concerned. In a regime of free competition and parliamentarianism, he predicted that Montreal would keep its place within the Quebec economy, but lose out to Toronto in the national economy, and that consequently the gap between Ontario and Quebec in industrial output would increase.

The decline of Eastern Ontario

We have already noted how the construction of the Rideau Canal contributed to the development of eastern Ontario. Kingston benefited from the canal, and also from its proximity to the Trent canal and its position on the Great Lakes-St. Lawrence system. It profited also from its importance as a garrison town, and (briefly, from 1841 to 1843) from being capital of the Union. Up to about 1830, Kingston was the biggest city in Ontario. The first branch of the Bank of Canada was opened in Kingston in 1819. Two years later Kingston had three banks, Toronto had none. As late as 1850, Kingston was still the major exporter to the United States among Ontario cities, although by that time Toronto (York) had a substantially larger population.

After 1850 the eastern Ontario economy went into a decline. The construction of the Erie Canal did not help, because one of the advantages of the Rideau canal had been that it linked Kingston and eastern Ontario to Montreal, and thus to Europe, by a route that had fewer complications than the St. Lawrence. The Erie Canal shifted the traffic from the St. Lawrence and Montreal to the Hudson River and New York. Thus eastern Ontario lost its transport advantage. What really killed eastern Ontario, however, was the railways. The latter half of the nineteenth century saw an explosion of railroad construction. In this period too the industrial heartland of the United States shifted to the Great Lakes. Toronto benefited from the combination. The railway system linked Toronto directly with American cities, and the Great Lakes, especially after the construction of the Welland Canal, linked her to Chicago, Detroit, Toledo, Cleveland, Buffalo, Rochester. By 1880 Toronto was the centre of an excellent railway system, while Kingston still had no link except to Montreal.

The Income Gap

The result of all these complex forces in Canada and North America was that in 1967 per capita incomes in Quebec were only some 10 percent below the national average. True, they were 25 percent below those of neighbouring Ontario, about 20 percent below those of British Columbia, some 10 percent below those of Alberta, and slightly below those of Manitoba; but they were higher than all other provinces. As regional disparities go in large countries, these are not enormous gaps. Why then so much dissatisfaction? In the Montreal region, since incomes were 10 percent above the provincial average, they were just about equal to the national average. Yet conflict, unrest, and tension were particularly apparent in Montreal. Why?

Among intellectuals, many of whom were concentrated in Montreal, among Quebec nationalists, among politicians, and among fair-minded people of all kinds, the fact that Montreal was about as well off as the country as a whole was not cause for comfort. On the contrary, the relative prosperity of the Montreal region within the Quebec economy was cause of grave concern. Something must be seriously wrong in the structure of the Quebec economy, when incomes in the metropolitan region were nearly twice as high as in Gaspésie/Bas Saint-Laurent.

But there was a deeper reason for discontent. It was the British and the Jews (as classified by the census) who were relatively well off in Quebec, and especially in Montreal. For the purposes of the Royal Commission on Bilingualism and Biculturalism (the "B and B" Commission), Statistics Canada undertook in 1961 a special study of incomes by ethnic group. For Canada as a whole, it turned out that French Canadians (outside of agriculture) earned about 12 percent less than the national average, while British Canadians earned 10 percent more than the national average, and the Jews 68 percent more than the national average. Of the ethnic groups distinguished, only the Italians earned less than the French. (Separate studies showed that French-Canadian farmers were considerably poorer than other farmers, too). What was even more dramatic, it turned out that the French were the poorest, after the Italians, in all provinces of Canada. But more germane to our immediate problem is the fact that in the province of Quebec, because of the peculiarly favourable status of the British (and Jews) in that province, the gaps between French and British or Jews were much wider than in the country as a whole. The British in Quebec had incomes 40 percent above the average; the French Canadians had incomes over 8 percent below the average. (Incomes of the relatively small Jewish population were nearly 80 percent above the average). Thus, in Quebec the average income of the anglophone population was more than half again as high as that of the French-speaking majority.

But that is not the end of the story. For the wealthy anglophone and Jewish populations of the province were heavily concentrated in the Montreal region. There the average income of the English Canadians was closer to being two-thirds above the average income of the French Canadians. A spread of that magnitude is highly visible, especially when two clearly defined social groups live in the same city. Thus Montreal, where alone in Canada large groups of francophones and anglophones were in daily contact, not to say daily confrontation or even conflict, was precisely the area where the contrast in standards of living was sharpest. Small wonder that Montreal was the centre of tensions between the two populations.

What was the reason for the continuing gap between the economic and social status of the two groups, after more than two centuries of living together? Table 39 provides a clue. The figures show the relationship of incomes of each ethnic group in a particular province and the average for each ethnic group in the country as a whole. Since most French Canadians live in Quebec, it is not surprising that their average incomes in that province were the same as the average for French Canadians in all Canada. But the anglophone population was far more prosperous in Quebec than anywhere else in Canada, even Ontario and Alberta. (The Jewish population was prosperous everywhere, although less so in Manitoba than in Ontario and Quebec). It could hardly be that anglophone Canadians, in particular occupations and with similar education and experience, were 22 percent more talented in Quebec than they would be elsewhere in Canada. It must be that they were a very select group in Quebec, an élite even within the anglophone population, doing special jobs and with special backgrounds. That was indeed the case.

The problem of "control"

One of the special things the English Canadians were doing in Quebec, and especially in Montreal, was owning and managing enterprises. A study undertaken especially for the B and B Commission revealed a heavy concentration of ownership by anglophone enterprises in Quebec (and so in Montreal). Moreover, the concentration was particularly marked in those sectors where productivity and incomes were relatively high. Table 40 shows the percentage of the Quebec labour force in establishments owned by francophone Canadians, by anglophone Canadians, and by foreigners. For all practical purposes the foreigners can be treated as anglophone; a large proportion of them were American, others were British; and even Japanese, Arab, Scandinavian, Dutch or other foreign enterprises that tended to operate in English rather

140

TABLE 39

Average Total Income by Ethnic Origin

Average total income index of the male non-agricultural labour force,
by province and ethnic origin — Canada, 1961

Canada	All origins (54,415) 100.0	British (54,852) 100.0	French (53,872) 100.0	German (54,207) 100.0	Italian (53,621) 100.0	Jewish (57,426) 100.0	Ukrainian (54,128) 100.0	Other (54,153) 100.0
						Income index by ethnic origin		
Newfoundland	67.3	61.0	71.7	*	*	—	—	*
Prince Edward Island	66.4	63.7	66.0	*	—	—	—	*
Nova Scotia	82.3	76.8	82.3	72.2	*	*	*	88.7
New Brunswick	79.2	76.5	77.5	98.4	*	*	*	85.7
Quebec	95.7	121.9	100.2	112.1	96.4	101.3	104.6	106.3
Ontario	106.6	103.7	105.7	105.9	100.7	86.7	104.1	113.7
Manitoba	100.4	99.1	94.4	99.2	*	104.2	90.4	93.9
Saskatchewan	92.5	92.0	89.6	88.2	*	*	92.5	87.7
Alberta	104.1	106.6	110.4	97.6	102.6	*	105.0	92.3
British Columbia, Yukon, and N.W.T.	108.1	105.1	117.3	99.6	101.0	*	102.4	100.7

SOURCE: Raynauld, Marion, and Béland, "La répartition des revenus."

* Statistically insignificant.

TABLE 40

Ownership of Establishments

Size of establishments owned by Francophone Canadians, Anglophone Canadians, and foreign interests in selected industrial sectors, measured by numbers employed — Quebec, 1961

| | Employees | Percentage of labour force in establishments owned by | | | |
	Number (thousands)	Francophone Canadians	Anglophone Canadians	Foreign Interests	Total
Agriculture	131.2	91.3	8.7	0.0	100
Mining	25.9	6.5	53.1	40.4	100
Manufacturing	468.3	21.8	46.9	31.3	100
Construction	126.4	50.7	35.2	14.1	100
Transportation and communications	102.4	37.5	49.4	13.1	100
Wholesale trade	69.3	34.1	47.2	18.7	100
Retail trade	178.7	56.7	35.8	7.5	100
Finance	62.2	25.8	53.1	21.1	100
Services	350.9	71.4	28.6	0.0	100
All industries[1]	1,515.3	47.3	37.7	15.0	100

SOURCE: Raynauld, "La propriété des entreprises au Québec."
1. Excludes forestry, fishing and trapping, the public sector, and unspecified industries.

than French. In agriculture, where productivity and incomes were low, 91.3 percent of the labour force was French Canadian. In middle-level sectors like retailing, construction, and general services, once again a majority of francophone workers appears. But when we turn to the high-productivity, high-income sectors we have the opposite picture: nearly 94 percent of mining employment, over 78 percent of manufacturing employment, over 74 percent of employment in financial institutions, about two-thirds of employment in wholesale trade, was in enterprises controlled by anglophones. And this in a province that was more than three-quarters French!

The contrast is even more striking if one looks at value added rather than employment. Francophone Canadian establishments produced an average value added of $790,000 per year, in comparison with $3,310,000 for anglophone Canadian firms and $5,640,000 for foreign firms. Value added by francophone Canadian firms was on average only one-quarter that of an average anglophone Canadian firm and only one-seventh that of an average foreign enterprise. Once again, the reason is that the anglophone ownership was larger scale and concentrated in high-productivity sectors. Francophones owned only 15.4 percent of the total manufacturing sector (measured by value added), less than 5 percent of precision instrument establishments, less than 1 percent in tobacco products, less than 12 percent in iron and steel, just over 6 percent in electrical products and transportation equipment, none at all in petroleum and coal products. The only sector where francophones predominated was in a traditional, low-productivity industry: 84 percent for wood products. The only other industries with a fair proportion of francophone firms were of the same type: leather (49.4 percent) and furniture and fixtures (39.4 percent).

Unfortunately, the story does not stop there. The concentration of ownership and control in anglophone firms had feedback effects both on the occupational structure and on patterns of education. Anglophone managers wanted in top positions around them people who were not only fluent in English — most educated French Canadians were that — but who were also *culturally* the same as themselves, preferably graduates of the same universities. (The writer remembers very well the deep suspicion of Laval University and the University of Montreal among top managers of his acquaintance in Montreal during the 1950s, something which, fortunately, has since changed a good deal.) The result was that

French Canadians were grossly under-represented in top managerial and financial posts. A vicious circle then emerged. Feeling that there was little chance of rising high in the ranks of the major industrial, financial, and commercial enterprises, French Canadians did not seek the kind of education and training that would fit them for those jobs. Anglophone management was confirmed in its suspicion that few French Canadians were qualified for top posts in their establishments.

In every province in Canada French Canadians were over-represented, relative to their share of the total labour force, in such activities as craftsmen, labourers, miners, fishing, and work in the forests; they were under-represented in managerial, professional, clerical, and sales occupations. As the Report of the Commission puts it,

> Those of British origin provided almost a perfect mirror image of this pattern. As managers they were above the average in all but one province; and as professionals, clerks, and salesmen, their participation was universally above average.[11]

Even more disturbing is the fact that the predominance of those of British origin was most pronounced precisely in those areas where they were in the minority: Quebec, and above all, Montreal. The proportion of British in managerial, technical and professional occupations was 21 percent for Canada as a whole, 30 percent in Quebec and 53 percent in Montreal. In the country as a whole there was an 8-point difference between British and French, in Quebec a 16-point difference, and in Montreal an 18-point difference. The Report remarks,

> Thus we have a rather remarkable — indeed a paradoxical — situation. In relation to those of British origin, those of French origin fare better on the occupational scale in Canada as a whole than they do in the one province where they form a majority of the population; and they fare better on the occupational scale in Quebec as a whole than they do in the industrial centre of the province, Montreal.[12]

The role of education

Differences in occupational structure are almost inseparably intertwined with differences in patterns of education. To begin with, as may be seen from Table 41, in 1961, French Canadians had *less* education than British Canadians. The proportion of British who attended university was twice as high as, and the

TABLE 41

Percentage Distribution of the Male Non-Agricultural Labour Force,
by Ethnic Origin and Level of Schooling — Canada, 1961

| Ethnic origin | Level of schooling | | | | | | |
	None	Elementary	Secondary 1-2 years	Secondary 3-5 years	University	Total
British	0.3	30.6	25.2	31.4	12.5	100
French	0.7	53.5	21.4	18.1	6.3	100
German	*	40.1	21.8	28.5	9.2	100
Italian	*	71.0	12.8	11.9	3.0	100
Jewish	*	26.8	15.2	31.5	25.5	100
Ukrainian	*	46.7	21.3	23.0	7.9	100
Others	1.5	42.6	19.3	25.7	10.9	100
All origins	0.6	41.0	22.5	25.8	10.1	100

SOURCE: Raynauld, Marion, and Béland, "La répartition des revenus."
* Statistically insignificant.

145

proportion with three to five years of secondary education 70 percent higher than, the proportion of French Canadians. Of the ethnic groups distinguished by the census, only the Italians were less well educated than the French Canadians — and only they were poorer than the French Canadians. In terms of the average number of years of education (last grade attended) the French Canadians were substantially below those of British origin in every province; but it is still more striking that educational levels of the French Canadians were lower in Quebec than anywhere else in Canada except in neighbouring New Brunswick. And of particular relevance for our analysis of the economic and social problems of Montreal is the fact that the educational levels attained by the French majority of that sophisticated city were barely above the provincial average, were well below that of the British in Montreal, and that the gaps between British and French were wider in Montreal than in either Toronto or Ottawa.

In 1961 only Prince Edward Island had a lower proportion of youths aged 15 to 19 in school than Quebec. However, Quebec had a higher proportion of young men 20-24 attending educational institutions than all of the Atlantic provinces, although lower than any of the other provinces. The B and B Commission calculated that some 60 percent of the differences in incomes between British- and French Canadians could be explained by differences in levels and patterns of education (remembering the strong relationship between education and occupation).

The Commission also conducted studies of university graduates in Quebec. They found that only 50 percent of graduates in commerce and administration and working in Quebec in 1964 received their degrees from French language institutions. In 1961 only 33 percent of the engineers and 38 percent of the scientists in the province were French Canadian. In the fields of science and engineering, only 15 percent of the bachelors degrees awarded by Canadian universities came from French-language institutions. For masters degrees and licentiates the figure was 13 percent and for doctorates, 6 percent.

Moreover, few of the French Canadians who did acquire degrees in management, science, and engineering challenged the stranglehold of the anglophones in the private sector. Graduates from McGill's School of Commerce went into industry; graduates of the University of Montreal's École des Hautes Études Commerciales went into government service and accounting firms. Even in the field of accounting, whereas more than 90 percent of chartered accountants employed by the provincial and municipal governments were francophone, in industry and commerce less than 40 percent were so. French Canadian engineering students tended to concentrate on civil engineering rather than electrical, mechanical, metallurgical, or chemical engineering; in 1963 in these latter fields only 20 percent were francophones. As a consequence most of the francophone engineers were employed by government. Only 25 percent were in private industry, compared to 70 percent for the anglophones.

The Commission report also provides some evidence that French Canadians had by and large given up trying to break into the Montreal world of top management, high finance, big industry and large-scale commerce. Feeling that their chances were slim, and disliking the necessity of becoming both linguistically and culturally anglophone if they were to succeed, many decided simply not to try. Accordingly they chose careers and types of education which did not rely for success on impressing anglophone owners and managers.[13]

Thus, behind the relative poverty of French Canadians was a vicious circle of interactions among ownership and control of enterprises, occupational structure, and patterns of education. It would seem, however, that it was the ownership and control of enterprises that was at the heart of this feedback organism. How is it that after more than two centuries of living side by side with anglophones the French Canadians had still not taken over the private sector of their own province and of "the second largest French speaking city in the world"?

The continuing ideological gap

In answering this question, in my view, we are forced back to the historical analysis which was presented above. In the century following the conquest, French Canadians in Quebec, and particularly in Montreal, gradually withdrew from the race with the British in the fields of industry, commerce, and finance. No doubt they were to some degree pushed out of the race; but it was less a matter of conscious exploitation and discrimination — at least in the beginning, as we have seen — than reluctance on the part of the French to accept the rules of the game as laid down by the conquerors, together, perhaps, with a somewhat lesser relish for the tough competitive game which the anglophones so obviously enjoyed. Consequently, they withdrew into their "superior culture," their family and their church, and ideologically if not physically "returned to the land." The anglophones did not object, just so long as the francophones provided them with a cheap and docile labour force.

One of the most startling of the studies undertaken for the B and B Commission showed that the ideological gap was still there in the mid-1960s. The study, by J. Dofny, undertook a comparative analysis of attitudes and values of francophone and anglophone engineers in Montreal. The contrasts with regard to those ideological traits which might be regarded as germane to entrepreneurial endeavours were striking. For example, one of the questions asked was, "At what level of income do you think a family can begin to save ?" The francophones put the figure much higher than the anglophones. Essentially the anglophones thought almost everyone should be able to save, the French Canadians found saving difficult. The anglophones were content with a significantly lower rate of return as a basis for investment than the francophones. Half of the anglophones thought 6 percent a good return. Only 21 percent of the francophones shared this view ; 40 percent of them felt that "a good investment" should yield more than 10 percent. There was also a pronounced difference in preferred fields of investment. The anglophones preferred shares in corporations, the francophones preferred bonds (especially federal government bonds !) mutual funds, and real estate near home. The French Canadians, in other words, were clearly less disposed to take risks than the anglophones.

The actual figures of investments undertaken at the time reflected these attitudes. In Montreal, where the anglophones were in the minority, as well as in Ottawa, where they were the majority, the largest number of investors were anglophone. Second in line among ethnic groups as investors in Montreal were "others"; the French Canadians came in the lowest rank.

The anglophones showed a strong preference for employment in the private sector, the francophones for employment in government and crown corporations. The anglophones preferred large enterprises, the francophones small ones. The francophone engineers were also less mobile than the anglophones, even within the province of Quebec. Their wives were even more reluctant to move.

Of particular interest is the fact that the francophones evinced much less regard for economic activity and business than did the anglophones. Indeed, essentially, one could say that the franco-phones regarded all business as "dirty business," justified only by the need to support one's family and play an appropriate role in the community. For the French Canadians there was a conflict between the welfare of society and industrial operations; the anglophones saw no such conflict. These attitudes led to mutual suspicion between top management and middle management in francophone firms; the francophones felt that doing a good job for the boss was inconsistent with serving society, the anglophones felt that society was served by serving the boss. There was consequently less devolution of decision-making power in the francophone firms. The attitude towards business in general may also be part of the explanation of the relatively small size of francophone firms. To exaggerate a bit, whereas the good West-mount Scotch Presbyterian or the good Outremont Jew, having made his first million, starts immediately to think of his tenth, the good French Canadian, having accumulated enough to take care of his family and be a respectable member of the community, wishes to wash his hands of the unpleasantness and the neglect of family and friends entailed in making an enterprise grow.

In short, in the mid 1960s there was still insufficient French Canadian entrepreneurship in Montreal. The concentration of ownership and control in the hands of anglophone Canadians and foreigners would have been irritant enough even if it had no repercussions in terms of economic and social status. But since it did have such repercussions, Montreal could not attain a stable or satisfactory social equilibrium until people who were both linguis-tically and culturally "Québécois" (or Québécoise, to avoid trouble) were basically in control of the economy in which they have a large majority. More nationalization would not be a simple answer; nationalized enterprises still need entrepreneurs. The success of Hydro-Quebec and the francophone financial institutions suggests that the entrepreneurial, managerial, scientific and technical skills needed to create large, efficient francophone enterprises in Montreal, capable of holding their own in competition with anyone in the world, might be more easily recruited for government owned and operated enterprises than for large private corpora-tions. More "recent evidence," however, suggests that the differ-ences between French and English may be disappearing in the private sector as well.

The Not So Quiet Revolution

During the 1950s and 1960s it was customary to speak of the economic and social transformation of Quebec as "la révolution tranquille," the "quiet revolution." In the late 1960s and 1970s with the "événements," bombings, lesser acts of violence, student strikes, and the noisily successful campaigns of René Levesque and his Parti Québécois, the characterization "quiet" no longer seemed to fit. But that there occurred a process of economic and social change of extraordinary rapidity, perhaps unique in history, there can be little doubt. In terms of relative incomes of francophones and anglophones, of productivity, of amount and type of education, of occupational structure, of French Canadian participation in the upper echelons of the industrial and services sectors, and of product-mix, the last two decades have brought a marked improvement, in Montreal and in the province of Quebec as a whole.

The diminishing income gap

It seems to be almost a sociological law that disfavoured social groups embark on their most noisy and violent protest movements just when the economic and social gaps between them and their "oppressors" are narrowing most rapidly. In the past two decades we have seen this "law" operating amongst the blacks of the United States, the aborigines of Australia, the Malays of Malaysia, the Indians and Inuit of the Canadian north, women everywhere, and French Canadians in Montreal. In a series of studies prepared for the Economic Council of Canada, Jac André Boulet presents persuasive evidence that the income gaps between anglophones and francophones in Montreal are in the course of disappearing.[14] To be sure, his figures relate to earnings from work and do not include investment incomes, where it is very possible that anglophones still have a greater advantage; but the figures are dramatic enough to suggest a strong and accelerating trend towards a diminishing income gap between the two major language groups in Montreal metropolitan region.

The 1961 census showed average earnings of anglophone males in Montreal 51 percent above those of francophones. The 1971 census revealed that for 1970 the gap had fallen to 33 percent, and the 1981 census that the disparity had decreased to 14 percent.[15] The allophones (those whose mother tongue was neither English nor French) had also gained on the anglophones, especially if they spoke both of the official languages. By 1980 the gap between bilingual francophones and anglophones (unilingual or bilingual) had virtually disappeared (Table 42). Among women too the income disparities among linguistic groups had narrowed. Indeed, by 1980 bilingual francophone women were the best paid of all (Table 43).

An important factor in the narrowing of income gaps was the pattern of emigration of anglophones after 1970. Between 1971 and 1981 there was a net loss of 22,000 male anglophone workers from the metropolitan region of Montreal. Most of the emigrants were relatively young and poorly paid unilingual workers; some 30,000 of these left. On the other hand about 10,000 more highly paid bilingual anglophones were employed in 1981 than in 1971. But these trends were by no means the only ones operative. More and more francophones were joining Montreal's upper income groups as well. In 1961 only 44 percent of these were francophone. By 1970 this figure had risen to 54 percent and by 1980 to 71 percent, a bit higher than the proportion of francophones in the total population. However, within this upper income group the average income was still 10 percent higher among anglophones than among francophones in 1980.

In Quebec outside of Montreal, the disparities were already relatively small in 1970. For males the gap between anglophones and francophones was 16 percent. By 1980 this gap had almost disappeared: 4 percent. Among women it is the bilingual allophones who do best, and their margin has increased from 2 percent compared to bilingual francophones and 7 percent compared to unilingual francophones, to 14 and 22 percent respectively. However, bilingual francophones were better paid than bilingual anglophones and considerably better than unilingual anglophones in both years. In Canada outside Quebec the bilingual allophones moved from second to first place between 1970 and 1980, the bilingual anglophones slipped from first to second place, bilingual francophones remained in fifth place, and unilingual francophones remained at the bottom of the heap in both years.

In his 1983 study Boulet divided differences in income between differences in hourly earnings and differences in hours worked. He made the interesting discovery that allophone males work more hours per year than anglophones, and anglophones more than francophones. Hourly earnings of anglophones remained 13.8 percent above those of francophones in 1980, but this gap was down sharply from 33.0 percent in 1970; and the hourly earnings of

TABLE 42

Average Income of Male Workers by Linguistic Groups,
Metropolitan Region of Montreal, 1970 and 1980

	1970		1980	
	Average income ($)	Rank	Average income ($)	Rank
Francophones	6,949	(2)	17,474	(2)
Unilinguals	5,636	6	14,351	6
Bilinguals	7,686	3	19,411	3
Anglophones	9,240	(1)	19,892	(1)
Unilinguals	9,123	2	19,840	2
Bilinguals	9,367	1	19,920	1
Allophones,[2]	6,564	(3)	16,150	(3)
Unilinguals	4,214	8	10,474	8
Bilinguals	7,155	4	17,213	4
French	5,316	7	13,531	7
English	6,809	5	16,203	5
Bilinguals	7,941	[1]	19,204	[1]
Non-bilinguals	6,678	[2]	15,285	[2]
Total	7,406	—	17,693	—

1, 2   See corresponding notes at bottom of table 1.
SOURCE: Special compilation taken from the 1971 and 1981 census, Statistics Canada.

TABLE 43

Average Income of Female Workers by Linguistic Groups,
Metropolitan Region of Montreal, 1970 and 1980

	1970		1980	
	Average income ($)	Rank	Average income ($)	Rank
Francophones	3,938	(2)	10,576	(2)
Unilinguals	3,604	6	9,627	6
Bilinguals	4,236	3	11,423	1
Anglophones	4,327	(1)	11,253	(1)
Unilinguals	4,342	1	11,291	2
Bilinguals	4,305	2	11,229	3
Allophones [2]	3,657	(3)	9,806	(3)
Unilinguals	2,846	8	7,278	8
Bilinguals	4,023	4	10,635	4
French	3,226	7	8,180	7
English	3,809	5	10,150	5
Bilinguals	4,229	[1]	11,288	[1]
Non-bilinguals	3,780	[2]	9,793	[2]
Total	3,994	—	10,599	—

1, 2 See corresponding notes at bottom of table 1.
SOURCE : Special compilation taken from the 1971 and 1981 census, Statistics Canada.

153

bilingual anglophones were only 2.6 percent above those of bilingual francophones in the latter year. Differences in hourly earnings between anglophone and francophone women were down to 0.8 percent by 1980, and bilingual francophone women were earning slightly more per hour than bilingual anglophone women in that year. In general, one can say that it paid to be bilingual everywhere in Canada by 1980, whatever one's original mother tongue.

Between 1971 and 1981 the proportion of francophones increased significantly in Montreal, the proportion of anglophones declined, and the proportion of allophones remained virtually unchanged. In the rest of Quebec the proportion of francophones increased, and the proportion of anglophones decreased, only slightly, while the small proportion of allophones was unchanged. In Canada outside of Quebec the proportion of both francophones and allophones declined slightly, the proportion of anglophones increased. Thus there is an increasing concentration of French speaking people in Montreal, sharpening the contrast between the city and Canada outside of Quebec; while Quebec outside of Montreal shows little change in language patterns.

Bilingualism

When it comes to bilingualism, however, a quite different pattern emerges : anglophones and allophones are becoming increasingly bilingual (in the two official languages) while francophones are gradually losing their superiority in capacity to speak both languages. In the metropolitan region of Montreal, the proportion of francophones in the work force who are bilingual fell from 54.6 percent in 1971 to 51.7 percent in 1980. In the latter year the proportion of bilingual anglophones was higher than the proportion of bilingual francophones for both men and women : 64.5 vs 61.7 percent and 61.0 vs 52.0 percent respectively. In Quebec outside of Montreal the proportion of bilingual anglophones was more than twice as high as the proportion of bilingual francophones. In Canada outside of Quebec, however, it is still a virtual necessity to speak English to earn a living, and the proportion of bilingual persons among francophone members of the labour force is very high. The proportion of bilingual anglophones is very low, but increasing.

Boulet noted in his 1977 study that significant differences in earnings of anglophones and francophones appear only after a certain threshold of income is passed, and that the threshold is moving rapidly upwards. In 1961, the threshold below which no significant difference in earnings appeared was $5,000; by 1970 it had risen to $10,750 and by 1977 to $19,000. Some 71 percent of all workers were below the threshold in 1961, 85 percent in 1970 and 76 percent in 1977. The greater part of the overall disparity — 86 percent of the total disparity observed in 1977 — can be explained by the over-representation of French-speaking members of the labour force in the lower income group that finds itself below the threshold. Only 14 percent of the discrepancy can be explained by income differences between francophones and anglophones with incomes above the threshold. Boulet insists that to understand the causes of the discrepancy this division of the labour market into two fundamentally different groups is essential.

Since the decline in the proportion of unilingual anglophones is considerably greater than the increase in proportion of bilingual anglophones, it seems that something more is involved here than anglophones deciding to learn French. Montreal has become less attractive to unilingual anglophones over the past two decades; fewer have decided to move to Montreal, and some who were there have decided to leave because of the changing situation. The ones who decided to come to Montreal were mainly those who were offered high positions with good salaries; and those who stayed were mainly those who already had such positions, and were not being transferred or attracted to equally good jobs elsewhere.

The increased bilingualism is greatly to be welcomed, but there is a fly in this particular ointment: younger French Canadians are becoming less bilingual, not more bilingual, than their older brothers and their parents. In 1971 only 47 percent of the francophones between 15 and 19 years of age were bilingual, whereas among the older age groups the proportion ranged from 63 percent to 73 percent. Yet 51 percent of the anglophones and 65 percent of the allophones aged 15 to 19 were bilingual. From personal observation, I believe that these trends continued through the seventies, but may be reversing again now. It would be a sad day for Montreal, and for Quebec, if once again, as in the years immediately following the conquest, most of the bilingual people in Montreal were those who were originally English speaking — especially since, in the remoter regions of the province, young Québécois seem less disposed to learn English than their contemporaries in Montreal.

Explanation of the continuing gap

What caused the gap between anglophones and francophones in Montreal in the first place, why is the gap diminishing, why is it still there? Boulet raises all of these questions, but does not really answer any of them. Basically, francophones were in 1961 and remained in 1977 (and 1981) poorer than anglophones in Montreal because they were overrepresented in the low-income group below the threshold where incomes are much the same, and by the same token, underrepresented in the higher income groups above the threshold. However, Boulet provides us with a very interesting division within the group above the threshold. His table is worth reproducing in full:

Boulet Table

Average Income from Work and Linguistic
Distribution of the Best Paid Workers (Top 15%)
Metropolitan Region of Montreal 1970 and 1977

Language Group	Avg. Income 1970	Avg. Income 1977	% Growth 1970-77	Percentage in 1970	Percentage in 1977
Francophones	15,997	30,459	90	57	70
Anglophones	18,058	31,595	75	43	30
Both groups		30,804	82	100	100

Boulet 1980, Table 4-10, p. 30

Here we see that within the top 15 percent of income earners, the francophones had just about caught up with the anglophones. The $1,100 gap might be regretted, but after tax the quality of life that can be attained with $30,459 per year is not significantly different from that attainable with $31,595. Moreover, with 70 percent of the total income earners in this bracket, the francophones were almost proportionately represented in it; Boulet estimated that to be strictly proportionate, the francophones should constitute 78 percent of the income earners in the bracket, and predicted that this proportion should soon be reached. Boulet argues that the "traditional" approach, which seeks to explain income differences by differences in the traits of the two groups, cannot be applied to the Montreal case because of this division of the Montreal labour market into two distinct groups, a majority group with no income differences and a minority group where some differences persist but are dwindling. In the first group the question is whether, with *different* attributes, French and English nonetheless earn more or less the same incomes. In the second group the question is whether the two groups, with *the same* attributes, are nonetheless paid differently.

I suspect that the remaining gaps, small as they are in comparison with the past, reflect a continuing disproportion of anglophone ownership and control of Montreal enterprises, especially those capable of generating high incomes; that this disproportion continues to influence relative incomes through the occupational structure by denying to francophones their share of the top jobs in industry, commerce, and finance; and finally that these vestiges of differences in opportunities still result in some difference in patterns of education and career ambitions as between anglophones and francophones. No doubt there is a strong trend towards convergence in all of these respects. But I would expect the convergence to slow down in the next few years, so that complete equality is approached asymptotically, for the simple reason that complete equality in ownership and control will be difficult to achieve — at least, if *all* the high-productivity anglophone firms do not decide to leave Montreal, in which case achieving equality of ownership and control of what is left in Montreal may prove to have a rather hollow ring.

One last point of Boulet's bears repeating. He believes that part of the progress made by francophones is to be explained by their taking over high level posts left vacant by departing anglophones. However, he suspects that they have not been granted salaries as high as those of the departing anglophones, either because they are less experienced than their predecessors or because the nature of the jobs has essentially changed as a consequence of the transfer of the head office. It may also be that the francophones, being less willing or less able to move to another province than the anglophones, have less bargaining power than their predecessors. Boulet also thinks it possible that the francophones who are taking over positions from departing anglophones are not paid so well as their predecessors. If so, we have here a partial explanation of the relative disadvantage of francophones above the threshold.

Values, attitudes, and occupational structure

There remains the question of the relationship between basic values and attitudes and the kinds of jobs French Canadians seek and get. In his 1977 study Boulet quotes N.W. Taylor, who seems to support my own conclusion regarding the role of values and attitudes in the retreat of French Canadians from competition with English Canadians for top administrative and entrepreneurial posts in commerce, industry, and finance.[16] But then he rejects this explanation on the basis of a single study made by A.A. Hunter, whom he quotes:

> There is a very high degree of agreement between Anglophones and Francophones in the prestige evaluation of occupations generally. Also, agreement seems to be somewhat higher for white-collar occupations.... This suggests that there is essentially no difference between the two groups in their evaluation of entrepreneurial occupations and casts some doubt on the value of Taylor's explanation for the underrepresentation of Francophones in Quebec in such occupations.[17]

He goes on to say that consequently the problem cannot leave the economist indifferent, which suggests that if indeed the gap were due to difference of values, attitudes, and ambitions the economist would have no interest in the problem, a conclusion which strikes me as curious indeed.

There are several things to be said on this issue. In the first place, one study cannot definitely disprove another unless the sample and the questionnaire are identical, which is not the case; in the second place, even if the population studied and the analytical framework were essentially the same, a study made in 1977 cannot disprove a study made in 1965, nor even one made in 1974, let alone cast light on what values may have been in 1800 or in 1900, since values and attitudes can change. Moreover, values of this kind can change very rapidly, even from one university generation to another. It would be very surprising if, in the light of enlarged opportunities for francophones in administration in the private sector, attitudes did *not* change. Certainly it could not be expected that young people in Quebec today would still believe that "Man is closer to God on the land," now that only 2.7 percent of Quebec's labour force is still engaged in agriculture. To the vast majority of younger Quebeckers living in a highly competitive urban society the traditional values of Quebec expressed in *Maria Chapdelaine*, or even the picture of Montreal presented in

158

Gabrielle Roy's *Bonheur d'occasion* (*The Tin Flute*) or McClennan's *Two Solitudes* must seem to belong to another planet. In my daily contact with young Quebeckers at the University of Montreal in the late 1960s and in my frequent contact with them at the University of Ottawa during the 1970s, I had the strong impression that attitudes were changing in the required direction. Now there is strong evidence that attitudes are indeed changing in such a way that the Montreal and Quebec economies can be taken over by Quebec's francophone entrepreneurs, managers, and professionals.

Quebec Catches Up — Almost. 1973–1983

The narrowing gap between French and English in Quebec would bring limited comfort if Quebec as a whole were slipping ever further behind the rest of the country. The reverse is the case. As may be seen from Table 44, in 1982 average family incomes in Quebec were $30,075, only 7 percent below the Canadian average and 8 percent below neighbouring Ontario. Nor do these averages hide markedly greater inequality of income distribution in Quebec than in Ontario or in Canada as a whole. If we take $1,000 per month as the "poverty line" for Canadian families in 1982, 13 percent of them were below the line in Quebec compared to 10.2 percent in Ontario and 12.5 percent in Canada as a whole. In that year, Ontario had a slightly higher percentage of families below $7,000 than Quebec. At the other end of the scale, 33 percent of Quebec families had incomes above $35,000, compared to 40.0 percent in Ontario and 37.6 percent in the whole country. More clearly than ever before, it is the Atlantic provinces, not Quebec, that emerge as the truly disadvantaged region in Canada.

Trends in wages present a similar picture. Prior to 1973, wages in Quebec were 4 percent below the Canadian average and 7 percent below Ontario. In the early 1980s they were equal to the average for the whole country and a bit higher than in Ontario.

Behind these improvements lies the fastest rate of increase in productivity of all major regions: +6.1 percent for Quebec (1973–80); +4.2 percent for the prairies; +3.6 percent in British Columbia; +0.3 percent in the Atlantic provinces; and for newly troubled Ontario, -4.9 percent.[18] One factor in Quebec's superior performance was a rise in the ratio of investment to gross provincial product from 10.5 percent in 1966–72 to 12.5 percent for 1973–80, 1 percent above Ontario and just 1 percent below the national

TABLE 44

Percentage Distribution of Families by Income Groups and Provinces, 1982

	Canada	Total	New-foundland	Prince Edward Island	Nova Scotia	New Brunswick Per cent	Quebec	Ontario	Total	Manitoba	Saskat-chewan	Alberta	British Columbia
Under $ 5,000	2.2	3.0	3.7	2.3	3.1	2.4	1.5	2.0	2.5	2.7	2.6	2.3	2.9
$ 5,000-$ 6,999	1.9	2.5	2.6	1.5	1.9	3.3	2.4	1.6	1.6	2.6	1.5	1.2	1.3
7,000- 9,999	4.2	6.9	7.5	7.7	5.6	7.9	5.3	3.4	3.5	4.0	4.6	2.7	3.5
10,000- 11,999	4.2	7.0	6.8	6.9	6.9	7.4	4.6	3.2	3.8	5.1	4.8	2.9	4.6
12,000- 12,999	2.2	3.1	2.8	4.4	2.9	3.4	2.4	2.1	2.2	2.6	2.4	1.9	1.8
13,000- 13,999	2.3	2.9	2.9	2.7	2.7	3.1	2.4	2.3	2.3	3.0	2.5	1.9	1.8
14,000- 14,999	2.3	3.4	3.4	3.9	3.7	2.9	2.7	2.1	2.3	2.6	2.7	1.9	1.6
15,000- 15,999	2.1	2.8	3.3	2.3	2.8	2.7	2.7	1.6	2.0	2.6	2.0	1.7	1.9
16,000- 16,999	2.2	3.0	3.8	2.4	2.8	2.7	2.1	2.4	1.9	2.0	2.2	1.7	1.6
17,000- 17,999	2.0	2.7	3.3	3.3	2.7	2.1	2.5	1.8	1.6	1.9	1.6	1.6	1.5
18,000- 19,999	3.9	5.0	4.8	7.4	4.8	4.9	4.4	3.5	3.4	4.3	4.5	2.6	3.7
20,000- 21,999	4.0	5.5	4.8	4.6	6.4	5.2	4.0	3.9	3.5	4.4	4.3	2.8	4.2
22,000- 24,999	6.9	7.9	6.1	8.8	9.3	7.4	7.2	7.4	5.8	6.6	6.7	5.0	5.9
25,000- 29,999	11.3	11.4	11.8	10.7	11.9	10.7	12.4	10.9	10.8	12.0	11.7	10.0	10.9
30,000- 34,999	10.6	9.2	9.1	10.5	9.7	8.5	10.5	11.5	9.9	10.3	10.0	9.8	10.2
35,000- 39,999	9.3	6.9	6.8	6.5	6.1	8.1	9.3	9.6	9.5	9.2	9.3	9.6	10.0
40,000- 44,999	7.5	5.2	5.4	3.9	4.9	5.5	6.5	8.5	8.3	6.3	5.8	10.2	7.4
45,000 and over	20.8	11.6	11.2	10.2	11.8	11.9	17.2	22.1	25.2	17.6	20.9	30.2	25.0
TOTALS	100.0	100.0	100.0	100.0	100.0	100.0	100.0	100.0	100.0	100.0	100.0	100.0	100.0
Average income $	32,447	25,994	25,554	25,113	26,412	25,988	30,075	33,716	35,305	30,554	31,586	38,834	34,501
Median income $	29,206	22,830	22,167	22,190	23,185	22,854	27,356	30,743	31,489	27,294	28,281	35,020	31,261
Number of records	27,901	6,911	1,904	763	2,022	2,222	4,338	5,334	8,365	2,275	2,784	3,306	2,953
Estimated numbers '000	6,474	563	139	31	214	180	1,713	2,327	1,114	257	248	608	757
Standard error of average income $	235	289	598	846	471	523	385	408	756	794	512	1,328	646

SOURCE: Statistics Canada. Family Incomes, 1982, Cat. 13-208.

average. Another was continued structural change. Farming, fishing and forestry, for so long sectors with pockets of low productivity and poverty, have dwindled to near insignificance in the Quebec economy, accounting for 3.6 percent of employment in 1981; and it is the less productive within these sectors that have tended to disappear (Table 45). The rise in productivity has been widespread among both traditional and modern sectors in Quebec, and among the sub-regions of the province.

Pierre Fortin attributes this rise in productivity to "the educational revolution." He considers and then dismisses the possibility that Quebec government policy may have been superior to that of other provinces, or that the liberal social welfare policies of Quebec may have compelled substantial improvements in technique to displace unskilled labour. Fortin writes:

> After reviewing all the possible causes of the relatively good economic performance of the Quebec economy in the last decade, I am left with the conjecture that this is all very much part of the process of modernization that Quebec society went through in the last quarter century, a sort of economic extension in the 1970s of the Quiet Revolution of the 1960s.

> It is very important to stress that Quebec's educational revolution since the early 1960's has been of an incredible magnitude and swiftness. It is almost without peer in the Western world. If one government policy did succeed, it is educational policy.

> While barely 50 percent of young Quebeckers — and even less, of course, among Francophones — reached grade 9 in 1960, now 95 percent do. Furthermore, in 1982 almost 15 percent go through the university, instead of only 4 percent in 1960. French Canadian university students no longer study only law, medicine or theology. They literally flood the economics departments and the business schools: while Quebec represents only about a quarter of the youth population in Canada, its business schools account for more than a third of all business students in the country. One out of six university students in Quebec is enrolled in a business school, compared to one out of ten in the rest of Canada. The business graduates do not crowd the government departments. At any rate, the recent sharp drop in government hiring would preclude this kind of absorption of graduates. Instead, most of them now enter the private sector and acquire business experience not only in French firms, but more and more in those English firms that were farsighted enough to accept the sweeping, and sometimes not so quiet, changes in Quebec demographics and language legislation.[19]

161

TABLE 45

Employment Distribution by Industry and by Province, Canada, 1961 and 1981
(in Percentage)

	Agri-culture	Forest exploi-tation	Fishing & trapping	Mines, quarries & oil wells	Manu-facturing	Construc-tion	Transport, communi-cations and other services	Commerce	Finance, insurance & real estate	Collective, commercial & personal services	Public adminis-tration & defense	All indus-tries[1]
1961 Newfoundland	1.5	6.3	7.7	3.9	11.2	8.8	14.0	17.4	1.3	16.3	11.6	100.0
Prince Edward Island	27.5	0.4	6.2	—	9.0	6.6	8.3	14.3	1.7	17.0	8.9	100.0
Nova Scotia	5.2	1.8	3.2	4.3	14.6	6.7	10.7	15.8	2.4	19.3	15.8	100.0
New Brunswick	7.2	6.0	2.1	0.9	16.3	6.3	12.4	16.7	2.2	19.8	10.0	100.0
Quebec	7.6	2.5	0.2	1.5	27.2	7.4	9.4	14.4	3.6	20.4	5.8	100.0
Ontario	7.2	0.8	0.1	1.8	27.5	6.6	8.3	15.8	4.2	20.0	7.7	100.0
Manitoba	17.7	0.4	0.4	1.7	13.9	6.2	11.9	17.1	3.6	19.1	7.9	100.0
Saskatchewan	37.5	0.4	0.4	1.3	4.8	5.4	9.5	14.3	2.2	18.5	5.7	100.0
Alberta	21.6	0.6	0.2	3.6	8.8	7.8	9.9	16.7	3.1	19.5	8.1	100.0
British Columbia	4.2	3.8	0.8	1.5	20.2	6.5	11.2	17.7	4.0	22.1	8.2	100.0
Canada[2]	10.2	1.7	0.6	1.9	22.3	6.8	9.6	15.7	3.6	20.0	7.6	100.0
1981 Newfoundland	0.6	1.8	4.6	3.1	17.0	7.6	8.8	16.8	3.0	27.6	9.1	100.0
Prince Edward Island	10.6	0.5	5.1	0.2	10.6	8.1	7.3	14.9	2.9	28.6	11.1	100.0
Nova Scotia	2.3	1.3	2.0	1.8	14.9	6.6	8.0	17.4	4.4	29.2	12.2	100.0
New Brunswick	2.5	3.2	1.2	1.4	16.7	7.4	9.2	17.1	3.6	27.8	9.8	100.0
Quebec	2.7	0.8	0.1	1.1	22.4	5.2	8.2	16.4	5.1	30.5	7.6	100.0
Ontario	3.3	0.3	0.1	1.0	23.8	5.7	7.2	16.8	5.9	29.0	7.0	100.0
Manitoba	8.5	0.3	0.3	1.4	14.1	5.3	10.3	17.4	5.1	28.6	8.7	100.0
Saskatchewan	19.4	0.3	0.1	2.9	6.2	7.0	8.1	16.9	4.3	26.8	7.9	100.0
Alberta	6.9	0.3	—	6.4	9.0	10.8	8.4	17.0	5.5	28.2	7.4	100.0
British Columbia	2.4	2.8	0.5	1.7	14.8	7.8	9.2	17.6	5.6	30.5	7.2	100.0
Canada[2]	4.2	0.9	0.3	1.8	19.2	6.5	8.0	16.9	5.4	29.3	7.6	100.0

1. With the exclusion of non-specified or non-defined activities.
2. With the exclusion of Yukon and the Northwest Territories.
SOURCE: Data from Statistics Canada. L'Ouest en transition, Economic Council of Canada, 1984, p. 170. Cat. EC 22-123/1984F.

Fortin adds that a good many young francophone graduates, after gaining a few years of experience, go into business for themselves, establishing new small and middle-sized enterprises. There seems to be a new wave of French Canadian entrepreneurship. The new generation is fluently bilingual, and so is not confined to Quebec in its business operations. As they perceive opportunities in the business world, they become interested in studying, and reading about, economics and business. "In the middle 1960s," Fortin writes, "the business sections of French newspapers did not really go beyond stock market quotations. Today they occupy something very close to center stage, and they are read by a proportion of subscribers which is exactly comparable to their English counterparts. It is a sign of changing times."[20]

But while times are changing, they are not yet completely changed. Fortin points to continuing problems of management, marketing, and distribution, and the atmosphere of confrontation in which business-labour-government relations are conducted. At the national level he fears that continued efforts to fight inflation will maintain the high level of unemployment, with particularly disastrous effects on unskilled workers and on small and middle-sized enterprises. Quebec's provincial and local tax burden, which is 25 percent above Ontario's, is a deterrent to growth. He worries too about the heavy burden of debt in the financial structure of French Canadian enterprises, and the high costs per manhour in the public sector.

So there is still some way to go. The "reconquest" of the Quebec economy is still not complete. French Canadians have *not* taken over the ownership and management of all the large anglophone firms in Montreal. Nor have they organized many enterprises of their own in the private sector, on a scale large enough and technologically advanced enough to rival the major anglophone firms. Boulet's income figures refer to wages and salaries. They tell us nothing about investment incomes, let alone who are running things in Montreal. The migration of highly placed anglophones to other centres — mainly Toronto — may open up entrepreneurial opportunities (as well as high-level jobs) to francophones. But French Canadians will need capital and skills to seize the opportunity to take over or create large-scale, technologically advanced, high-growth enterprises to fill the gap left by migrating anglophone enterprises. I predict that in time they will. But it may still take some time.

CHAPTER 6

PROGNOSIS FOR MONTREAL:
"FALL" OR RENAISSANCE?

We have come full circle. We have seen Montreal grow from a tiny trading post and jumping-off point for saving souls and exploring the west into Canada's leading metropolis. We have observed its recent decline. With the wisdom of hindsight we can now see that the decline was inherent in the reasons for the rise. Montreal got its headstart among Canadian cities from the dubious advantage of being at the crossroads of four systems of rivers and lakes — lower St. Lawrence, Richelieu, Ottawa and upper St. Lawrence — with a barrier between the first three and the fourth. "Dubious," because a barrier to traffic is not a long run advantage, and it was ultimately overcome, so that Montreal was no longer a natural point for breaking journeys and trans-shipment; dubious because once the canal system was completed shippers who wished to take advantage of the greater economies of "lakers" could do so at Trois-Rivières, Quebec City, or Sept Iles just as well or even better than at Montreal; dubious because the Port of Montreal had no natural advantage over Halifax, Vancouver, New York, Boston, Baltimore, and Portland and had the great disadvantage of being frozen over much of the year; and finally because water transport was destined to decline in importance.

We have followed the transformation of Montreal from North America's fur trade capital to Canada's leading centre for commerce, industry, finance, communications and culture. We have seen the city change from French to British and back to French again, but with an economy dominated by anglophone enterprises. We noted the vicious circle by which francophones, finding themselves disadvantaged in the competition with the British and other essentially anglophone communities, retreated from the competition in industry, trade, and finance, and sought education more suitable to their cultural values and to other kinds of economic activity. We have shown how this vicious circle was related to the income gap between those who speak French and those who speak English in Montreal. The ascendency of Montreal was intertwined with the ascendency of the English language in the economic sphere.

We examined the interactions of growth and change in Canada, Quebec, and Montreal. We have seen how Montreal's fate has been affected by the winds of change throughout the country, and indeed throughout North America and the world. We have seen that Quebec has followed the same pattern of structural change, with consequent industrialization and urbanization, as in Ontario and in Canada as a whole. Quebec has always been somewhat more urbanized than Canada as a whole, and has never been far behind Ontario in either respect. The growth of Montreal, its reconversion into a French city, but with two sharply divided linguistic and cultural communities, was the result of this conjuncture of growth and change. We also underlined Quebec's failure, in comparison with Ontario, to develop a hierarchy of dynamic and prosperous middle-sized cities with which the metropolis could interact, a major element of the growing strength of Toronto and the increasing weakness of Montreal.

We have seen that, contrary to natural expectations, Montreal is not a powerful "development pole" for Quebec, generating as it grows "spread effects" in the form of increased employment and income throughout the province. Neither is it so powerful a "centre of attraction" that it is drawing to it enterprises that might just as well have been established elsewhere in the province, and thus "stifling" industrialization and urbanization in other Quebec regions. Most of the enterprises that choose to locate in the Montreal region are of a kind which would not go to smaller cities

166

in the province, and which would go outside of Quebec altogether if Montreal were not an attractive alternative. As "centre of attraction" Montreal is bringing enterprises from the outside world, not from elsewhere in Quebec. Moreover, it is clearly in a phase of decentralizing, moving industries from the city proper to satellite towns within its zone of influence. But the fact that Montreal operates in a vast "economic space" where smaller centres cannot compete also means that its expansion does not create jobs and incomes where they are most badly needed in Quebec. Montreal enterprises import raw materials, equipment, and entrepreneurial, managerial, scientific and technical skills from all over the world; and they export goods and services all over the world. To be sure, Montreal is a large market for Quebec farmers, textile manufacturers, boot and shoe makers, and the like. But even the smallest Quebec cities — Sept Iles for example — may have far more important markets outside of Montreal than in Montreal itself.

Montreal's importance for Quebec — and for Canada — is not that the city serves as a vital development pole for a larger Canadian region. Its importance is first of all that it is a very large economic and social entity, more than half the Quebec economy; and no organism can be healthy if more than half of it is sick. Secondly, Montreal is a late twentieth century "central place" for an urban hierarchy that includes all cities in Quebec and in eastern Ontario, even Ottawa. In other words, while Montreal may not be *buying* enough from her greater peripheral region (Quebec and eastern Ontario) to solve problems of retardation in this region, she is *selling* vital goods and services which are the foundation of today's economic activity: consulting services, large-scale financial services, research, higher education, specialized legal services, electronics, telecommunications, an international airport, computer software and hardware, scientific instruments — the whole gamut of sophisticated services of the "quaternary sector," plus scientifically oriented and technologically advanced manufacturing activities. These are not yet present on a scale sufficient to assure the future health of Montreal; but they are there in quantities which can contribute a great deal to the healthy functioning of the smaller cities within Montreal's urban system.

Montreal is also, because of the concentration of this kind of activity in the city, a source of innovation. Whatever doubts one may have about the importance for the rest of Quebec, and of

Canada, of Montreal as a place where innovations are made and from which they are diffused, there can be no doubt that Montreal is the only city in Quebec with the potential to become a diffuser of innovation in the future.

Finally, Montreal is important for all the reasons stressed in Chapter 1, as a city where people like to live, a city where people can find fun and excitment, intellectual and artistic stimulus, fresh ideas and creativity, as well as good restaurants, good theatre, good music, good universities and secondary schools, street life and churches. As the one truly bilingual metropolitan centre in Canada, bicultural as well, with all the other languages and cultures of importance in Canada well represented in the city, Montreal continues to have a special sparkle which no other Canadian city can match. It would be a pity to lose it.

The "Fall" of Montreal ?

Is it excessively melodramatic to raise the question of the possible "fall" of Montreal? The Empire of the St. Lawrence is hardly comparable to the Roman Empire. What could "the fall of Montreal" mean, and how would it come about? If there is real danger of a fall, how could it be averted?

Before allowing ourselves to speculate a bit on the answers to these questions, let us make a few pertinent observations solidly founded on fact. First, as we saw in Chapter 3, there are clear signs of Montreal's *relative* decline during the past decade. Montreal is no longer Canada's leading centre for industry, commerce, communications, or finance. With any sensible definition of boundaries of metropolitan regions, Montreal is no longer Canada's biggest city. Many Torontonians would be prepared to argue that their symphony orchestra is better, their universities superior, their English theatre more lively, their restaurants as good as Montreal's. English-language radio-television and film making have moved to Toronto, as have many individual writers, painters, and poets who once preferred Montreal. Even culturally, Montreal's position at the top of the totem pole is no longer unchallenged.

Second, there is a good deal of evidence that a city, like any other social organism, tends to follow almost biological laws of growth and decay. When growth ceases and stagnation sets in, rot is likely to follow. A city, like any species that loses out in the evolutionary race, is likely to be replaced by another.

168

Third, the threshold of size at which certain types of activity appear in a city, which we have noted above, work in both directions. Just as one new activity after another tends to appear as a city thrives and grows, so one activity after another tends to disappear when decline sets in. A "dominoes" effect takes place. It is not even necessary for total population to fall. It is necessary only for certain categories of population, or certain types of operation, to leave a city in order to induce other groups and other operations to follow. If major financial institutions leave a city, for example, purveyors of computer hardware and software are likely to follow. And so on. A movement of this kind can become cumulative.

What kind of city could Montreal become if such a cumulative process were to set in? Obviously Montreal will not become a "ghost town" such as one sees in the neighbourhood of exhausted mines. It is unlikely to become a "museum town," like Manaus or Oro Preto in Brazil, whose inhabitants packed up and left when the natural rubber bubble burst and the minerals gave out, but which now attract tourists because of their architecture and their charm. Montreal has moved too far from its natural resource base to suffer such a fate. With luck it might become a North American Vienna, a city which slipped a few notches down the European totem pole in terms of military power, and perhaps as a world centre for music, psychology, economics and general culture, but remains a beautiful and lively city nonetheless, a "metropolis" as defined in Chapter 1. There are many instances of cities losing their position as leader in population, industry, trade and finance but remaining more attractive than the city which displaced it: Rome versus Milan; Surabaya versus Jakarta in Indonesia; Penang versus Kuala Lumpur in Malaysia; San Francisco vs. Los Angeles. But once a city starts to slip it is hard to predict where it will stop. Returning to Brazil, Recife, Salvador, and Belem were all at one time or another the leading urban centre of the country. They remain large and important cities today, and their very stagnation has helped to preserve the Dutch and Portuguese architecture and town planning which make them such pleasant cities to be in. But the same stagnation has converted them from thriving centres of rapidly developing regions to poor cities in the poor northeast region, the object of the government's major effort at reduction of regional disparities.

Turning closer to home, Edgar Rust points out that in recent decades there have been in the United States seventy-two metropolitan areas which have stagnated or declined in population. These are mostly former boom towns which "grew on temporary, localized advantages," such as coal, iron, railways, cotton and beef in the case of the older cities, and petroleum, defense industries, and aero-space programmes, in the case of the newer ones.[1] We cannot say "it can't happen here." The seventy-two cities include New York, Chicago and Los Angeles. Some might say that to suffer the fate of these cities would not be so bad for Montreal. But if we look at stagnant or declining American cities closer to Montreal's size, like Buffalo, Cleveland, and Detroit, with depressed incomes, high unemployment (especially among youth), an increasing proportion of low-wage industry, and wide-spread downward mobility — without the gracious town plans and lovely architecture that relieve the poverty of Belem, Salvador, and Recife — one may justifiably hope that Montreal will not go the same route. There are solid reasons for viewing Montreal's current situation with concern, and seeking means of reversing unfavourable trends.

The Urban Hierarchy, Urban Growth and Regional Development

Let us therefore review briefly the literature on urban and regional economics to see if there are some "laws," tools of analysis, theories or concepts that may be useful in designing a strategy to revigorate Montreal. This book is obviously not the place for a general survey of recent progress in the field of urban and regional economics, and such is not our intent. Rather we shall limit ourselves to well-known theories which fall into at least one of three categories:

1. Theories that can legitimately be tested by comparing them with the experience of a single city;
2. Theories that might help in making a prognosis for that city;
3. Theories that might be the basis for formulating a prescription for that city that would improve the prognosis.

The subject matter of urban and regional economics covers a wide range, and the range is wider still if we include urban and rural sociology, political science, and city and regional planning. We shall focus on those areas of discussion which seem most relevant to the three types of considerations listed above. One of these areas is the urban structure, or hierarchy, of a region, country, or larger unit, and the ways in which such structures change and why. Another is concerned with interactions between urban growth and regional development. A special branch of this field of analysis is the role of cities in the widening or narrowing of regional disparities. Another special field of inquiry is the inter-actions between cities in the same structure, and the impact of these interactions on growth or decline of those cities. Ultimately, we are concerned with the whole complex feedback system of city-region-nation.

It must be stressed that urban and regional economics is a relatively immature branch of the discipline, and we will not find ourselves on such firm ground as we would if concerned with monetary, fiscal, and trade policy. Urban and regional economics have only recently become a focus of attention for the economics profession, and the amount of "received doctrine" in the field is still very limited. Nonetheless, some regularities have been dis-covered and some useful concepts have emerged. Let us look at some of the better known of these, with the specific case of Montreal in mind.

Neo-Classical Location Theory and Regional Balance

Let us begin with the prevailing neo-classical paradigm, which is at the core of mainstream economic thought in the western world, although increasingly under attack. The neo-classical theory of location of industry and the theory of regional balance grew up as offshoots of the theory of equilibrium of the firm, and are cast in essentially the same form. Both are theories concerning decisions made by the managers of enterprises, or entrepreneurs, and assume that the same general considerations apply to the choice of entrereneurs as to where to locate their enterprises, as to their decisions regarding what to produce, how much to produce, what combination of labour, capital, and natural resources to apply, and where and how to market the output. Basically, the idea is that entrepreneurs make choices which they believe will maximize the long-run profits of the firm. Prices are usually assumed to be given for the firm, although the "theory of monopolistic competi-tion" does take account of decisions regarding advertizing, packaging, and other aspects of marketing, which may alter prices. The main factors in decisions about location are therefore those pertaining to costs: wages for various types of labour skill;

prices of various types of equipment; prices of raw materials; and cost of transporting the final product to the market. The forces of competition are supposed to bring prices of factors of production, as well as prices of final products, into equilibrium, apart from transport costs. Thus no net advantage remains on that score in one site as compared to another. Consequently transport costs, of getting inputs to the site and outputs to the consumer, become the major factor determining choice of location in neo-classical location theory.

In the neo-classical theory, regional disparities cannot persist. If wages are lower in one region than in another, capital will flow to that region, thus raising labour productivity and wages. Labour on the other hand will flow from the poor to the rich region, reducing wages there. If returns to capital are higher in one region than another, capital will flow from the low-return to the high-return region, making capital more scarce and raising returns on it in the low-return region, and making it more abundant and lowering returns in the high-return region. If either the entrepreneurs or the workers want to stay in a particular region, despite a lower level or productivity of labour and capital, or higher transport costs, a free market will reduce wages and returns to capital enough to permit the disadvantaged region to compete, and thus to maintain full employment of both labour and capital. In some versions of the theory, it is not even necessary for labour or capital to migrate for incomes to be equalized among regions or nations; it is necessary only to have freedom or interregional and international trade.

If we could accept this theory at face value, it would not be very comforting for those who are concerned about the future of Montreal. It does provide a partial explanation for the early growth of Montreal; the city did have an advantage in terms of transport costs when the rivers were the main highways, and for a long time Montreal was near the centre of the main Canadian market. But these advantages in transport costs and markets are long since gone, and Montreal does not have an across-the-board advantage in terms of basic production costs over other North American cities. However, there are two reasons why we need not take the neo-classical theory too seriously when making a prognosis for Montreal. The first is that the theory is "true" only when hedged in by a host of simplifying assumptions which are in fact highly unrealistic: identical technology and production functions in all regions; an infinite range of choice of combinations of labour and capital; perfect competition; perfect knowledge; perfect foresight; complete, costless and instantaneous diffusion of information, including information about new techniques; no economies or diseconomies of scale; no indivisibilities or discontinuities of factor inputs, outputs, or decision making; no government interference with the working of the free market; no external costs or benefits, no public goods. The second is that today, in a metropolis as large and as sophisticated as Montreal, other considerations weigh more heavily in location decisions than cost of production and cost of transport. The service enterprises which provide most of the employment, and many of the scientifically-oriented manufacturing enterprises as well, are "footloose," so far as production and transport costs are concerned. Consequently, more weight can be given in location decisions to such elements as the general attractiveness of various possible urban centres, especially to upper-income personnel such as managers, scientists, and engineers; presence of universities, research institutions and consulting firms; comparative tax burdens on the higher income groups; the social, cultural, and political environment; access to communications facilities and to convenient air transport. On grounds such as these, as we shall see in more detail below, the prospects for Montreal are considerably brighter, although there are a few problems.

There are by now many books attacking the neo-classical theory, its application to urban growth and regional development included. A book is what is required to do a satisfactory critical analysis of it. But we may allow ourselves one observation. In the market economies of Italy, West Germany, and France, per capita output in the richest region still ranges from 2.1 to 2.6 times that of the poorest region. The United States is frequently held up as an example of a successful free market economy. Yet it took that country 120 years to reduce the gap in per capita income between the richest and the poorest region from over 400 percent, as it was in 1860, to about 30 percent today, which might be regarded as tolerable. I doubt that the inhabitants of the poorer regions in Canada are in a mood to wait that long for their relative positions to be improved. Moreover, in the United States, as Harry W. Richardson has pointed out, there is at least a possibility of the gaps being reversed and becoming cumulatively worse again:

> In the relatively near future, an opportunity will develop to test the appropriateness of the neo-classical compared with the cumulative causation model. The key question is whether regional per capita

income will stabilize close to equality (i.e. an approximation to neo-classical equilibrium) or whether they will cross over, with the four lower income regions (South Atlantic, East South Central, West South Central and Mountain) then becoming progressively richer than the four regions of the northeast and midwest. The latter development would be more consistent with the cumulative causation model. The competing hypotheses or interregional income equilibrium and the "cross over" is the most intriguing question in contemporary regional economics.[2]

Translating Richardson's question into the Canadian context is not altogether simple because current trends are not clear. Quebec, we have seen, has made remarkable gains in the past two decades, and the gains seem to be accelerating. Alberta and British Columbia have also made rapid progress in the past ten years, surpassing Ontario in per capita income, but now show signs of slowing down if not actually stagnating. The Atlantic provinces show little sign of catching up with the other provinces. Is Quebec on its way to becoming Canada's richest province? With the new dynamism displayed by the French Canadian population of that province it is not beyond the realm of possibility.

Economic base theory

One chapter in the neo-classical theory of establishment and growth of cities is "economic base theory." The argument is that different regions have different resource endowments (natural or human) which give them a comparative advantage in the production and export of different goods and services. Economies of scale result in many of these productive activities taking place in urban centres. Cities grow as a consequence of the "multiplier effects" of the expansion of their exports.

There is obviously a large chunk of truth in this theory, but two words of caution are needed before an attempt is made to apply it to a particular case. First, increasing exports from one city depends upon growing income of other cities that are buying the exports; and growing income of other cities, according to this theory, depend upon expanding exports to other cities, which in turn depend upon rising incomes of other cities, which depend —. There is a basic circularity in the argument. Somewhere within the system something must happen to cause expansion of population and income of some of the cities, in a way that does not depend upon the rise of population and income of other cities. Second, the major exports today of cities like Montreal are services, and comparative advantage in export of services depends upon human resources, not natural resources. Montreal has long since moved away from dependence on any natural resource base, in her own hinterland, for her future growth. And human resources, being just people with particular training and skills, are highly mobile. About the only way to demonstrate a comparative advantage of a particular city in particular services is to point to the fact that the required human resources are available in the city, and that the services are being produced and exported — which is circular reasoning once again. The fact that so many sophisticated services have moved from Montreal to Toronto and elsewhere is proof that Montreal has lost some of her comparative advantage in these fields. The fact that many sophisticated services are still there means that Montreal has not lost her comparative advantage altogether. The economic base theory does not help us much in making a prognosis for Montreal, without detailed information on future comparative advantage in a wide range of economic activities.

Cumulative Causation and the "Knife-Edge Balance"

Several economists in recent decades have argued that, far from there being a tendency to return to equilibrium when the economy is disturbed, there is instead a tendency towards cumulative movement away from equilibrium. Roy Harrod of Oxford University has demonstrated that when the results of past investment decisions are more favourable than expected, entrepreneurs will raise their level of investment, stimulating further expansion of the national economy, bringing still higher profits, and another round of increased investment.[3] Unless brought to a halt by some unforeseen shock or by government policy, this process leads to cumulative growth and ultimately to hyperinflation. Conversely, disappointing results lead to reduced investment, further contraction of the economy, falling profits, successive rounds of cuts in investment, and deeper and deeper unemployment.

Evsey Domar of the Massachusetts Institute of Technology, in a work often linked to Harrod's, demonstrated that for an economy to remain in dynamic equilibrium, with steady growth, full employment, and stable prices, the percentage rate of growth of investment must equal the percentage rate of growth of national income, and both must equal a particular number; that is, the marginal propensity to save (increase in saving with a given increase in national income) multiplied by the accelerator (response of investment to a given increase in consumer spending).[4] The chances of any market economy staying on this "knife-edge" are obviously small. Indeed one economist, John Cornwall, felt called upon to write a whole book attempting to explain how the comparatively steady growth of the industrialized market economies between 1950 and 1970 could possibly have happened.[5]

Gunnar Myrdal applied similar reasoning to regional disparities.[6] Regions with an initial advantage will tend to attract both labour and capital. Investment in the advantaged region will tend to raise both wages and profits there, leading to further inflows and further expansion. The accelerated population growth in the more prosperous region will itself encourage investment there. Because of linkages between advantaged and disadvantaged regions, expansion of the more prosperous region will generate both "spread effects" (favourable impacts) and "backwash effects" (unfavourable impacts) on the less prosperous ones, but the backwash effects will prevail. For example, emigration from the lagging region will discourage investment there. So the rich regions get richer and the poor regions get poorer, and regional disparities get worse and worse.

Whether industrialized market economies are characterized by constant movements towards equilibrium in the wake of any disturbance, or, in the absence of favourable shocks or effective government intervention, by cumulative movements away from equilibrium, is a question of fact that cannot be settled by any exercise in pure theory alone. The answer is probably "sometimes the one, sometimes the other." There is a whole set of theories of economic fluctuations, or business cycles, of different durations, which depend upon alternations of movements towards with movements away from equilibrium. These can be applied to regional disparities as well as to national economies as a whole. It can be shown that regions with a slow rate of long run growth tend to have as well longer and deeper depressions than regions with faster long run rates of growth. This interaction helps to explain the lag of Quebec behind more prosperous provinces until recent years.[7] The catching up of Quebec has lasted too short a time for us to be sure that a new long run trend has set in. But there is reason to think that it has, based mainly upon a new wave of technological advance, upgrading of skills, and improvements in product-mix and occupational structure, as evidenced by the rapid rise in productivity. If all that is true, we can expect an improvement in the pattern of Quebec business cycles too, and the whole catching-up process could become cumulative. Perhaps Quebec really will be Canada's richest province by the time the century ends. Human-resource-based development is a much more reliable source of continued progress than natural-resource-based development. Montreal cannot help but participate in any such new wave of progress in Quebec, if only because a large part of the progress is bound to take place in the metropolis itself.

Bi-Modal Production and Regional Dualism

Closely related to Myrdal's concept of cumulative causation in relations among regions is the theory of regional dualism, which grew out of the theory of bi-modal production or technological dualism, developed at M.I.T. in the late 1950s. The latter theory in turn was an effort to explain why very large-scale investment and rapid expansion of exports in developing countries failed to bring generalized prosperity in its wake, and brought instead the division of the national economies into two distinct sectors: a modern sector using advanced, capital-intensive technology, where output per manyear is high; and a traditional sector, using small-scale, labour-intensive techniques and traditional modes of production where output per manyear is low. In developing countries the traditional sector is consecrated mainly to peasant agriculture, fishing, and handicrafts. Industry, plantation agriculture, mining and forestry, with heavy equipment, and services related to these, are in the modern sector.

This situation came about because European settlement was associated with a population explosion, and because techniques became increasingly capital-intensive in the modern sector as time went by. Large-scale though the investment in the modern sector was, it did not create enough jobs to keep up with the growth of the labour force, compelling the bulk of the increase of the population to seek their livelihood in the traditional sector, resulting in severe population pressure on the land and "shared poverty."

From this analysis it is an easy step to regional dualism. The advanced regions are simply those in which the modern sector is concentrated, often in a few major cities, plus some plantation, mining and forestry areas. The traditional sector is concentrated in the retarded regions, mainly in the countryside, although an informal sector that is mainly traditional may exist in cities too. Thus the large regional disparities that are associated with underdevelopment are the outcome of the geographical spread of the modern and traditional sectors.

Does this analysis have anything to do with Canada, Quebec, and Montreal? The answer is yes. Of course, the disparities in technology, occupational structure, and product-mix are less glaringly apparent in Canada today than they are in developing countries, just as the regional gaps are less wide. But historically regional gaps in Canada, as elswehere, have been associated with differences in the things people were doing to earn a living, and in the techniques they used to do them. Even today, a part of the relative poverty of areas like Gaspésie/Bas St-Laurent and northeast New Brunswick is explained by the numbers engaged in relatively traditional fishing and forestry and in marginal farming, and the failure of more technologically-advanced enterprises to grow fast enough to absorb all the population growth. In other lagging regions, such as the Cantons de l'Est in Quebec, the explanation lies rather in the numbers still engaged in traditional manufacturing activities, such as textiles, boots and shoes, clothing, furniture, etc. And when we come to Montreal itself, we have seen that not so long ago the discrepancies between the Montreal economy and that of Toronto could be traced to the smaller number of modern, hi-tech enterprises, and the larger number of those that were comparatively traditional in their product mix and their techniques.

Now, happily, Montreal seems to be on its way out of this comparatively unfavourable position of being located in a region where productivity is comparatively low because of a relatively high concentration of traditional undertakings. But it is not all the way out of it yet.

Dependency Theory and Uneven Development

At the end of Chapter 4, in analyzing Montreal's role within the Quebec economy, we considered briefly the question of whether or not Montreal should be regarded as a neo-colonial enclave, dependent upon decisions made by multinational corporations in the United States, Europe, Japan and the Middle East and stifling growth in the rest of Quebec. Now we must raise this question again with respect to Montreal's future.

The last three decades have seen a massive revival of neo-marxist theories of economic development and social change. One group of authors, mainly American, has labelled themselves Radical Political Economists. Another, overlapping school, which began in Latin America and spread to Africa and Europe, is called the *dependentistas*, or dependency theorists. The various theories take a wide range of forms, and there are lively debates among the neo-marxists themselves. This diversity of ideas means that summarization in short compass will satisfy no one; but the neo-marxist framework of analysis has recently been applied to urban growth and regional development, and the ideas that have emerged are too important to ignore. For those who may not be acquainted with the voluminous literature on Radical Political Economy, we shall present a rough sketch (some will no doubt say caricature) of the basic ideas, proceed to their application in the field of urban growth and regional development, and then relate these ideas to the case of Montreal.

There are two main versions of dependency theory, which I have labelled the "conspiracy" theory and the "black box" theory. Both assume that power is concentrated in the hands of the capitalist class in industrialized capitalist countries (ICCs) typified by the multinational corporations (MNCs). In the conspiracy theory this power is used consciously and deliberately to keep wages down, in developing countries and in retarded regions of ICCs, in order to protect profits. Incomes of peasants and farmers are also kept down, for two reasons; the capitalists need cheap food in order to keep wages low, and rising incomes in the rural sector would tend to raise the wages that must be offered to lure workers from the farms to the factories.

The way in which the system works is illustrated by figure A. The capitalists at the "Centre" (metropolitan centres and rich regions of ICCs) exercise their power in several, mutually support-ing ways. First, they bring pressure directly upon workers and peasants at the periphery (developing countries and retarded regions of ICCs), utilizing the superior bargaining power inherent in their monopoly and monopsony positions. Second, they require the weaker capitalist class of the periphery, which they dominate, to do the same directly and through their governments of ICCs. Third, they direct the governments of ICCs, which are mere creatures of the capitalist class, to put pressure on the govern-ments, and on the capitalist classes, in the periphery to compel them to carry out policies favourable to the capitalist class at the

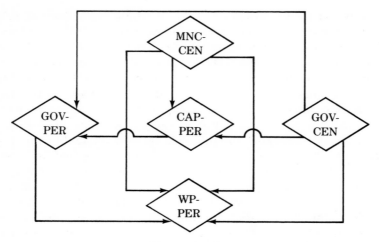

Figure A Key

MNC-CEN	Multinational Corporations in the Centre
GOV-CEN	Government in the Centre
WP-PER	Workers and Peasant in the Periphery
CAP-PER	Capitalists in the Periphery
GOV-PER	Government in the Periphery

centre; and also to execute policies themselves which help to keep workers and farmers poor. Fourth, they bring pressure of their own on the governments at the periphery (governments of developing countries or provincial and local governments in ICCs) to make sure that their interests are protected.

The "black box" version makes some allowance for good intentions on the part of the capitalist class, admitting that some capitalists really think that they are improving the lot of workers and peasants through their operations. However, the basic structure of capitalism, with all of its "contradictions," is such that good intentions produce evil results. The analysis of this basic structure is perhaps the weak spot in dependency theory; the logic of the "conspiracy" version is at least clear. The theory of bimodal production, or technological dualism, outlined above, would put analytical content into the black box; but on the whole dependency theorists have shied away from the concept of dualism, insisting on the monolithic nature of international capitalism.

180

Since the system involves inter-related decision making by so many widely scattered groups, it is very hard to test empirically. Most dependency theorists tend to support their arguments merely by citing examples of the *results* of the operation of the system in particular cases. The typical case study takes this form of logic:

> The MNCs are big, rich, and powerful
>
> The MNCs want profits
>
> The MNCs must keep wages and peasant incomes down in order to maintain profits
>
> The MNCs earn big profits in the retarded region of Esperanza
>
> The workers and farmers of Esperanza are virtuous, hard working, and abstemious, but poor
>
> Therefore the poverty of the Esperanza region is to be explained by capitalist exploitation.

Note that the logical structure of this argument is the same as in the following sequence:

> Bill Smith is big, strong, and handsome
>
> Bill Smith likes girls, and does what he must to get them
>
> Bill Smith is dating Mary Jones
>
> Mary Jones is a nice girl but pregnant
>
> Therefore Bill Smith raped Mary Jones.

One can only hope that such an argument would not stand up in court, if Mary Jones's angry father pressed charges. In fact, both Mary and Bill feel that theirs is a "meaningful relationship," they want to marry and raise a family eventually, and Bill is more sorry than Mary that she became pregnant too soon.

One of the "contradictions" of capitalism is that the capitalists want the workers to do their jobs for low wages, but they also want the workers to buy a lot of their products. In the United States, and to a lesser degree and a bit later in the United Kingdom, Scandinavia, and western Europe, the system actually worked in such a way as to bring substantial increases in real wages, leading eventually to mass consumption. To what extent this development resulted from conscious decisions of the capitalists is perhaps debatable; the famous story of Henry Ford suggests that at least some of them saw the advantages of high wages. But in the developing countries the imperialist powers (including the United States with regard to Latin America and the

Philippines) seem to have been more interested in getting cheap labour than in selling their products to the indigenous population. True mass consumption has yet to emerge in any of the former colonies except Australia, Canada, New Zealand and the United States.

I have myself endeavoured to test the dependency theory by analyzing the relationship of levels of living and improvements in these, in a large sample of countries, to foreign investment, foreign trade, terms and balance of trade, exports to and imports from ICCs, dependence on ICCs for food and energy, and similar factors to which importance is attached by dependency theorists. The results are not very conclusive, but show that on balance countries which are more dependent on the ICCs in terms such as these tend to be better off than those which are less dependent.[8] To make a convincing test of the theory, one would need to study the decision-making process of all the groups in the diagram above — without being oneself observed by them, lest awareness of your presence might alter their behaviour — and then study the mechanisms by which their decisions are implemented and the impact upon the welfare of workers and farmers — an enormous undertaking.

There are debates among the Radical Political Economists themselves as to whether or not the relative poverty of lagging regions should be regarded as the product of neo-colonial capitalistic exploitation. The current trend seems to be rather to treat regional disparities as the product of another feature of capitalist development, namely "uneven development."[9] A recent and typical expression of this theory is that of Columbia University economist Neil Smith, who writes in his recent book on *Uneven Development*:

> ... capital is like a plague of locusts. It settles in one place, devours it, moves on to plague another place. Better, in the process of restoring itself after one plague the region makes itself ripe for another. At the very least, uneven development is the geographical expression of the contradictions of capital.[10]

 The process of capitalistic accumulation leads to concentration of wealth, not only in the hands of a particular social class, but in particular places as well, leading to polarization of development. Underdevelopment in some regions and cities is the opposite side of the coin of development in others. Cities are "the most accomplished geographical expression of centralization of capital."[11] Geographic space itself is not something that is given; the geographic landscape is the product of capitalistic development. But

182

powerful as they are, capitalists face constant threats to their profits, in the form of rising costs of labour, transport, and rents. They are consequently constantly on the lookout for new and cheaper locations for their operations, and will move at the drop of a hat, inhibited only by their inability to move fixed physical capital. Development is uneven both in time and in space, and the incessant and frenzied efforts of the capitalist class to protect their profits and accumulate still more capital leads to disruptive restructuring of geographic space.

So where does all that leave Montreal?

There can be no doubt that the "capitalist class," including multinational corporations — American, Canadian, Japanese, European — has played and will play a major role in determining Montreal's fate. And even if we may doubt that the decisions of high salaried managers of particular enterprises have much to do with maximizing profits of that enterprise (they may not be major shareholders, and they may be more concerned with outselling rivals and expanding output) there can be little doubt that they are keenly interested in the preservation of the capitalist system and the maintenance of the profitability of private enterprise as a whole. Whether they believe that this objective is best attained by grinding down the faces of the poor or by encouraging reasonable increases in wages and salaries, so as to improve the market for their products, is a question open to research. That they will on occasion pull up stakes and move somewhere else, whether to increase their profits or to live in a better climate, without much concern for the social impact of their decision on the places they leave, is scarcely open to question at all.

So we can agree that what happens to Montreal depends a good deal on what the capitalists at the centre want to happen. But even within the framework of the dependency theory itself, two major questions arise: Is Montreal centre or periphery? And what do the capitalists at the centre, whoever they are and wherever they are, want to happen?

In my view, neither of these questions can be answered in the black and white terms so favoured by the dependency theorists. Montreal is neither at *the* centre nor on the periphery. It has a certain status within a very complex urban hierarchy which extends beyond Canada in all directions, with equally complex ties to a host of non-urban regions scattered in global economic space. More thorough research could no doubt isolate the decision-making centres most important for a prognosis for Montreal; but the list would certainly include Toronto, Ottawa, Calgary, Vancouver, Quebec City, New York, London, Paris, Zurich, Brussels and whichever city is the site of the next OPEC meeting. In answer to the second question, it can be safely stated that while the capitalist class clearly needs profits to survive, they want a lot of other things too, including life in a pleasant place without too much tension and friction. Whether one believes that governments and even trade unions in capitalist countries are mere creatures of the capitalist class is partly a matter of observation and partly a matter of faith; but I believe that at least on occasion they can take decisions and actions that are inimical to the short-run interests of the capitalist class, so that what happens to Montreal depends on what they want too. Who dares to predict the decisions of management, labour, and government, all three, in a dozen countries or so, over the next two or three decades?

The Urban Hierarchy

When we speak of "reversing trends," and generating a "renaissance" in Montreal, preventing further deterioration of Montreal's position in the Canadian urban hierarchy, we are speaking of intervening in the urban structure. All that we have learned in the past few decades about urban growth and regional development suggests that the forces determining the relative positions of cities within an economy like Canada's are very powerful, and that redirecting them by government policy is far from easy.

The concept of a "hierarchy of cities" has two aspects, one essentially quantitative and the other more qualitative. The first of these relates to relative size of cities, usually expressed in terms of population, although in principle it could be expressed in terms of income, employment, or some other measure. The question here relates to the degree of stability in the size-distribution of cities in any economy. The second aspect relates to the kinds of economic activity or occupations that are likely to be found in cities of various sizes. One principle states that, as certain "thresholds" of size (usually measured by population) are passed, additional economic activities, appropriate to cities of the newly attained size, become possible. Given the close association of occupational structure with levels of per capita income, and the tendency for the "quality" of economic activity to improve with size of city, a corollary of this proposition would be that average productivity and incomes will tend to rise with size of city.

The Rank-Size Rule

A frequently cited "quantitative" principle regarding urban structure is the "rank-size rule." The rule implies that the second city in the hierarchy should have a population half that of the bigger city, the third city one third the population, and so on.[12] This principle also implies that as a national or regional economy grows, cities in all size-groups will grow more or less proportionately, so that the relative sizes, or the shape of the size-distribution curve (slope of the straight line on double log paper) remains more or less unchanged.

This "rule" stands up surprisingly well to empirical testing, at least for advanced countries and for large or prosperous less developed countries (LDC's) such as Malaysia, China and India.[13] In small LDC's a different structure frequently emerges, with a primate city as centre of the "rich" region, and "the rest of the country" which is usually the poor region (Sri Lanka, Salvador, Greece, Senegal). It should be emphasized, however, that the rank-size rule applies to groups of cities, and does not tell us what will be the fate of any particular city. Some cities may grow rapidly while others decline and still the rank-size rule could be maintained. Particular cities may change rank considerably over time, as in the case of burgeoning Atlanta and Houston and declining Cleveland and Detroit in the United States, or in the case of slipping Quebec City, Halifax, and Saint John in Canada, without violating the rank-size rule.

Increasing Rigidity of Urban Structure: "Lasuen's Law"

It has been argued, by José Ramon Lasuen among others that urban structures become more rigid as national development proceeds.[14] Data on European nations show an increasing stability in the urban structure over long periods up to 1970. The process is even clearer in the U.S., where the dramatic shifts within the urban hierarchy of cities like those of Chicago and Los Angeles in the late nineteenth and early twentieth centuries disappeared in the decades following World War II. A study of urban growth in the United States by William Alonso and Elliott Medrich points to similar conclusions.[15] It shows that between 1900 and 1965 an increasing share of metropolitan growth is accounted for by the larger and faster growing centres. The study also shows that cities with above-average rates of growth in recent decades have usually been high-growth centres for several decades.

Lasuen explains the increased rigidity of urban structure in terms of the changing nature of innovation and of the "dynamic" enterprises. The very fact that the new-style, innovating, dynamic enterprises are "footloose," rather than tied to natural resources, energy, or transport, means not only that the dynamic enterprises can move if they wish, but also that they can stay where they are if they do not want to move. And, says Lasuen, they do not want to move; the top level entrepreneurs, managers, scientists and engineers prefer to stay in the dynamic metropolitan centres where such enterprises are already located. As Lasuen puts it:

> Of late, the production engineering revolution has initiated an entirely new type of management and drastically changed the organizational structure of the leading corporations... They operate plants all over the world, market thousands of products, produce many, assemble others, subcontract all sorts of functions, have footholds in agriculture, industry, services, and so on. In brief, to realize the change in corporation structure which has occurred in the last thirty years, just compare the tremendous rigidity of Krupp with the stupendous flexibility of Litton."...[16]

Lasuen concludes that the rise of new enterprises is much less likely now than in the past to lead to the rise of new cities. The new scientifically oriented undertakings are likely to go to the cities where existing scientifically oriented enterprises already are, attracted by the same characteristics: research institutes, universities, sophisticated cultural and recreational facilities, physical beauty, pleasant residential districts, good schools, and a large and diversified group of sophisticated, highly trained, creative, and interesting people.

Increasing instability of urban structures: The 1970s and '80s

The ink was hardly dry on these "proofs" of long-run trends towards increasing rigidity of urban structures when patterns of migration of labour and capital, and thus of regional development and urban structure, began to change drastically. In the United States the dramatic shift was towards the sunbelt and the west, leading the U.S. Census Bureau to predict that by the end of the century 60 percent of the American population would be living in these two regions. As a result of these shifts the established

186

metropolitan centres of the north declined in relative importance. In fact the northern metropolitan regions with populations above 2.5 million, as a group, actually declined in total population during the 1970s. The northern metropolitan regions with populations between 1.0 and 2.5 million continued to grow, but at a rate less than one third the national average. The most rapid urban growth in the 70s occurred in small and middle-sized cities. In Canada too net immigration into established metropolitan centres (core regions) declined abruptly during the 1970s, not only in Montreal but in the "golden horseshoe" of southwestern Ontario as well.

Similar patterns emerged in Europe. Northwestern Europe experienced declining net immigration into core regions even in the 1950s, which turned into net emigration in the 1960s and '70s. Japan also registered a sharp drop in net immigration into the larger metropolitan areas in the '70s. In France, the Paris region is losing population to the south and the west. Even in the United Kingdom emigration from the northern periphery fell during the '70s, and the southeast (London) had net emigration. West Germany too had net emigration from the Rhine/Ruhr industrial heartland, mostly to the south. Belgium registered net emigration from the Brussels metropolitan region to the less prosperous region of Wallonia in the south. In Spain there was reduced migration from the peripheral regions of the south and west to the four core regions.

This experience gave rise to predictions of de-industrialization, counter-urbanization, polarization reversal and new patterns of polarization, a new "post-industrial" and "post-metropolitan" era. Thus Gregory Jackson and George Masnick write:

> Between 1940 and 1970, regional demographic growth rates were converging. Since 1970, however, the nation has become increasingly polarized between regions where high levels of natural increase (the excess of births over deaths) combine with high levels of in-migration to produce rapid growth and regions where low natural increase combines with out-migration to produce low or negative growth. Our research indicates that, contrary to some influential estimates, this polarization will continue throughout the 1980s...

> ... The nation faces, therefore, a continuing shift of employment, income, and population away from the "older" (that is, economically mature), industrialized, and densely settled regions of the north towards the "newer", less industrialized, and more sparsely settled regions of the south and west. Within the sunbelt and frostbelt, growth differentials are taking a new form. Within all regions, the shift is from metropolitan to nonmetropolitan areas.[17]

187

Similarly, A. Fielding concludes from a study of nine European countries that "'Urbanization', used in the sense of a positive relationship between net migration and settlement size, has ceased in almost all of the countries of western Europe in the period 1950–1980"; and adds "In seven of the nine countries in which it can be shown that urbanization has ceased, the metropolitan and principal industrial cities showed, during the 1970s, signs of net migration loss, and rural regions containing small and medium-sized towns showed signs of net migration gain." [18] Brian Berry, one of America's leading economic geographers and regional scientists, also concluded that "counterurbanization has replaced urbanization as the dominant force shaping the nation's settlement patterns." [19]

Back to Lasuen's Law?

For the early 1980s the data are of course a good deal less comprehensive than census data for 1970 or 1971 and for 1980 or 1981. But the figures available so far suggest another turnaround. The experience of the 1970s may have been an aberration from longer run trends, and Lasuen may have been right after all.

The United States figures, for example, show that in 1980-81-82 there was a decrease in immigration to the south and also a mirror-image decline in emigration from the northeast and the midwest. The picture for the west is even more blurred: immigration into the region declined in 1980-81 but increased again in 1982. The shift towards small and middle-sized cities has also been reversed. [20] Of particular importance for Montreal, the population of the northeast, which had been declining for a decade, increased in 1981 and 1982. Even more heartening is the rise in population in the northern areas of Vermont, New Hampshire, and Maine, although this phenomenon seems to reflect movements for residential and recreational purposes rather than migration of industry.

In Japan too a process of "reconcentration" has set in during the 1980s, especially in the Tokyo area. Western Europe shows a strong trend towards zero net migration among regions, suggesting that a species of at least temporary equilibrium has been reached. [21]

Altogether it is not very clear what is going on in the world with regard to urban structures, and it would be a bold social scientist who dared predict what will happen in the future. What emerges most clearly is that the new technology has introduced a new fluidity and flexibility with respect to location of economic activity. Hansen points out that the relative decline of the northern U.S. metropolitan areas during the 1970s is in itself somewhat illusory.[22] While it is true that these areas either declined in population or grew less rapidly than the average rate for the country as a whole, the same is true of the northern non-metropolitan areas. In the south and west, by contrast, *all* size classes of cities grew at rates above the national average, and metropolitan areas as a group grew more rapidly than non-metropolitan areas. In fact the highest rates of growth in the south and west were registered by the largest cities, in the 2.5-5.0 million category. Thus the relative decline in northern metropolitan areas was a by-product of the more general shift of economic activity to the south and the west. It is not easy to discern what is going on in the world right now with regard to urban structures, and it would be rash to interpret it in terms of any general law. It would be still more rash to make a firm forecast of what will happen in future.

What emerges most clearly is that there is a new fluidity and flexibility with respect to location of economic activity. Most observers attribute this tendency for enterprises to become increasingly "footloose" to the new technology, including improvements in transport and communications. Niles Hansen writes:

> Various explanations have been given for the relatively recent changes in the spatial division of labour. In the U.S. context they have included improved transportation and communications accessibility, changing life styles, weather differences, air conditioning, a growing number of footloose retirees, changing energy relationships, differing "business climates", and regional differences in federal taxation and spending policies.

He adds, "However, the *sine qua non* is technological change."[23]

One of the arguments made is that the new Hi-Tech industries are of a sort that can be efficiently conducted by small or middle-sized enterprises (SMEs), and that SMEs can operate effectively in small and middle-sized cities, and are more mobile than the vast industrial complexes that dominated an earlier generation of industrial and urban growth. Questions arise, however, regarding all of these propositions, and indeed with respect to all aspects of the relationship between the pace and pattern of innovation and the location of enterprises. Probably the most thorough survey of accumulated knowledge of this subject is that conducted by

Philippe Aydalot for the Group on New Technologies and Space, in Paris.[24] After studying a vast amount of literature, Aydalot reports the following findings:

1. New technologies are often the work of new enterprises which are created in and by the milieux where they are located, rather than choosing a location for production after the event. "L'entreprise n'est pas un agent tombé du ciel qui 'choisirait' librement son environnement: elle est secrétée par son environnement: ce sont les milieux qui entreprennent et qui innovent".

2. Research-and-development (R & D) is still heavily concentrated in the largest metropolitan centres: 52 percent in the 10 largest centres in the U.S., 30 to 40 percent in the Tokyo area of Japan, 50 percent in the greater Paris region of France.

3. In the United States, apart from a tendency for Hi-Tech enterprises to stay in Massachusetts, they are migrating to the south and west.

4. Hi-Tech industries can also be very resistent to changes in location desired as a matter of government policy. This statement applies with special force to non-production workers. Thus while the share of telecommunications employment in assisted regions in the U.K. increased from 28 to 37 percent in twenty years, the employment was in the more mature types of production where less advanced technology was applied and lower skills required.

5. The innovations that do take place in retarded regions tend to be less advanced than those that appear in more prosperous regions.

6. In the U.K. the share of innovations undertaken by SMEs is increasing but still small, and nearly a third of them fail.

7. Large companies are capable of introducing innovations anywhere, but SMEs which are in large metropolitan centres innovate more than those in small and middle-sized cities.

8. SMEs do not suffer from lack of *access* to new technology.

9. In the U.K., the U.S.A., and Italy, the old, established industrial regions adopt innovations sooner than the others. In Italy the adoption of robots follows the classic model of "seeping down" from the top to the bottom of the urban hierarchy, but SMEs were often the first to adopt them.

10. The speed of transmission depends on the structure of individual enterprises. Decisions on technology are largely a matter of "conflict resolution" among different members of top management. The older men who are often in power tend to fear and distrust new technologies that they do not know, younger and more recently trained members of the management team are more eager to innovate.

190

11. To innovate an enterprise needs more than technical and scientific skills; it also needs skills in finance, marketing, feasibility studies, etc.
12. The new information technology reduces the importance of information as a factor in location. However, this fact may strengthen either SMEs in small and middle-sized cities, or top management in the head offices of large companies in large cities.
13. There is a tendency for Hi-Tech industries to concentrate in the neighbourhood of university centres (Route 128 near Boston, Silicon Valley near San Francisco, Research Triangle Science Park in North Carolina, Science Park near Cambridge, England, the southern suburbs of Paris). Yet other evidence suggests that the ability to consult the scientific community of *the same* region is not a major factor in location decisions. (It may be that managers, scientists and engineers trained in an exciting and pleasant city like to stay there after graduating; or it may be that the same environment which attracts top flight people to universities also attracts them to Hi-Tech industries).
14. Both the residential environment and the socio-cultural environment are important factors in the location of Hi-Tech enterprises.
15. More generally, there has been a sharp shift during recent decades in the factors determining location of industry. Traditional factors such as access to raw materials, transport, markets, energy, and infrastructure now play a relatively minor role. According to a study of 691 Hi-Tech enterprises in the United States, the most important factors in location were availability of technicians, skilled labour, and professionals, followed by tax burdens and the level of wages and salaries. Further down the line but still important were transport facilities for persons, cultural facilities, presence of a university, and cost of living.

Aydalot's main conclusion, however, is that there is just too much uncertainty about this whole issue, and his research institute is now launched upon a vast project to get some more clear cut answers to the questions still hanging fire.

What we can take from Lasuen and Aydalot is that enterprises in the vanguard of scientific and engineering progress and industrial expansion today, the innovating, impulsive enterprises whose presence characterizes a development pole, are more "footloose" than ever before. They do not need to be near to sources of raw materials, because transport costs of raw materials is a minor consideration. They do not *need* to be close to their final markets, because transport costs of their final products are low relative to the value of these products (the cost of transporting a computer *program* is a postage stamp). Being close to the market is still an advantage but it is not essential and other things count more. For the top level managers, scientists and engineers, a very important consideration is being in or near a city in which it is pleasant to live. Perhaps even more important is being where the action is, in daily contact with the mainstream of scientific and technological progress. The conclusion is on balance a cheerful one. It is not only the megalopolis that can attract new, dynamic, high-productivity enterprises. Middle-sized metropolises can do it too, — provided they have some special advantages.

In comparison to the United States and Europe, Canada's urban structure seems still to be somewhat "immature." As may be seen from Chart 4, there were no dramatic changes in overall structure between 1961 and 1981, and the cities that grew rapidly during these two decades were for the most part cities that were growing rapidly before. But both Edmonton and Calgary overtook Winnipeg during these twenty years, while London, Windsor and Charlottetown registered small declines in population (perhaps through movements to suburbs beyond the city limits) and Moncton and Niagara-St. Catharines were virtually stagnant. These demographic trends, of course, reflect the resource boom in Alberta which has made it Canada's wealthiest province, the continued relative stagnation of the Atlantic provinces, and the recent tarnish on the formerly glittering economy of Ontario's "Golden Horseshoe." It seems likely that the new wave of frontier development based on oil and other minerals will continue to play a major role in Canadian development for some years to come, bringing consequent further shifts in distribution of population among regions and cities, and in relative levels of income.

Explanation of the Urban Hierarchy

What explains the apparent regularity in the size-distribution of cities? The only honest answer, probably, is "We don't yet know."

One view is that the regularity of the size distribution of cities of "stochastic"; that is, a simple byproduct of the law of large numbers, with no particular causal significance.[25] Other social phenomena (income distribution, for example) seem to obey the same law, and the principle seems to stand up less well where the number of cities in a country or region is small. Most urban and

CHART 4

Metropolitan Regions of Canada, 1961, 1971 and 1981

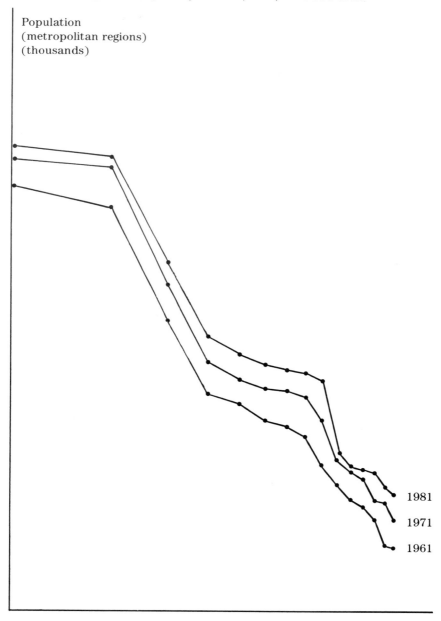

Population
(metropolitan regions)
(thousands)

1981

1971

1961

regional economists, however, feel that there is a causal process at work in the phenomenon of urban structure.

Another idea, attractive to economists because of its analogy to the concept of equilibrium, is the concept of "spin-off" or the "seeping down process." As cities grow, diseconomies as well as economies of scale appear; the balance of economies and diseconomies is not the same for all economic activities. As various thresholds of city-size are reached, the diseconomies of scale for some activities outweigh economies, and it becomes profitable to transplant certain enterprises, or certain aspects of their operations to smaller centres. Thus, automobile assembly has been widely diffused throughout the North American economy in recent decades; "sophisticated" enterprises like I.B.M. set up manufacturing plants in small towns, like Bromeau, Quebec, while maintaining head offices in large metropolitan centres. Scientific instruments and consulting service and research firms establish themselves in middle-sized cities like Palo Alto and Santa Barbara, California; Austin, Texas, etc., which have universities and other research organizations, although these are usually close to large metropolitan centres.

A factor which has received too little attention is simple differences in taste. Some people prefer large cities, some middle-sized ones, and some like small towns. People will tend to establish themselves in towns of the size they prefer, whenever their field of specialization permits. They may even choose their field of specialization in terms of the kind of city in which it can be practised successfully. With the increasing concern with pollution, congestion, organized violence and crime in large cities, more and more people may seek the sophisticated smaller city. Yet, the lure of the metropolis remains. And as Prof. Lloyd Rodwin, Director of M.I.T.'s Special Program in Urban Studies and Planning has pointed out, we do not really know when a city is too big or too congested, rather than merely poorly organized.[26]

Another clear cut conclusion arising from studies made to date is that there exists in any country or region a "critical size" or "threshold" in the size of cities for each category of economic activity.

It will be easier to create new growth centres near Montreal or Toronto than in areas far from any true metropolitan centre. The principle applies both to manufacturing and to services; the quality of both (in terms of technology, skills, growth, productivity, and outlet for talent and training) tends to rise with city size.

194

There is, however, also a phenomenon of "borrowed size." High-quality activities may be found in middle sized, or even small, cities if they are near enough to metropolitan centres.

Central Place Theory

As originally formulated by Walter Christaller, "central place theory" was related to density of agricultural population and the impact on urban growth.[27] The theory was designed to "explain the size, number and distribution of towns." The urban hierarchy is viewed as a system of "central places." An interesting question is "How does the area/density relationship change with overall growth of an economy? Is this relationship affected significantly by geographic factors? These questions can be tested empirically by putting numbers into the simple identity, $P_t = AQ_t$ where P_t is the total population served by a central place, A is the area served, and Q_t the (average) population density of the area served.

This identity does not tell us, of course, how the population of an area served by a particular "central place" is divided between the city and the peripheral region. But a part of the concept is that the larger the area served or the greater the population density of the area, the more specialized functions will be found in the central place, and the larger its population will therefore be. Thus, there is also a conception of dividing lines between "zones of influence" of several cities in a system.

In the "central place" theory it is the region that creates the city, not the city that creates employment and income in the region. The city grows by providing services to the population of its zone of influence. Urban growth is limited by the growth of population (and perhaps of per capita income) in its peripheral region. The metropolitan centre, of course, will have other cities within its system, for which it serves as "central place" for higher level services, while smaller towns serve as "central places" for the population of their more restricted zones of influence. A small market town, for example, may provide farmers with a place to sell their products and to purchase other consumers' goods.

We see here the importance of the higher population density in Toronto's peripheral region than in Montreal's peripheral region. According to the central place doctrine, it is to be expected that the range, quantity and quality of economic activities in Toronto should be superior to those of Montreal.

Growth poles

The concept of "growth poles" was introduced into the literature by the distinguished French economist François Perroux.[28] The basic idea behind the "growth pole" doctrine is just the opposite of that behind the central place theory. Here it is the expansion of the metropolitan urban economy which generates "spread effects" in the form of employment and income elsewhere. The theory enjoyed enormous vogue during the late 1960s and early 1970s and is now somewhat in disarray because of misunderstanding or misapplication of Perroux' ideas. There is probably not a retarded region of any importance anywhere in the world where some planners or politicians have not proposed the creation or strengthening of a "growth pole" to take care of the problem. In addition, the disillusionment with highly aggregated development planning cast in terms of growth of national income during the 1950s and 1960s led to a wide-spread search for ways of disaggregating development planning; and many governments found that the easiest way to disaggregate is in space. For planning purposes, it became common practice to break the "growth pole" concept in two: "development poles" generating spread effects and "growth centres" reacting strongly to them. It is probably fair to say that the majority of developing countries have experimented in recent years with development planning which proceeds from the urban hierarchy, treated as a system of development poles and "growth centres" adding up to a desired pattern of national development.

It has been found, however, that even where policies powerful enough to influence the urban hierarchy have been instrumented, and new industrial and other economic activities have been pulled or pushed into cities selected as "growth poles" or "development poles" in retarded regions, the hoped-for "spread effects" have refused to spread. Certainly, people can be attracted to cities to take jobs created there, reducing population pressure in the surrounding countryside, and bringing structural change of a kind which has been associated with development everywhere in the past. Montreal has served as a centre of attraction in this way, too, as we have seen. But most of the planners and politicians who have dumped their eggs into the "growth pole" basket were hoping that industrial expansion in selected "growth poles" would create jobs and raise incomes *outside* the selected urban centre but *inside* the peripheral region. By and large this hoped-for result was not realized. Where it was, the explanation was simple: the industries in the "pole" were using raw materials produced region. It is easy to see that industrial growth in an iron and town that grew up close to iron and coal deposits will create j in the mines, or that expansion of the basic industry of a pulp and paper town will create jobs in the forests. But how can the installation of an electronics firm or a computer firm in Montreal create jobs in Gaspésie/Bas Saint-Laurent? Thus we arrive at a curious contradiction: a city like Sorel or Trois-Rivières (at least so long as they were using raw materials from their own region) might serve as "development poles" in this sense, whereas Montreal does not.

An interesting question arises here. Was Montreal ever a development pole for its own peripheral region, generating spread effects to that region? The answer is yes, so long as its industries included some that depended importantly on raw materials produced within the region, and so long as the region depended importantly on production of those raw materials. As "fur trade capital" Montreal provided employment and income for Indians and for some white men as well. As a wood products centre it provided income and employment in the forests — so long as the forests were there. But as Montreal grew, as its economic activities became more diverse and more sophisticated, as its economy became more integrated with the Canadian, North American, and world economies, the relationship of the city with its hinterland was broken.

In the light of experience with development poles, one might wonder why the theory ever enjoyed so much vogue. But in defence of Perroux, the originator of the concept, three things must be said. First, Perroux was primarily interested in explaining unbalanced, disequilibrated, polarized growth, to combat the excessive faith in tendencies towards spatial "equilibrium" among his colleagues at the time. Second, Perroux himself never expected the "spread effects" of expansion of a development pole to be concentrated in its own region. On the contrary, he underlined the distinction between "banal space" and "economic space," and expected the spread effects of the truly large metropolitan centres to be scattered over a very large economic space indeed. Obviously, the policy implications are totally different if the spread effects of growth of Montreal are felt in Tokyo, Bahrein, Lichenstein, and London, rather than in Quebec. Third, Perroux stressed the role of development poles as aggregations of innovating enterprises more than their role as markets for the output of enterprises outside the pole but inside the peripheral region. It was Perroux's own "cluster of followers," eager to use the concept for practical purposes of decentralizing industrial activity and reducing regional disparities, who made the unjustified intellectual leap of expecting spread effects to be concentrated in the pole's own peripheral region. And it took another intellectual leap, even more unjustified, to identify Montreal's peripheral region in this sense with the whole of the province of Quebec.

Finally, when Perroux first published his ideas in the early 1950s, France had not yet recovered from World War II and the Great Depression. It's industrial structure was still essentially that of the inter-war period. It was, accordingly, a country in which many industries were located so as to be close to their raw material supplies, and where cities specialized to a considerable degree in industries utilizing nearby raw materials. In that context, it was reasonable to expect a substantial share of the spread effects of industrial expansion of the pole to be felt in its own peripheral region. Today the major development poles of the world, in the sense of large urban centres where the decisions are made and the innovations introduced, have largely broken away from the natural resource base of their own region, and their spread effects are felt in an "economic space" that is essentially global.

The unfortunate truth is that when a city matures to the point where it can serves as a "development pole" in the sense of a concentration of innovating enterprises and a diffuser of technology, it is no longer a development pole in the sense of a centre of diffusion of spread effects in the form of employment and income creation in its own region. A large city like Montreal may, of course, generate dormitory suburbs, and these may move further and further from the urban core as the metropolis grows. As the metropolitan population grows opportunities are provided for producing vegetables, fruit, eggs, dairy products, etc., in whatever neighbouring agricultural areas remain, and demand for recreation facilities in the neighbourhood of the metropolis also grows. But it cannot be expected that this kind of increase in demand in the Montreal metropolitan region will turn Gaspésie/Bas Saint-Laurent or the Cantons de l'Est from a relatively poor to a relatively rich subregion of Quebec. Even for food, moreover, as a metropolis grows an increasing proportion will consist of processed and packaged foods coming from other cities, and as a metropolitan population becomes more affluent it seeks an ever larger

198

proportion of its recreation facilities outside its own per
region.

Montreal's importance for Quebec and for Canada does 1
in the fact that it is a development pole for Quebec, nor does
Montreal need to be a development pole in order to be important
for Quebec. Apart from being in itself over half of the Quebec
economy, and the intellectual and cultural capital of the province,
Montreal's importance lies in being the only city in Quebec that
can hope to attract and to hold certain types of sophisticated
services and certain types of technologically advanced manufacturing activities. If policy at all three levels of government is
directed towards assuring that Montreal remains an attractive
location for this kind of propulsive enterprise, the city can play an
increasingly important role as "central place" for the whole urban
hierarchy of Quebec, and for other Canadian cities as well.

Two Way Interactions: Gravity Models

Interactions between cities can be analyzed by use of "gravity
models," which borrow concepts from the science of physics and
apply them to urban growth. The models show that the force of
attraction between cities as measured by various flows (sales by
residents of City "A" to residents of City "B," for example), varies
directly with the populations of two cities and inversely with the
distance between them. Thus as cities grow, the interactions
between them are less affected by distance. In other words, as
Montreal, Quebec and Ottawa/Hull all grow, while distances
between them remain unchanged (or perhaps fall in terms of time
or cost) interactions between Montreal and each of the other
cities should tend to expand. On the other hand, there is also
evidence (largely unexplained) that with technical, social, and
economic development the unfavourable effects of distance tend
to increase. This evidence is supported by other findings which
suggest that with the passage of time urban economic activities
have become more "footloose," so that cities become less specialized
and more autonomous for any given size of population.

The "Shadow Theory"

A special form of gravity model has been developed by Dr. Michael
Ray of Carleton University in Ottawa. His "shadow theory" is
designed to explain why so many of the branches of United States

firms located in Ontario have been established in or near Toronto. For example, Ray shows that nearly 90 percent of the Ontario subsidiaries of companies with head offices in the New York metropolitan area are in or near Toronto. The basic idea is that branch plants tend to be located between the centre where the head office or major plant is located and the city which constitutes the major market of the region under consideration — in the case of Ontario, Toronto. Any other Ontario city suffers an "economic shadow" whenever Toronto constitutes an alternative location lying between the other city and the United States centres. Thus Toronto casts an economic shadow on all of eastern Ontario for all United States cities except Boston and other New England cities. The same reasoning applies to Montreal, for all markets west of the Quebec border.[29]

Ray also points out that directors of the United States companies like to establish branches in locations which provide easy access to their head offices. In terms of time, Toronto is "near to" New York, Chicago, Detroit, and the other Great Lakes manufacturing centres. Branch plants often draw upon the head office or main plant for the more complicated machinery parts, engineering and technical services, supervisory services and top management. Ease of access is therefore of primary importance.

"Access" is mainly a matter of time, and is measured primarily in terms of jet travel and telecommunications. The greater the total distance between office and branch plant, the less important is marginal distance. Nearly 90 percent of the 33 Los Angeles firms with operations in Ontario are in Toronto. In terms of miles, Windsor would have been closer; but Toronto is easier to reach from Los Angeles than is Windsor. On the other hand, when branch plants are so close as to be accessible by road, jet travel and telecommunications become less important. Thus, less than one third of the Buffalo subsidiaries in Ontario, were in Toronto, since in that case the branches could be situated just over the Canadian border, a short drive away.

In general, what Professor Ray's analysis implies for Montreal is that any United States firm considering a branch operation in Canada is better off in Toronto than in Montreal unless it is primarily interested in the Montreal market itself or in a market east or north of Montreal.

The recent shift to the sunbelt is bad news for Toronto as well as for Montreal, but somewhat worse for Montreal than for Toronto, as a glance at a map of North America will show. The recent relative decline of the Great Lakes industrial region, with the diffusion of the automobile industry and the reduced relative importance of heavy industries such as iron and steel, certainly means that Toronto can expect less stimulus in future than in the past from proximity to these centres. But for Montreal the southward and westward movement means that the extreme northeast corner of the continent that might be regarded as being under Montreal's "shadow" and within Montreal's natural zone of influence is becoming more and more isolated. With what cities should Montreal interact, without interference from larger or stronger urban centres?

The "shadow" and "central place" theories fortify conclusions derived from gravity models. Between what major American or Canadian industrial centre and another potential location of an industrial enterprise does Montreal intervene? If distance is measured by rail and water miles, to be sure, Montreal imposes a "shadow" between European centres and Canadian cities further west. But for air travel and telecommunications, which today may be more important considerations for sophisticated enterprises, there is no significant difference. As for central places, we have already noted that Toronto is central to a larger population than Montreal, and that the higher density of population in Toronto's urban system is accompanied as well by higher productivity than in Montreal's urban system. Once again, such tendencies, unless interrupted by forceful policy or dramatic events, could become cumulative.

Polarization Reversal?

There is in economics a number of "laws" which, true to the grand tradition of "the dismal science," say in effect "things are going to get worse before they get better." One of these is the "law" of polarization reversal: concentration of economic activity and population in a few large urban centres will tend to become aggravated in the first stages of development, but will be followed by deconcentration, decentralization, and dispersal in the later stages. As we have seen, in the United States, western Europe, and Japan it is not yet clear that a definitive stage of polarization reversal has set in; indeed, there are signs of "polarization reversal reversal." What of Montreal, Quebec, and Canada? For Montreal itself, a distinct pattern emerges. Looking first at the administrative regions of Quebec, we see that between 1971 and 1981 the share of

TABLE 46

Population and Regional Distribution, 1971, 1981 and 2006

Region	Population (thousands)					Distribution (in percentage)				
	1971	1981	2006 weak	2006 average	2006 strong	1971	1981	2006 weak	2006 average	2006 strong
01	232,6	234,0	252,8	240,0	247,9	3.9	3.6	3.8	3.4	3.3
02	280,0	300,8	315,3	340,1	351,8	4.6	4.7	4.7	4.8	4.7
03	941,5	1,032,1	1,099,1	1,093,4	1,124,8	15.6	16.0	16.4	15.3	15.1
04	420,7	441,4	470,4	485,8	500,8	7.0	6.9	7.0	6.8	6.7
05	224,2	239,1	242,7	255,4	265,8	3.7	3.7	3.6	3.6	3.6
06	3,423,5	3,631,4	3,725,4	4,048,7	4,254,2	56.8	56.4	55.5	56.8	57.2
6N	392,5	532,2	680,0	740,0	769,3	6.5	8.3	10.1	10.4	10.3
6L	228,0	268,3	309,5	336,1	349,6	3.8	4.2	4.6	4.7	4.7
6M	1,959,1	1,760,1	1,523,4	1,579,3	1,680,7	32.5	27.3	22.7	22.2	22.6
6S	843,9	1,070,8	1,212,6	1,393,2	1,454,6	14.0	16.6	18.1	19.5	19.6
07	243,3	273,7	309,1	329,2	343,6	4.0	4.3	4.6	4.6	4.6
08	147,3	153,1	169,4	172,6	179,9	2.4	2.4	2.5	2.4	2.4
09	100,5	115,2	107,4	137,9	143,1	1.7	1.8	1.6	1.9	1.9
10	14,4	17,6	16,0	24,1	25,0	0.2	0.3	0.2	0.3	0.3
QUEBEC	6,027,8	6,438,4	6,707,7	7,127,2	7,436,8	100.0	100.0	100.0	100.0	100.0

SOURCES: — 1971 Bureau de la statistique du Québec, 1984b.
— 1981 Bureau de la statistique du Québec, 1984c.
— 2006 Projections du Bureau de la statistique du Québec.

01 Gaspésie/Bas St-Laurent
02 Saguenay/Lac St-Jean
03 Québec
04 Trois-Rivières
05 Estrie

06 Montréal
6N Nord de Montréal
6L Laval (île Jésus)
6M Île de Montréal
6S Sud de Montréal

07 Outaouais
08 Abitibi-Témiscamingue
09 Côte Nord
10 Nouveau-Québec

the Montreal administrative region in the total Quebec population remained virtually unchanged, declining insignificantly from 56.8 percent to 56.4 percent (Table 46). Total population of the region grew by a mere 208,000. However, the share of the *island* of Montreal in the Quebec total fell from 32.5 percent to 27.3 percent, while the share of north Montreal, south Montreal and Isle Laval all increased. The shares of Gaspésie/Bas Saint-Laurent and Trois-Rivières declined. Estrie remained unchanged, and all other administrative regions registered increases in their shares of Quebec population, although in some cases very modest ones. These figures suggest deconcentration from the centre of Montreal to the rest of the province.

Table 47 shows the pattern of migration among regions of Quebec. The pattern is striking, and except for the conversion of Côte Nord and Nouveau Quebec from areas of net immigration to areas of net emigration, is the same in 1976-81 or 1981-83 as it was in 1971-76. North Montreal, south Montreal and Isle Laval are all areas of net immigration, all the other regions are area of net emigration. The mining boom in Côte Nord and Nouveau Québec is tapering off; otherwise what these figures show is a movement towards the Montreal region, but away from the island of Montreal.

Table 48 and Chart 5 show population movements within the administrative region of Montreal broken down in a different way. Here we see that between 1971 and 1976 the island of Montreal lost fewer people than the City of Montreal, indicating some movement from the core city to other parts of the island. Between 1976 and 1981 the loss of population of the island slightly exceeded the loss in the city, indicating some movement *back* to the central city from the suburbs. Otherwise the pattern is the same in both periods: a movement out of the island to the "suburban crown" on both the north and south shores (and Isle Laval), a much smaller movement to the satellite cities, and a larger and increasing movement to Montreal's "hinterland" (all of the administrative region not included as part of the metropolitan region or the satellite towns). The new population of the hinterland has settled for the most part in localities around the metropolitan centre or around the satellite cities, including the recreation areas of the Laurentians, De Lanaudière, and the Cantons de l'Est. Martial Fauteux explains this new phenomenon by the flight from the city, people converting their weekend and vacation chalets

TABLE 47

Interregional Migratory Balance, by Region and Sub-region,
1996-1971, 1971-1976 and 1976-1981 (Population 5 Years and Over at end of Period),
and 1981-1983 (Population of all Ages, Analyzed on a Five-Year Basis)

Region and Sub-region	1966-1971	1971-1976	1976-1981	1981-1983[a] (five-year basis)
01	-12,486	-13,317	-3,745	18
02	-13,023	-351	-4,695	-3,800
03	-3,009	-22,090	-3,935	-570
04	-13,515	-9,164	-940	-2,058
05	-1,950	-6,491	-2,175	-2,548
06	50,730	49,748	24,980	27,693
6N	—	38,287	38,960	42,985
6L	—	14,639	8,600	9,265
6M	—	-89,232	-68,335	-49,413
6S	—	86,054	45,755	24,855
07	2,064	441	285	3,193
08	-7,505	-6,083	-1,660	-200
09	-1,303	7,307	-6,180	-12,035
10	-3		-1,935	9,693

Note: In order to facilitate the comparison with other five-year periods, we multiplied by five the estimated
average for the years 1981-1982 and 1982-1983.

Sources: BSQ compilations based on unpublished data from Canada Census (for periods 1966-1981) and on
annual estimations of the constituents of population growth of the census divisions, produced by
Statistics Canada (for the period 1981-1983).

01 Gaspésie/Bas St-Laurent	06 Montréal	07 Outaouais
02 Saguenay/Lac Saint-Jean	6N Nord de Montréal	08 Abitibi-Témiscamingue
03 Québec	6L Laval (Île Jésus)	09 Côte Nord
04 Trois-Rivières	6M Île de Montréal	10 Nouveau-Québec
05 Estrie	6S Sud de Montréal	

TABLE 48

Distribution of Regional Population Growth,
1- 1971-1976

| | Population | | Increase | |
	1971	1976	Number	Distribution
Metropolitan region [1]	2,743,208	2,814,070	70,862	59.4%
— City of Montreal [2]	1,218,210	1,083,372	-134,748	—
— Island of Montreal (CUM) [3]	1,959,143	1,869,641	-89,502	—
— Northern and southern parts (suburban crown)	784,065	944,429	160,364	—
Satellite towns [4]	270,752	282,916	12,164	10.2%
Hinterland (zone of resources and towns) [5]	409,498	445,835	36,337	30.4%
Administrative region of Montreal	3,423,458	3,542,821	119,363	100

1. Metropolitan region of census (RMR) 1971 definition.
2. Including Saint-Jean-de-Dieu.
3. Pertains to the territory of Montreal's urban community, including Bizard island.
4. A gathering of 7 towns ranging from 30,000 to 50,000 inhabitants each: Saint-John, Saint-Hyacinthe, Granby, Saint-Jérôme, Valleyfield, Sorel, Joliette.
5. The territory of the administrative region of Montreal minus the metropolitan region (RMR, 1971) and the satellite towns.

SOURCE: OPDQ compilation based on the data of the 1971, 1976 and 1981 census.

TABLE 48 (*con't.*)

Distribution of the Regional Demographic Increase,
II- 1976-1981

	Volume of population		Increase	
	1976	1981	Number	Distribution
Metropolitan region [1]	2,814,070	2,835,759	21,689	23.8%
— City of Montreal [2]	1,083,372	982,339	-101,033	—
— Island of Montreal (CUM) [3]	1,869,641	1,760,122	-109,519	—
— Northern and southern parts (suburban crown)	944,429	1,075,637	131,208	—
Satellite towns [4]	282,916	296,132	13,216	14.5%
Hinterland (zone of resources and towns) [5]	445,835	501,925	56,090	61.6%
Administrative region of Montreal	3,542,821	3,633,816	90,995	100

1. Metropolitan region of census (RMR) 1971 definition.
2. Including Saint-Jean-de-Dieu.
3. Pertains to the territory of Montreal's urban community, including Bizard island.
4. A gathering of 7 towns ranging from 30,000 to 50,000 inhabitants each: Saint-John, Saint-Hyacinthe, Granby, Saint-Jérôme, Valleyfield, Sorel, Joliette.
5. The territory of the administrative region of Montreal minus the metropolitan region (RMR, 1971) and the satellite towns.

SOURCE: OPDQ compilation based on the data of the 1971, 1976 and 1981 census.

CHART 5

*Distribution of Population, 1971, 1976, 1981
in the Administrative Region of Montreal*

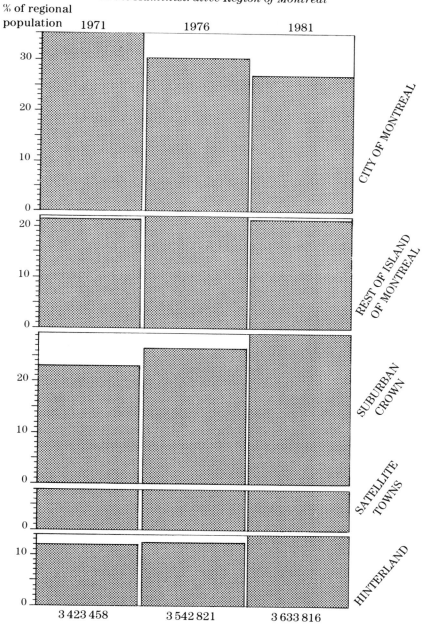

Population of region 06

into their principal residence, the growth of tourism, and some resurgence of farming in the area.[30]

Does the overall pattern support or deny the "law" of polarization reversal? It is by no means clear. There is an undoubted movement away from the island to suburbs on the mainland and on Isle Laval, and a smaller movement to satellite towns a few miles further out. But the suburbs are part of the Montreal economy, and so in varying degrees are the satellite cities. The share of the whole Montreal administrative region in the Quebec economy seems to be stabilizing, and within the Montreal region there is a process of decentralization under way. The combination might be regarded as a healthy one from the Quebec point of view, but it is doing little to alleviate the extremely high rates of unemployment in Abitibi-Tamiscamingue and Gaspésie/Bas St-Laurent. Even within the Montreal region the rate of unemployment is uncomfortably high (12.0 percent in 1984), and in some of the satellite cities it is higher still. But even if this very mixed picture were accepted as a case of "polarization reversal," it does not seem to be the product of any generally applicable economic law alone. Many of the enterprises that have left Montreal for Toronto and elsewhere were of the type that occupied premises in the central city, and the movement out of the island of Montreal is in part a movement out of Quebec altogether. To the extent that it was a movement *to* a metropolitan region even bigger than Montreal, and one growing faster than Montreal, the whole process was one of polarization, not polarization reversal. It does not seem to have much to do with diseconomies of scale of metropolitan regions as such. The Montreal metropolitan region can still grow without loss of efficiency.

The Need for Further Structural Change

Any economy that continues to grow will arrive sooner or later at a point where further improvement in levels of welfare requires sharp structural change. This statement applies to urban and regional, as well as to national, economies. Most nations, regions, and cities face this need more than once. If technological progress happens to coincide with repeated new resource discovery related to the new technology, as has been the case in the United States, Canada, and Australia, the structural change needed for further development can take place through a shift from one kind of natural-resource-based pattern of output and employment to another. The difficult cases are those where growth on the one set of natural resources comes to an end, while no sav__ the form of new resource discovery and technological change appears on the horizon. In these cases, further development requires a discontinuous quantum leap from a natural-resource-based to a human-resource-based pattern of development.

Canada, Quebec, and Montreal, as we have seen, have all made the transition from primary production economies to economies based on industrial and service activities. But that transition is not enough for continuous progress. It is necessary now to make the shift to more human-resource based activities (those requiring advanced technology and high-level skills) in *each* major sector, as Switzerland, Sweden, West Germany, Japan and (to a lesser degree) the United States have done. Canada, Quebec, and Montreal still rely too much on our "rich natural resources" in all three sectors. To move from wheat to flour, from lumber to newsprint, from beaver skins to textiles or boots and shoes, does not suffice to assure high levels of productivity and income on today's world standards. If Canadians want to continue living as members of an affluent society we must compete in electronics, scientific instruments, computer technology, metallurgy, and the like. But one aspect of the development pole theory that remains valid is its insistence that structural change and scientific advance of this kind cannot take place at the same pace everywhere. The urban centres, and particularly the metropolitan centres, must take the lead. It is here above all that Montreal, together with Toronto and Vancouver, can make its biggest contribution to Canadian development as a whole.

The substitution of technology and human skills for natural resources is never easy. It is especially difficult where a relatively rich natural resource base, in comparison with the size of the population, seems to make the development of increasingly advanced and ever-more-widely-applicable skills unnecessary. Australia faced this problem early in the 1920s when the good land became fully occupied. The thirty years that followed were ones of near stagnation in per capita output and income, as industrial import replacement proceeded painfully behind a very high protective tariff wall. Only the extreme homogeneity of the Australian population at the time, together with a society remarkably free of tensions, saved Australia from social and political upheavals during this period. The process is still not completed, and recent resource discoveries, while attracting capital and earning foreign exchange, delay further the required transition, at a time when the population has become less homogenous and less tension-free. Cuba and Argentina, facing the same problem at about the same time as Australia, were less lucky; there is as yet no assurance that the social and political upheavals that followed stagnation in those countries have put their economies on a smooth new road to development or that their social and political system will be stable over the next few decades. Malaysia, having attained one of the highest standards of living in Asia on the basis of one pattern of development (rubber, oil palm and tin) which has now run its course, is now undergoing transition under conditions of severe tension between the Chinese and Malay populations. Quebec also faces the need for further structural change under conditions of continuing tension.

The need for the leap from natural-resource-based to human-resource-based development may come at any level of per capita income, depending on the wealth of the natural resource endowment in relation to the population. Canada, being richly endowed in natural resources, came a long way without moving far from the natural base. The Canadian pattern of maintaining an export sector based on natural resources while shifting the labour force from farm to factory and office, and developing manufactures behind a protective tariff wall, worked reasonably well. But the time for the transition has come. Montreal reached the point where the quantum leap was necessary during the 1960s. It did not make it — only a hop, a skip and a modest jump. The decline of Montreal outlined above is the direct result of this failure. Genuine progress in future requires the development of high-productivity occupations not directly tied to the resource base. Canada, and especially Montreal, must become a purveyor of brains, not only to its own people but to the world market as well.

It is too seldom realized that this situation may arise even if there are natural resources left to exploit. When we talk of "economic development" we talk of raising the general level of welfare by creating new jobs where man-year productivity is above the present national average for all occupations. Accordingly, it is below what the national average will be if economic development continues.[31]

André Raynauld, then Chairman of the Economic Council of Canada, has pointed out that growth of the labour force accounted for nearly two-thirds of Canada's recent growth, rising productivity barely one-third. But in the 1980s population growth could shrink to a mere 1 percent, and in the 1990s it may disappear altogether. For Canada to stop its slide downwards among nations on the economic ladder, new economic activities must be developed. Dr. Raynauld asks:

> But then, which activities? What will we do tomorrow if ultimately there is no other wealth than men, and if we hardly have the numbers? The answer lies in the accumulation of knowledge. This is where our comparative advantage is to be found. Thus, while less developed countries are capable of increasing and improving knowledge, the source of science is in the modern world. Therefore, all our strategy of the future rests on a new international division of labour, and it must be analysed in such a context. Tomorrow's Canadian industry will consist of enterprises capable of mobilizing knowledge, technology, and innovation, or else it will fade away.[32]

Conclusions

What can we glean from this review of theories on urban growth and regional development, in terms of the three questions posed at the beginning of our discussion of them? Is any theory irrefutably proven or rejected by Montreal's experience? Does any of them, or even all of them together, permit us to predict with certainty what will happen to Montreal during the next few decades? Do they provide clear and concrete guidance for the formulation of policies that will assure the kind of future we want for Montreal? It is hard to formulate enthusiastic answers to such questions. Let us look quickly at the theories again, moving from right to left in the political spectrum.

On the extreme right we have the neo-classical, "leave everything to the market" school. The more apolitical and analytical facets of this body of thought, like the economic base theory and the neoclassical theory of location of industry, are becoming less and less relevant as technologies and societies change, and the reasons for economic activities being in a particular city change with them. If the policy recommendation is interpreted literally to mean that the role of government in the economy should be limited to keeping law and order, the school has virtually no adherents today. But there are certainly a good many economists of neoclassical persuasion who believe quite honestly that pandering politicians and bungling bureaucrats do more harm to the economy, and bear more responsibility for lagging regions and declining cities, than monopolistic multinationals or treacherous trade union leaders. Many of these also believe in a natural tendency towards economic growth balanced in space, just as they believe in a natural tendency towards "equilibrium" in the economy as a whole. From them we can take at least this much: before introducing new urban and regional policies it is a good idea to try to figure out what would happen if the outcome were left to the market, as it is, or with obvious improvements in its structure and functioning; and it is also a good idea to look at existing policies, to see whether or not they are hampering rather than helping the market in doing its job.

Moving slightly to the left we come to the "knife-edge" theorists, who believe that steady and balanced growth can be achieved only by astute, continuous, and flexible management of the economy through monetary and fiscal policy. Whether they say so or not, a major implication of this school's recommendations for policy is a good deal of administrative discretion in the timing of changes in monetary policy, and in both the timing and the placing of changes in government spending and taxing patterns.

Perroux takes us one move to the left again. His theory of polarization, domination, and dependency leads to the conclusion that the encouragement and guidance of the polarization process requires planning, at the level of the individual enterprise, the city or region, the nation, and ultimately the global economy. It should be added that Perroux himself is proposing only French-style "indicative planning," not Soviet-style centralized planning. Perroux does not think that polarization is bad in itself. It is the form that progress takes under capitalism. But the progress can also be disruptive, and needs to be managed.

With Myrdal the faith in the market mechanism becomes still more attenuated. For him regional disparities are distinctly unhealthy, a clear sign of malfunctioning of the economy. Left to themselves they will get worse, finally undermining the economy and the society. Thus regional gaps, and by implication urban decline, are problems that need to be tackled head on, diagnosing the causes of the malady and treating them directly.

The analysis of regional dualism is not really a theory, and it has no implications in itself for the future. It is rather a description of how existing structures of national economies came into being; it says only that if the same kinds of decisions are made in the future as in the past, in the private and public sectors, regional disparities are likely to increase. By the same token, different decisions could bring reductions in regional gaps, including differences in relative degrees of prosperity of metropolitan regions.

The various theories of the urban hierarchy do not fit well into our political spectrum. They are concerned with the mechanics through which urban structures are created and changed, and have little implication for organization of the economic system as a whole. Perhaps for that very reason they are more useful tools than some of the more general theories. However, their usefulness lies more in indicating things to look for, and ways of looking at them when you find them, than in providing clear and unique conclusions as to what policies should be applied in particular circumstances.

Finally, when we arrive at the extreme left hand end of the spectrum, among the orthodox, neo-marxist dependency theorists, "The Market" is the very instrument by which the international monopoly capitalists wreak their will, exploiting poor people in poor countries and poor regions, maintaining a state of "development of underdevelopment," so that disparities among countries and regions, including metropolitan regions, continue to grow. This group of social scientists sees little hope within the capitalist system. By the same token the help that they can give to those who want to find solutions to problems without overthrowing the capitalist system altogether, is limited. It is not, however, zero. It is always useful for the policy-maker to know what the power structure is and how it operates.

Our brief survey of the literature on urban growth, regional expansion and national development has not turned up any one theory which explains why things are as they are today or how they got there. Still less do we have a theory which enables us to predict the future for any particular nation, region, or city, although the aggregation of all of them can help a good deal in guiding our thinking on the matter. Nonetheless, returning to the specific case of Montreal, we can state some significant conclusions:

1. There is nothing we know for sure that allows us to predict that if we just let nature take her course, Montreal will continue to thrive as a dynamic metropolis, characterized by economic and social progress, and playing a leading role in the continued progress of both Quebec and Canada as a whole.

2. It is therefore necessary to design policies that will assure that the desired prognosis for Montreal is achieved.

213

3. Our accumulated knowledge of the forces of urban growth and regional development leads to the conclusion that palliatives ("band-aids") applied to Montreal alone will not suffice to achieve the desired prognosis.

If the reader will think back over the content of chapters 2 to 5, he or she will recognize that the history of the rise and decline of the metropolis, and the analysis of its role in Quebec and within Canada, was not conducted within the framework of models of the sort outlined in this chapter, although elements of all of them cropped up from time to time with regard to particular aspects of the story. But the factors, forces, and events determining the fate of Montreal have been nationwide, and ultimately world wide. There is therefore little reason to think that its fate in future can be shaped merely by some improvements in the landscape or organization of the city itself. Montreal got its start through a unique and favourable conjuncture of geographical and historical variables. It is on this scale that we must think if we wish to launch Montreal into a renaissance. In our final chapter an attempt is made to outline a strategy, that will do for Montreal in the twenty first century what four rivers and some rapids did for it in the seventeenth and eighteenth centuries.

CHAPTER 7

A STRATEGY FOR THE RENAISSANCE
OF MONTREAL

> Montreal's cultural vitality is unrivalled
> in Canada; it is the only city in the
> country which can fairly be described as
> an international metropolis, and the
> diversity of its cultural and ethnic cha-
> racteristics has produced a cosmopolitan
> blend of Latin flair and European
> architecture.
>
> *George NADER
> *Cities of Canada*

In the preceding chapters we have seen how Montreal, from
Jacques Cartier's arrival at Hochelaga to the present day, has been
buffeted by the winds of change. Sometimes the changes shaping
Montreal's destiny have been close at hand, sometimes very far
away. Among the more dramatic events which have changed the
course of Montreal's history have been the conquest of Quebec by
the British, the American Revolution, the industrial revolution in
Europe and later in the United States and Japan, the opening up
of the west and the development of the wheat economy, the shift

of the United States industrial heartland from the Atlantic seaboard to the Great Lakes, the shift of Canada's centre of gravity with respect to population and industrial activity to the "Golden Triangle" of western Ontario, the great depressions of the 1930s and of the 1880s and '90s, the rise of Toronto, and the more recent treck of American enterprises to the west and to the sunbelt in the south. It is necessary to mention also the world recession of 1973–83 and the Quebec elections of 1976 and 1981.

Viewed in this fashion, the economic and social history of Montreal is seen as a vast chess game in four-dimensional space (with time as the fourth dimension) and with many simultaneous players. Once the nature of the game is understood, it should be apparent that it cannot be won by any simple moves confined to the Montreal scene itself: industrial parks, new freeways, anti-pollution devices, housing projects, recreation facilities, although all of these might help. In order to win the battle to save and resuscitate Montreal, the city and its region of influence must be put into the entire urban hierarchy of North America and conditions created to enable them to play their optimal role within the hierarchy.

The task is complicated by the fact that not all of the players in the game are Canadians. The influence that Canada can have on governments and private investors in the United States, in Europe, in Japan, in the Middle East, in Latin America, is obviously limited. Yet even there we are not powerless. Within Canada we have five strong players: the federal government, the provincial governments, the municipal governments, the private employers, and the trade unions. Together these should be able to determine the outcome of the game, with respect to Montreal, to Quebec, to other provinces, to Canada as a whole. And the pleasant aspect of this kind of game is that all players can win: there need be no losers.

What we are proposing for the reinvigoration of Montreal is nothing less than a national policy of urban growth and regional development. Lest this concept seem far-fetched, let us point out that the Canadian government has already taken long steps along this path. The Department of Regional Economic Expansion was committed to reducing regional disparities, and regarded urban planning as an integral part of this process; the department was highly aware of interactions between urban growth and regional development. In the late 1970s Public Works Canada was also thinking along these lines, with respect to the regional allocation of its activities. All the provincial governments have regional development strategies, which imply policies with respect to urban growth within their own borders. The Trudeau government in the late 1970s announced a policy of land management, which would require all federal departments having an influence on patterns of land use to plan, not only in terms of services to clients, but also in terms of the broader social, economic, and environmental objectives of the government. The government also announced a strategy with regard to "Urban Pattern"; essentially, the government wished to restrain the growth of large metropolitan centres and encourage the growth of small and middle-sized cities, but it recognized that discouraging the growth of Montreal could be dangerous for Quebec, and that encouraging further growth of middle-sized cities within the Toronto system, like London, Windsor, and Kitchener, could be dangerous for Toronto. Progress was made towards formulation of an "Urban Form" strategy as well, one which would be concerned with quality of like in our cities. There was also the policy of "sensitivity of government," or decentralization of federal government activities. Finally, there was growing recognition that tackling inflation and employment simultaneously requires regionalization of public spending policy in general. Add all these policies together, and we were already a long way towards a national strategy regarding urban growth and regional development. The Mulroney government, elected in September 1984, had not, as at time of writing, explicitly renounced any of these policies.

Let us underline the point that we are *not* proposing a strategy of promoting Montreal *at the expense of* Quebec City, or Rimouski, or Halifax, or St. John, or Moncton, or Toronto. On the contrary, it is our contention that a strong Montreal can only strengthen other urban economies in Canada, and *vice versa*, because of the increased interactions that such strengthening entails. The trick is to enable Montreal to play her proper role within her own region, within Quebec, and also within Canada as a whole, by building on Montreal's capacity to make a *unique* contribution to Canadian development, by adding to the quantity and quality, the number and diversity, of innovating, propulsive industries in Canada. Some of these no doubt belong in Toronto, in the sense that they can operate more efficiently from there. Rather, it is a matter of identifying such enterprises that belong in Montreal, in the sense that Montreal is the most attractive place for them in Canada, rather than having them establish themselves in the United States, Europe, Japan, or elsewhere.

General principles

Certain basic principles or guidelines may be stated at the outset to assist in the formulation of such a strategy.

1. The renaissance of Montreal does not require it to become once again Canada's biggest city, nor — in the aggregate — its major commercial, industrial, and financial centre. With appropriate specialization in each sector Montreal can do very well as Canada's second city. A possible model (for illustrative purposes only) would be for Montreal to aim at being Canada's amalgam of Boston and New Orleans while Toronto becomes Canada's amalgam of New York and Chicago. Given the choice, many if not most people would probably prefer the first amalgam to the second. Boston benefited enormously from the emigration of its traditional boot and shoe, textile, and pulp and paper industries and their replacement by scientifically oriented enterprises. Its institutions of higher learning have a better reputation than New York's. Many regard its symphony orchestra as superior to New York's. Even its night life has its special style. Its financial centre, if smaller than New York's, is no less sophisticated, and some would insist that it is more sophisticated within its range of specialization (especially its bond market, its insurance companies, and banks). New Orlean's "vieux carré" is much like Montreal's, and both cities combine old world charm with modern technology. One need not go so far as to insist that "small is beautiful" where cities are concerned to appreciate that a Montreal that combined the best characteristics of Boston and New Orleans need not suffer much from being second biggest in Canada.[1]

2. That being said, it should be added that the federal and Ontario governments have agreed on the desirability of restraining the growth of Toronto, and indeed of all the cities in the Golden Triangle, while luring industry and population into nearby but almost empty eastern Ontario, and holding in the Ontario north the natural growth of its population. The development of eastern Ontario is a key element in the strategy for a Montreal renaissance, and we shall deal with it at some length below. Let us note here simply that from the stand-point of Montreal's

natural urban system or zone of influence, the border between Quebec and Ontario is totally artificial. Much of the francophone Canadian population outside of Quebec is to be found in the St. Lawrence and Ottawa River valleys to the west of Montreal and in Ontario, spilling over into the mining areas of northern Ontario. The other major francophone area outside of Quebec is in the Atlantic provinces, particularly in northeast New Brunswick.

3. In short, as emphasized by the University of Montreal's Centre de Recherche en Développement Économique (CRDE), the expansion of the Toronto and Montreal economies needs to be planned together. However, the "bipolar" strategy stressed by the CRDE does not go quite far enough. Montreal and Toronto need to be put into the entire Canadian (and North American) urban hierarchy. In particular, the national strategy should include measures to extend the axis of urban development which begins at Chicago and extends through Detroit and Windsor to Toronto (and which despite recent developments in Kingston and other cities along the seaway, still ends essentially at Oshawa) eastward to Montreal and then onwards towards Quebec City, building up interactions along the way.

4. The Montreal-Ottawa/Hull axis should not be neglected. The Ottawa River, let us remember, was once the main highway from Montreal to the west and contributed to Montreal's economic expansion. It could do so again.

5. Plans for Montreal itself should be ambitious but realistic. In the North American context Montreal has little comparative advantage. Its geographic location is bad, and getting worse as the centre of economic activity in North America continues to move west and starts to move south. It must be recognized too that in various fields Montreal competes with highly specialized cities, each with complementary advantages : publishing in New York, finance in New York and Boston, petrochemicals in Houston, iron and steel in Pittsburgh, meatpacking in Chicago, optics in Rochester, aircraft in Seattle and Texas. Montreal must find its own niche within each field, building on its own assets. What are these ?

a) Montreal is unique in North America as a bilingual and bicultural city (despite the efforts to resurrect French in New Orleans, and the large Spanish-speaking populations of San Antonio or Los Angeles, all three cities are essentially anglophone-American cities in "ambience"). This fact makes Montreal an attractive setting for international activities in Canada. It is no accident that the only United Nations agency in North America outside New York City — the International Civil Aviation Agency — is in Montreal.

b) While Montreal is no longer significantly closer to Europe than Toronto in terms of jet travel or telecommunications, it is nonetheless true that Montreal "looks to Europe" in a sense that is true of no other Canadian city. Halifax looks to New England, (still called "the Boston states" in that part of the world), Toronto looks west and south, Vancouver looks south and to Asia. Where "the European connection" is concerned, Montreal still has an advantage over other Canadian cities.

c) Montreal has a splendid physical setting and is within easy reach of dramatically beautiful countryside both to the north and to the south.

d) Montreal is close to the national capital in the one sense that counts — time — closer than any other major Canadian city, and could be made closer.

e) Montreal is closer to Boston than any other major Canadian city. Moreover, the large French-Canadian population in northern New England, and indeed even as far south as Rhode Island, with French-language newspapers and radio, provides a cultural bridge between Montreal and Boston. The Maine coast is increasingly becoming *Quebec's* seaside resort.

f) Montreal and Toronto are, for all practical purposes, equidistant from New York where air transport and telecommunications are concerned, but Montreal is closer by rail and road.

g) Montreal is, obviously, closer to Quebec City than is any other major Canadian centre. This advantage may not seem of great importance, but nonetheless it gives Montreal an advantage where Quebec government activities are concerned, including provision of consulting services, finance, etc.

h) Despite the shift to Toronto, Montreal retains financial, commercial, industrial, and research activities with a great deal of sophistication. The essential aim now must be to retain these and attract others.

i) Montreal has four excellent universities, two francophone, two anglophone but increasingly bilingual. Their effectiveness in the community is greatly enhanced by the fact that the former "two solitudes" — or four — are breaking down. More and more reciprocity in recognizing each other's courses for credit, joint research projects, etc., exist among Montreal's universities. If this trend continues Montreal will have few rivals on the North American continent as a centre for higher education and research. Nothing could be more important for the attraction of sophisticated enterprises, as Boston's experience demonstrates.

j) Finally, there are all the attributes of Montreal which make it a "metropolis" in Dean Burchard's sense, as outlined in Chapter 1 above: a sparkling, "mouvementé" city with a wide range of recreational and cultural activities, a sense of fun, a place where *bon vivants* can feel at home.

When all these advantages are added up, it is quite a lot. The problem, obviously, is to find ways of building on them. Doing so is clearly not a one-man job. Putting detailed content into the strategy is a job for the federal, provincial, municipal governments and the private sector combined. We can, however, make some suggestions as to the sort of thing that needs to be considered.

The measures to be taken fall generally within four categories: those relating to the administrative region of Montreal itself; those relating to the rest of Quebec; those relating to eastern Ontario; and those relating to the outside world.

Montreal

The measures to be taken within the Montreal region seem fairly straightforward. The recommendation of the HMR Report that the powers of the federal government be used to attract sophisticated services and scientifically-oriented industry to the smaller cities within the Montreal urban system, beginning with those in the "couronne" and gradually moving outward, is still valid. It should be borne in mind, however, that in implementing such a policy, the Montreal region can expect little more growth from structural change in the large. The primary sector has virtually disappeared already, and what remains of it is probably there for good reasons. The manufacturing sector is also about as small, and the services sector about as big, in terms of share of total employment, as is consistent with healthy development of the Montreal economy in the long run. Montreal cannot become a predominantly services city to the degree that capital cities like Ottawa and Quebec can; a thriving industrial sector is an essential component of a reinvigorated Montreal. Borrowing a term from the biologists, who speak of "climax vegetation" when stability of the mix of plants and trees in a region is reached, we might describe Montreal as a "climax economy" where the mix of economic activity in terms of broad sectors is stabilized. In other words, further increase in output per manyear must come from improvements in the quality of activity *within* each sector, and particularly, of course, within the service and industrial sectors.

The CRDE has recommended as part of their proposed strategy for Montreal building upon the city's character as an *international* centre and concentrating within the Montreal region as many as possible of the Canadian institutions, public or private, which have a distinctly international flavour. As part of the federal government's program of decentralization, for example, the Canadian International Development Agency and the International Development Research Centre might be moved to Montreal. So might the Trade Commissioner and other international activities of the Department of Industry, Trade, and Commerce. Whether the CRDE's proposal to move the Department of External Affairs to Montreal merits serious consideration is debatable. Ottawa without its diplomatic corps might resurrect stories about "The Twin Cities of Hull and Dull."

Multinational firms wishing to establish a Canadian headquarters should be encouraged to choose Montreal whenever there are no clearcut advantages to them of some other Canadian city. Professor Ryba proposes the establishment at Montreal of an International Financial Centre. This Centre would bring together in an autonomous institution the stock exchange, the money market, and the bond market. It would offer a highly advanced communications system and a completely computerized system of transactions. It would include an International Finance Institute to promote sophisticated research on financial affairs. The Centre would develop particularly close relations with European financial centres.

There are of course aspects of the physical planning and development of Montreal that would help: improved traffic circulation, pollution control, housing projects for various income groups, etc. These are, however, fairly obvious and better left to the experts in physical planning.

Mirabel

The Montreal region has within it one very expensive resource that is currently grossly underutilized: the new international airport at Mirabel. Why is that, and what can be done about it? Was the airport put in the wrong place?

Three major considerations underlay the recommendation of the Special Task Force, set up by Ottawa, Quebec City and Montreal, to build the airport at Saint Scholastique, rather than at Vaudreuil, Saint-Jean, or Saint Hyacinthe–Drummondville.[2] First, because of the greater width and depth of the river to the south, and the presence of the Saint Lawrence Seaway to the south, the cost of access to the airport was very much higher from any site on the south shore than from a site on the north shore. Vaudreuil was situated in a high income residential area, making cost of land acquisition high and introducing the risk that a curfew might be imposed on night time operations, as had already been done at Dorval. Second, the configuration of spatial relationships was such that the Saint Scholastique site was best designed for pushing and pulling urban growth and regional development towards the east, in conformity with the objectives of all three governments. The third set of considerations related to the general quality of the four zones in terms of attracting sophisticated enterprises, hotels, convention centres, and the like. It was felt that the possibility afforded by the Saint Scholastique site for people working at or near the airport (especially top managers, engineers, and scientists) to live in the Laurentians and still be within a few minutes of their offices and half an hour from Montreal made it virtually unique among major airports in North America. The same considerations applied to hotels and convention centres.

Nothing which has occurred since the Mirabel airport was completed has proved this analysis to be wrong. But if the right site was chosen, why is Mirabel so generally regarded as a failure, and what can be done about it?

When Mirabel was planned, it was expected not merely to serve the growing needs of Montreal in terms of transatlantic air service, but to meet those needs for the whole of Canada, and in so doing to become a major "propulsive industry" for the entire

Montreal economy. The planners had visions of a bustling airport, with neat, clean, well-designed modern factories and offices, occupied by hi-tech manufacturing firms and purveyors of sophisticated services, surrounding the airport and lining the freeway and the high-speed railway into the metropolis. Hotels and convention centres would be located near the airport and in the nearby Laurentian mountains, where too would be found the mansions of the executives, scientists, and engineers of the enterprises locating near the airport.

Anyone who has flown into or out of Mirabel knows that nothing like that has happened. Those who visit Mirabel for the first time must be astounded by the miles of empty fields and patches of forest as they come into the airport, and the blocks of empty corridors and acres of empty lounges when they get inside it.

Mirabel is, as Fernand Martin puts it, "a small airport."[3] In terms of total passengers moving through the airport, it is scarcely more important than the airport of Halifax, a city whose metropolitan area contains less than 250,000 people. Even Dulles airport near Washington D.C., often cited as a failure, handled in 1979 more than twice as many passengers. Montreal's other airport, Dorval, handles four times as much. Toronto, which was supposed to be a secondary airport by comparison, has a volume of passenger traffic nearly nine times as great. When one comes to really big airports like Chicago, Kennedy, and Heathrow, there is just no comparison. For cargo, Mirabel comes out a bit better, but not much. It handles more cargo than Dorval or Halifax, but less than half as much as Toronto and a tiny fraction of the volume of giants like Kennedy or Heathrow. For airmail, the comparison is equally unfavourable.

When the airport was planned it was expected to create, directly and indirectly, 75,000 jobs, thus building up an Airport City of some 200,000 people or adding a similar number to an existing nearby community, such as Saint Jerome. These estimates were based on the well established fact that sophisticated enterprises like to locate near major international airports, less because they expect to ship by air freight than because being in the neighbourhood of a major airport ensures the availability of hard flat ground for building, rapid access to the city, first class telecommunications, and time-saving for fast-moving executives. Certainly the industrial development encouraged by Mirabel has not "spilled over the Ontario Border into Cornwall," as spokesmen for the Union Nationale government of Quebec predicted at the time. The trouble is that it hasn't "spilled over" at all. What went wrong?

There are several answers to this question. Most important, perhaps, is the fact that the Toronto International Airport was opened up to direct flights from Europe across the Atlantic. When Mirabel was planned it was stated unequivocally that it would be the only Canadian airport open to transatlantic flights. It was to serve Toronto as well as Montreal, Ottawa, and Quebec City. Since today Toronto is the final destination of many more transatlantic passengers than Montreal, the volume of traffic at the Montreal airport is a fraction of what was expected. Obviously, if all the scheduled transatlantic flights now going to Toronto went to Montreal instead, Mirabel would be a busy airport indeed.

Another reason for the overestimation of the economic impact of Mirabel is that at the time it was planned it was not fully appreciated that Montreal was already losing out to Toronto as an industrial, commercial, and financial centre. It was not just that enterprises did not settle near Mirabel as expected, they did not settle in the Montreal region at all. Needless to say, the threat of Quebec independence has been a further deterrent to the choice of a site near Mirabel by enterprises wishing to establish themselves in Canada.

A third factor is the failure of supersonic transatlantic services to develop as expected. The new airport at Montreal was designed to deal with supersonic jets, as well as jumbos. It was thought that because of the congestion at Logan Field in Boston and Kennedy in New York, many residents of those cities would prefer to catch their supersonic jet at Mirabel after a short flight from their domestic airport. The Department of Transport spoke grandly at the time of Montreal as the major supersonic jetport in North America. Clearly nothing like that has happened.

A fourth factor has been the delay in providing rapid transport by road to Dorval and the city centre, and the total failure to provide the rapid rail transport that was promised at the time. (One of the reasons for choosing Saint Scholastique was that it already has a rail link with the centre of Montreal that could be upgraded to carry highspeed trains). The consequence is that Mirabel has remained an inconvenient airport, the exact opposite of what was originally planned.

Of these four factors, it is the loss of Montreal's attractiveness as a location for sophisticated enterprises, rather than any technical factors pertaining specifically to the airport itself, that is most important for the explanation of Mirabel's failure as an industrial centre.

In retrospect, it seems clear that a serious error was made in the planning of Montreal's airport facilities. As things stand, far from being an asset favouring the growth of Montreal, the extreme inconvenience of getting from one airport to the other, or even of getting to Mirabel from the city centre, results in people avoiding Montreal as a "turn-table" for getting from one place to a third place, and may well be a factor in location decisions for enterprises which demand a good deal of international travel for their top managers, scientists, and engineers. At the time of writing, the federal government was offering land expropriated for industries and services near Mirabel to its former owners, at 15 percent below market price, which is already well below the price originally paid by the government.

What to do, now that Mirabel is there? Clearly there is no possibility now of revoking the decision to allow overseas flights into Toronto. Passengers heading for Toronto cannot now be told that they must fly to Montreal and change to a domestic flight for Toronto. The original estimates of volume of transatlantic air traffic at Mirabel can never be achieved. The effort must be directed rather at building up activities that do not depend directly on the flow of transatlantic air traffic.

One suggestion is that Dorval should be abandoned and that all air services of Montreal should be amalgamated at Mirabel. Such a move would eliminate most of the problem of interflight connections, so troublesome now with two airports having no good communication between them. The land at Dorval is enormously valuable for residential and related uses, and no doubt alternative uses could be found for most of the existing structures. Closing the Dorval airport would relieve some of the pressure on the Metropolitan freeway between the city centre and the suburbs in the western part of the island. It is more difficult to think of good ways of using the land and facilities at Mirabel if all air services were concentrated at Dorval, and congestion between the centre and the western island would then be further aggravated. But concentrating all air services at Mirabel would make all the more necessary the provision of rapid transport between the airport and the city centre, whether by road, by rail, or both.

Prof. Fernand Martin is of the opinion that if the purpose of the airports is to provide necessary air services to the metropolis, and no more, it is scarcely worthwhile to fuse them into one.[4] However, if Mirabel is to serve as a "pôle de croissance" as originally envisaged, Dorval would have to be amalgamated with it, and other things would have to be done in the neighbourhood of the airport as well. For example, if an International Trade and Finance Centre is established in the Montreal region, as has been suggested by the University of Montreal's Centre for Research on Economic Development, perhaps a site near Mirabel would be appropriate.[5] Busy executives are increasingly taking to airport meetings to avoid the waste of time involved in going into the centre of the city and back again. For meetings involving executives from Canada, Europe, and the United States, Mirabel is the ideal meeting point. If Dorval were closed, provision should be made for the best possible facilities for such meetings at Mirabel, together with attractive hotel accommodation and large conference halls and convention centres. If and when such facilities are available, the world should be told about them.

As Mirabel approaches its tenth birthday (October 1985) the debate still rages on what to do with it. Air traffic experts in the Department of Transport still predict that the volume of traffic will one day require the use of Mirabel at full capacity, and some of them suggest "putting Mirabel in mothballs," relying on Dorval, until that day arrives. The president of Air Canada has suggested that it might be used for industrial and military purposes meanwhile. Another idea is to use it as a maintenance station and as a school to train pilots and maintenance personnel.

Mayor Drapeau has a bolder idea. He is convinced that Mirabel could be made viable by provision of high-speed trains from Mirabel through the centre of Montreal to the centre of New York. An initial technical pre-feasability study made by two French railway engineers reached optimistic conclusions; the centre of Montreal could be put within less than three hours from the centre of New York by rail. This report was submitted in the summer of 1983. An economic and commercial prefeasibility study by a well known private consulting firm was undertaken for the governments of New York and Vermont and submitted in the fall of 1984. A third study by the same firm was launched early in 1985 for the governments of New York, Vermont, and Quebec. Meanwhile the Director of the University of Montreal's Centre de recherche sur les transports has declared the whole idea "rubbish."[6] He may well be right; but when one sees Japan's "bullet trains," each several cars long, leaving Tokyo every fifteen or twenty minutes for Nagoya, Kyoto and Osaka, one wonders if Mayor Drapeau's idea is necessarily mad.

Meanwhile there are other proposals for high-speed trains to Ottawa, Toronto, and Quebec City. Obviously I cannot pronounce on the feasibility of any one of these proposals. But they are in keeping with the sort of broad strategy outlined in this final chapter. I would only add that I would like to see a direct link from Mirabel to Hull/Ottawa, and a high-speed spur to Boston as well.

Finally, the DRIE powers could be used to attract an entire complex of sophisticated, inter-related enterprises to Mirabel. Once a few such enterprises are established there, others would follow. Of course, DRIE incentives alone may prove insufficient to attract industries and services of the desired type, unless the decisionmakers involved have confidence in both the economic and the political future of Montreal and of Quebec.

Measures to be taken elsewhere in Quebec

When the Special Task Force recommended the Saint Scholastique site and argued that putting the airport in Drummondville or Saint Jean was not an effective strategy for solving the economic and social problems of the Cantons de l'Est, they urged at the same time that the federal and provincial governments mount a joint program for the reconstruction of that region. Once the "couronne" and satellite cities have been strengthened, high priority should be given to transforming the old industrial towns of the Eastern Townships. As pointed out above, the Economic Council of Canada has already proposed that the federal government's powers be used to smooth the transition in that region from the low-productivity and stagnant traditional industries (such as textiles and boots and shoes) to high-productivity and dynamic ones (electronics, scientific instruments). The example of assisting IBM to establish a branch operation in Bromeau is a good one. If head offices of companies like IBM can be attracted to the Montreal region, arrangements might even be made simultaneously for establishing branch activities in one or another of the relatively retarded regions of Quebec, especially those within easy striking distance of Montreal.

Quebec City and the East of Quebec

In retrospect it is unfortunate that the terms of reference of the Bureau d'aménagement de l'est du Québec, which was assigned the task of preparing a regional development plan for Gaspésie/Bas Saint-Laurent, required the team to find a solution for the poverty and unemployment in the east of Quebec within the region. Too little attention was accordingly paid to the role of Quebec City in the region, and to the possibility of strengthening interactions between Quebec and Montreal. We have argued above that Montreal cannot be expected to serve directly as a "development pole" for the east of Quebec, generating through its own expansion income and employment in that retarded region. But within a more broadly defined strategy it might do so indirectly via Quebec City. Where the largest city of a geographical and political entity like a province or state is not its capital, a natural symbiosis tends to develop between the two. Examples are Austin, Texas and Houston; Albany, New York and New York City; Baton Rouge, Louisiana and New Orleans. Much can be learned from these examples because in all of them growth of the major city and of the capital city are mutually reinforcing. The same could be true of Montreal and Quebec City, in much larger measure than can be observed today. The HMR Report maintained that Quebec City could not serve as a development pole for the entire province; but it could serve as a growth centre and pole of attraction for the east of Quebec. It has attained a mass where it can certainly serve as a regional centre. It has an excellent university, enormous charm, an active night life, first rate restaurants, and the provincial government — much like Austin, Texas. Many people — and not only born Québécois — prefer it to Montreal. It is time for Quebec to branch out and develop more sophisticated manufacturing and service activities of its own. But this should be done in such a way that Montreal and Quebec City do not compete with each other for identical activities (except for those that are aimed at a strictly local market and need to be close to that market). The objective should be to maximize the interactions between the two cities, not the competition between them. One element in such a strategy would be improved transport.

The National Capital

More should be made also of the interactions between Montreal and the National Capital, on both sides of the river. In particular, the freeway from Hull to Mirabel should be completed as soon as possible. Rail services should be improved on both sides of the Ottawa. Surely we in Canada are capable of a level of technology equal to that of Japan; why should we not have a 200-kilometre-per-hour train from Ottawa/Hull to Mirabel/Montreal like Japan's "bullet" linking Tokyo with Nagoya, Kyoto, and Osaka? It would be an excellent idea also to reintroduce the STOL Air service between the National Capital and Montreal, linking the centres of the two cities directly by air, even if it required further subsidization for some period. The social benefits of such linkages cannot be measured in terms of fares collected. It may have been a mistake ever to have moved Canada's capital away from Montreal; but fortunately they are close together in distance and could be made much closer together in terms of time, increasing the interactions between them in accordance with the "gravity models" outlined above.

Eastern Ontario

We have indicated above that an essential component of any strategy for the renaissance of Montreal is the reactivation of eastern Ontario and the establishment of appropriate interactions between Montreal and the small industrial towns of that region.[7] These cities belong naturally within the Montreal urban system, and a triangular development pattern with Montreal, Toronto, and Ottawa/Hull as the poles could strengthen the economies of Ontario, Quebec, and Canada as a whole. It is not often that the objectives of the three governments concerned are so clearly complementary. The Ontario government wishes to restrain the growth of Toronto and the other cities of the Golden Triangle, to conserve rich agricultural land, to preserve the natural beauty of the region, and to limit congestion, pollution, and conurbation. The Liberal government agreed. For Montreal, it is of fundamental importance to have in its hinterland, in all directions, dynamic small towns with which it can interact. It is also important to extend the axis of development now running from Chicago to Oshawa on to Kingston and then further along the Saint Lawrence to Cornwall and Montreal. Such a strategy should be of interest to Quebec, not only because strengthening Montreal means strengthening the Quebec economy as a whole, but because a large proportion of the population along the way on the Ontario side is francophone.

230

Eastern Ontario is not a distressed area in the sense that the east of Quebec or northern New Brunswick are distressed. Unemployment has been above the national average in some of the cities of the region and a few people are clinging to marginal farms, while others have been abandoned. But the character of the region is rather that of one which has been stagnant for a century than of one which is poverty-stricken by Canadian standards. The University of Ottawa team argued that the region should be regarded, not as a problem but as an opportunity — an opportunity to help solve the problem of conurbation in the southwestern part of Ontario, and in so doing to strenghten simultaneously the Montreal and Quebec economies. The University of Ottawa Report states:

> Viewed from this angle, the century-long doze of Eastern Ontario may be regarded as a blessing in disguise. The region is a valuable reservoir of attractive residential space. Population densities remain very low; except for Ottawa no city reaches even 100,000 population. Most of the area is pleasant, rolling, partially wooded countryside, dotted with lakes and rivers that led to the early nineteenth century development of the region. For those whose tastes do not require constant immersion in the hustle and bustle of great cities, it is a very agreeable place to live, — if you have an interesting and pleasant way of earning a living.[8]

The Report calls for measures designed to lure up to one million people into the region over the next twenty years. Combined with a "stay option" strategy for northern Ontario, this approach would permit the limitation of population growth and industrialization in the Golden Triangle, making it possible for that area too to remain a pleasant place in which to live. It would also mean, in conjunction with the policies proposed for strengthening the Quebec cities within the Montreal urban system, that instead of being situated in an industrial desert, Montreal would be surrounded by vigorous small industrial towns, as Toronto is, and through them would be linked to Toronto as well.

The University of Ottawa team which prepared the Report on Development Strategy for Eastern Ontario at the request of the Ministry of Treasury, Economics and Intergovernmental Affairs, found few linkages among the industrial towns of the region. Indeed they found few even with Ottawa and Montreal; and while there were more interactions with Toronto, the enterprises operating in eastern Ontario towns were not there primarily because the towns are "near Toronto." The establishment of linkages must be a matter of planning and policy, after the manner suggested by Jacques Boudeville shortly before his death, and outlined above. Individual entrepreneurs do not always think in terms of possible linkages with other enterprises in neighbouring towns. But a consortium of federal departments involved in land management and industrial development, together with their counterparts in the two provincial governments and in the municipal governments, could do so. The combined powers of these departments are certainly enough to have a major impact on patterns of regional development. The right combination of incentives, investment in infrastructure, and dissemination of information could do a great deal.

Important in this connection is the urban economist's concept of "borrowed size." Sometimes a small or middle-sized city can have many of the attributes of a metropolitan centre, including the presence of sophisticated services and scientifically oriented manufacturing, by "borrowing size" from nearby big cities. Examples are Austin, Texas; Santa Barbara, California; Palo Alto, California; Madison, Wisconsin; Ann Arbor, Michigan; Geneva, Switzerland; Brighton, England; London, Ontario. (Note that all of these cities are university towns in attractive physical settings, as well as being close to one or more metropolitan centres). The "size" borrowed by smaller cities from nearby metropolitan centres is not only, and perhaps not even primarily, the provision by the metropolis of a market for output of the smaller towns, or a convenient location for branch offices of enterprises with head-quarters in the metropolis. More important may be ready access to urbane living, with its concert halls, theatres, and restaurants; and also to high level banking and other financial services, computer facilities, telecommunications, consulting services, research institutes, and the like. It is mainly in this sense that "proximity to Montreal" can help Cornwall, Hawkesbury, Trois-Rivières, Saint Jérôme and Sherbrooke.

Eastern Ontario has fresh air, clean blue water, green fields and forests, and uncluttered space, a combination becoming increasingly rare and precious the world over. A million more people can be easily accommodated in the region without losing any of these assets. But to create half a million jobs in high-productivity, rapid-growth services and industry, and to attract people into them, something more than these physical attractions will be needed. The cities of eastern Ontario, which will still be small after the migration of one million people to them, will need to "borrow size" from somewhere. From where? Obviously, for cities east of Kingston, the answer is: Ottawa/Hull and Montreal. The National Capital Region will have well over one million inhabitants by the end of the century, and with the special attribute of a national capital, can certainly serve as a "central place" for a system of nearby small towns on both sides of the Ottawa River. Montreal can perform the same function for towns closer to it, and for more specialized and "rare" services and industry, act as "central place" for all Canadian cities from Kingston to Quebec City.

Each of the cities in Montreal's greater sphere of influence has special characteristics, and the Grand Design we are suggesting requires a tailor-made program for each of them. This study of Montreal is not the place for a detailed exposition of these programs, even if we were in a position to provide them. It is rather a matter of illustrating an approach.

With its location midway between Toronto and Montreal on the Chicago-Montreal axis, Kingston is obviously an important link in the chain. With one of Canada's finest universities, together with the Royal Military College and the National Defence College, with a pleasing physical setting and retaining much of its colonial charm, Kingston is an attractive alternative as a place to work and live to overcrowded southern Ontario. With good air feeder line services to Montreal, Toronto, and Ottawa/Hull, together with improved rail services, Kingston, once Ontario's most important city, could attract scientifically oriented industries and sophisticated services with only limited use of government incentives. Kingston might be encouraged to grow to a population of about 250,000 by the end of the century, as a specialized quaternary sector town with some scientifically oriented industries. It could then serve as a secondary central place for the region. The Report of the University of Ottawa team suggests that Kingston could become a "little Geneva," with live theatre, music, good restaurants, and an attractive intellectual life.

The Report also has suggestions for each of the centres along the Toronto-Montreal axis which we shall not repeat here. Let us, however, have a look at Cornwall. A vigorous Cornwall is needed to complete the process of extending the southern corridor to Montreal. The city has enjoyed rapid growth in the past few years and is still attracting new enterprises. However, the industry is not very high quality and the city has the ambience of a mill town or company town. Its problems are physical and social. The core city is ugly and the population consists mainly of relatively unskilled workers. Yet the physical setting is excellent, the industrial park is spacious and attractive, and to the east of it is some high land overlooking the river that is potential upper income residential territory, suitable for the managers, scientists, and engineers who must be attracted to Cornwall if its industrial structure is to be upgraded. The waterfront has excellent possibilities, and fortunately most of it is in the hands of government at one level or another, extending to Saint Lawrence College to the east. There is a score of federal government offices in the city and another score of provincial government offices. There is a splendid opportunity here for a joint federal, provincial, municipal and private enterprise land management project. In short, what Cornwall needs most is a facelift to make it as physically attractive as it could be; and then the nearness to Montreal should make it possible to attract sophisticated enterprises.

The Northern Axis

Eastern Ontario's prosperity and expansion during the first half of the nineteenth century resulted from its position between two major transportation routes : the Saint Lawrence to the south and the Ottawa River to the north. This situation created a triangular field of attraction with Bytown (Ottawa/Hull), Montreal, and Kingston at the corners. To recreate eastern Ontario as a thriving and growing industrial region it will be necessary to restore to both of the major transportation axes some of their former importance. As it is, there is no city of importance between Montreal and the National Capital on either side of the river. The strongest candidate for becoming a secondary "central place" along this route is Hawkesbury, with Grenville on the other side of the river. It is about equidistant from Ottawa and Montreal, one hour's drive from either, and could be closer by train. It has a very attractive physical setting. Moreover, since the only bridge across the Ottawa between Montreal and the capital is there, Hawkesbury is closest to Mirabel of all eastern Ontario cities. The city's recent stagnation springs from the fact that its employment base is narrow and limited to traditional industries : pulp and paper and textiles. Building on its special location, government agencies could attract some high technology industries to the area, perhaps on the Quebec side. A research institute concentrating on the paper industry and related activities is an obvious possibility.

234

There is also need for an urban renewal program, particularly in the city core.

The Montreal-Ottawa axis that developed eastern Ontario did not end at Bytown, but extended far to the west. Pembroke would need some attention as part of the strategy of recreating this axis. Further west still is Chalk River, a strong point because of its high technology research facilities and the superior quality of its workforce. Moving on west we come to North Bay, already a vigorously expanding small town. Then come Sudbury, Sault Sainte Marie, and Thunder Bay, all of which need new life blown into them if the Montreal-Winnipeg corridor is to become a dynamic one. The solution to the problem of eastern Ontario, and thus of Montreal, lies partly in northern Ontario.

Conclusion: A nation-wide strategy

We have probably said enough to indicate the kind of nation-wide strategy of urban growth and regional development which may be necessary to restore Montreal to its former state of robust health, while at the same time relieving congestion in the Golden Triangle and stagnation in eastern Ontario and in the Eastern Townships of Quebec. Planning for Montreal should also take into account the impact of policies to reduce disparities between the Atlantic provinces and the more prosperous provinces, or to stem agglomeration in Winnipeg and provide a "stay option" (the possibility for Manitobans to earn a decent living without having to emigrate to Winnipeg). Ultimately, the entire urban hierarchy of Canada is one unit and must be planned as such.

Montreal and the Outside World

At several points in this study we have underlined the fact that from the very beginning Montreal developed as an international rather than a merely national centre. The set of linkages and interactions we have suggested above, which can be brought into being by appropriate policies at all three levels of Canadian government, in collaboration with private enterprise, would do much to restore Montreal to its former status as Canada's metropolis. But to become once again Canada's major cosmopolitan centre, old links must be strengthened and new links forged with metropolitan centres abroad as well. Once outside

Canada's borders the impact of Canadian government policy is obviously less direct, and the collaboration of the private sector becomes all the more important. But given imaginative policy at all three levels of government, plus the cooperation of private enterprise, much can be done even abroad.

The French connection

Montreal's position as "the world's second biggest French-speaking city" has never been fully exploited. More could be done by way of cultural and professional exchanges, with international congresses of French-speaking scientists, artists, managers, financiers, etc. Film festivals and music festivals concentrating on French-speaking countries could be a regular feature of Montreal life; Man and His World as a continuing institution could become somewhat less of an amusement park and return to something closer to what Expo '67 originally was. International trade fairs concentrating on francophone countries would be another possibility, perhaps held at an International Finance Centre near Mirabel. Out of such exchanges could come an expanded flow of goods, services, and capital between Montreal and other francophone centres.

In thinking of French-speaking communities, the organizers of the various events and institutions — and the founders of enterprises — should remember, in addition to France, Switzerland, Belgium, and the francophone countries of Africa, Asia, and the Carribean, the French-speaking populations of the Atlantic provinces, New England, and Louisiana. In all of these areas a recrudescence of interest in the French language is occurring, even and perhaps especially among young people. This fact gives Quebec and Montreal a foot in the door for whatever kinds of interactions they may wish to build up with these communities. The French-speaking areas of New England provide a bridge to Boston, and the French-speaking society of Louisiana provides a doorway to the sunbelt, for Montreal and Quebec.

There is room for debate as to how important the cosmopolitan atmosphere of Montreal may be in the location decisions of hi-tech industries and sophisticated services. On this point, Mario Polèse first waxes lyrical about the city where he lives and which he obviously loves:

Montreal also offers a point of cultural contact between Anglo-North America and Francophone Europe and Africa. From an economic standpoint, Montreal would appear to offer a unique location for firms doing business in more than one continent. The life-style which Montreal offers is no less unique, some would say a combination of the Old World and the New: side-walk cafés beneath skyscrapers, Latin "joie-de-vivre" and American efficiency, French elegance with North American informality, superb restaurants and fast food parlours. Montreal is undoubtedly the most European of North American cities. Montreal certainly offers a very attractive urban environment with a vibrant downtown and an active night-life, all within a comparatively crime-free setting by North American standards, and even by recent European standards.[9]

At least one favourable byproduct of the emigration of anglophones from Montreal is that it has contributed to the blurring of geographical lines between French-speaking and English-speaking residents of the city. As anglophones moved out of Westmount and Mount Royal, francophones have moved in. Some anglophones have discovered the charms of Vieux Montreal, Lafontaine Park, and other areas in the east of the city. Some have deliberately moved into such areas in order to be in a French-speaking neighbourhood. In the upper echelons of Montreal society more and more people make a point of belonging to both French-speaking and English-speaking clubs. Not only are more French Canadians going to McGill, but more English Canadians are going to the Université de Montréal and Laval. More than ever before, parliamentarians make a point of presenting speeches in both languages — and these days this has to be more than a gesture; it has to be a show of genuine bilingualism. At the level of decision-making in both the private and public sectors, Canada seems at long last on the road to becoming a truly bilingual country, with the Montreal community leading the way.

But Polèse concludes that Montreal's cosmopolitan atmosphere, and especially the insistence upon preserving its "Frenchness" is not an unmixed blessing. It is

probably viewed negatively, constituting a constraint rather than an opportunity, given the limited importance of French language within this continent...

... Linguistic capacities are only relevant if they are tied to existing or potential economic opportunities and markets. One must clearly distinguish between the international flavour of a city, as characterized by its population mix and life-style, and the international business functions it performs and the markets it must serve. International financial centres such as Zurich, Frankfurt, and even the City of London are, after all, quite homogeneous and unilingual in character compared to many other places around the globe.[10]

The point is, however, that it is not necessary for *all* decision-makers of *avant-garde* enterprises to be attracted by Montreal's glamour and charm. It is only necessary for *some* of them to be attracted. I have no doubt that a good many of them would be, once the uncertainty about the future of Quebec and Montreal has been dispelled. The characteristics described by Polèse are a distinct asset, and Montreal, Quebec, and Canada should build on that asset to restore the metropolis to its former vigour.

The Eastern Seaboard

As we have seen, Montreal retains some advantage with regard to communications with the eastern seaboard of the United States. We have suggested that Boston, with its unrivalled concentration of scientific, intellectual, and cultural activities, its sophisticated financial centre and its scientifically oriented industries, is a good model for the future development of Montreal, with a judicious touch of New Orleans added. If Boston is to be a model, it becomes of special importance to develop interchanges of various kinds with that city. It is less than one hour away by air. Once again, the policy might be to start with cultural exchanges of various kinds, using these to open up linkages in the fields of industry, commerce, and finance. Possibilities should be explored in other eastern seaboard cities as well, such as Portland, New York, Philadelphia, and Baltimore.

The Sunbelt

While Montreal may not be in a highly strategic position for developing relations with the rising cities of the sunbelt, neither is it in markedly disadvantageous position in comparison with other Canadian cities, especially for the sunbelt cities further to the east, such as Atlanta, New Orleans, and Houston. Why should Canadian policy not be for once farsighted and imaginative, so that we could climb onto this particular bandwagon before it is moving too fast to catch?

Latin America

Moving on south we come to Latin America, a rapidly developing area with some 200 million people, in our own hemisphere. Canada has never fully exploited its excellent relations with Latin American countries. The seat in the Organization of American States (OAS) has been kept warm for Canada for decades, but never occupied, presumably because of fears that in an organization where the United States is now the only non-Latin-American country, Canada would play second fiddle to the United States, or risk conflict with our most powerful friend and ally. There can be no doubt that most Latin American countries would welcome our presence in the OAS. Some years ago, at a joint meeting of the Canadian Institute of International Affairs and the World Peace Council of Boston, concerned with the United States-Canada-Latin American Relations and held in Quebec City, leading Brazilian economist and now Senator Roberto Campos (former ambassador to the USA and the United Kingdom), and leading Mexican economist Dr. Victor Urquidi (now president of the Collegio de Mexico) were among the distinguished Latin Americans who urged Canadians to recognize that their country is not only in the western hemisphere but is one-third "Latin," and accordingly should join the OAS.

Few Canadians, perhaps, recognize the possibilities entailed, especially in Latin America, in being one-third "Latin American." But French is a Latin language and French Canadians are Latin Americans in the literal sense of that term. It is no accident that most of our ambassadors to Latin American countries have been Québécois. A "Latin Canadian" has a better chance — other things being equal — than an Ontario "wasp" of becoming "sympatico" to Latin Americans, quickly enough for his acceptance by the people of the country where he is posted to be useful to him during his term of office. Moreover, any educated person whose first language is French can easily learn Spanish or Portuguese. Here again, cultural and similar exchanges could lead to economic relationships. Particularly attractive, perhaps, are Brazil, the "colossus to the south," with a population of 130 million people and a per capita income of over $2,500 per year, and Mexico with 75 million people and a per capita income of $2,500 per year, both rapidly growing. The potential for the Montreal economy of opening up relations with countries such as these is enormous.

Montreal in a Sovereign Quebec

And so we arrive at the question, "What would be the fate of Montreal in an independent Quebec?" Clearly, this question cannot be answered without first answering the question, "What kind of independence?" There has been a good deal of ambiguity in the Parti québécois statements regarding their concept of the economic aspects of independence, and even more uncertainty as to what the federal government and the other provincial governments would be prepared to accept.[11] This book goes to press shortly after the resignation of René Levesque as leader of the Parti québécois, and all the signs point to the defeat of the party in the next election. But Quebec nationalism is not dead, nor should it be; and if things go badly in the province, separatism too may have a resurgence.

No one can predict what might emerge from a negotiation as emotional, complex, and delicate as one between an independent Quebec and the federal government plus the nine provinces would be. Any objective analysis, however, leads to the conclusion that the other governments would be likely to drive a hard bargain and that Quebec's bargaining position would be weak.

In the field of manufacturing, no other province is so dependent on the rest of Canada for markets as is Quebec. Nearly 30 percent of Quebec's shipments of manufactured goods goes to other provinces. Goods shipped from Quebec to Ontario alone constitute nearly one-fifth of the total, while Ontario's shipments to Quebec are just over one-tenth of the total Ontario shipment. One study concludes that "Quebec would be severely affected by any change, however moderate, in the freedom of trade that exists within the Canadian Federation." [12] The study also points out that in the whole pattern of Quebec's balance of payments the only favourable item is its trade in manufactured goods with the rest of Canada; all other items, including all aspects of international trade and inter-regional trade in raw materials and services appear to be deficit. Another study shows that "there is a dramatic difference in the degree of interdependence between Quebec and the rest of Canada." [13] This Report concludes that "the realities of interprovincial trade place the rest of Canada in a very strong bargaining position. Given these circumstances, the best an independent Quebec might be able to negotiate is an arrangement similar to the General Agreement on Tariffs and Trade (GATT) under which a restructured Canada would treat Quebec simply as another country in terms of trading relations." [14]

The withdrawal of Canadian protection for Quebec industries and the imposition of tariffs on Quebec exports to Canada would be only part of the losses suffered by Quebec. Independence would certainly accelerate the exodus from Montreal of top level industrial, commercial, and financial firms. Nervousness regarding Quebec's future, already displayed in New York, Washington, London, and Paris, would be enhanced. Enterprises considering the establishment of an operation in Canada would be less likely than ever to choose Montreal. Quebec has long relied heavily on the American bond market to finance her deficits, and has enjoyed a good rating in that market. That rating slipped with the election of the Parti québécois and with independence it would slip more. Perhaps after an initial unfavourable reaction, the outside financial world would once again become interested in Quebec, as happened in Mexico some years after the 1934 revolution and the nationalization of United States enterprises. But Mexico was already a heavily populated country on the verge of a takeoff into very rapid growth. Quebec would be a small country in terms of population, and one which only recently suffered stagnation and showed signs of decline. The danger is that exodus of sophisticated enterprises would proceed at such a speed that Quebec entrepreneurs, scientists, and engineers would not be able to take over fast enough to prevent an absolute decline in economic activity in Montreal. And as we have noted above, the thresholds of city-size and scale of activity at which various kinds of operations can be expected in any city work in both directions. The exodus could become cumulative; and as we have also seen above, once an enterprise has moved, particularly if its head office is concerned, it is very difficult to lure it back.

It is not possible to predict in detail how a cumulative decline might take place, but one can see some of the more obvious possibilities. For example, it is most unlikely that Montreal's universities would continue to draw so many students from elsewhere in Canada and abroad once Quebec becomes independent. Even the status of the degrees, especially in professional fields like law and medicine, may be in doubt. Moreover, without the federal grants for education, Quebec would find its present system of tertiary education difficult to maintain. The universities would also find it more difficult than before to attract top level people from outside of Quebec. Some loss of size and quality seems inevitable. The international reputations of Montreal's universities would suffer in the process. In that case, it would be just that much more difficult for Montreal to follow the course of Boston, replacing low-productivity traditional industry and services with scientifically oriented industry and sophisticated services, attracted by the city's universities and other research institutions.

Finally, it is obvious that the kind of strategy outlined above for generating a renaissance in Montreal as part of a national policy regarding urban growth and regional development is out of the question if Quebec were another country. It would be absurd to imagine that the powers and the budgets of federal departments could be made available to promote the prosperity of a city in another country. Rather than moving more federal government activities to Quebec, and especially to Montreal, as part of the decentralization program, Canada would have to move out of Quebec what is already there. It is unlikely that the International Civil Aviation Organization would stay in Montreal, or that any new international organization would come. The idea of making Montreal a major *international* centre would lose all reality. The international airport at Mirabel, and similar properties of the federal government in Quebec, would presumably have to be bought by the new nation (a heavy financial burden in itself) and operated by its government. Any remaining hope of making Mirabel a major North American airport and attracting to its environs a package of scientifically oriented enterprises would be gone.

Montreal would not disappear in an independent Quebec. It could even develop a new charm, with gentle reminders of past glory and the ambience of earlier times, while becoming a more purely French city than it has ever been since the conquest. But it could become a rather sleepy provincial town, instead of the throbbing national and international metropolis that it was at the time of Expo '67. If on the other hand a strategy like the one outlined in this chapter is carried out, the "Spirit of Expo '67" can once again dominate the metropolis.

NOTES

Chapter One

1. For a somewhat more detailed treatment of these agencies of the 1960s, see Benjamin Higgins, "Growth Pole Policy in Canada," in Niles Hansen, editor, *Growth Centres in Regional Economic Development* (New York: The Free Press/Macmillan 1972), pp. 204-28; R.A. McClarty, "Government of Canada Policy for Regional Development," in R.C. Mathews, editor, *Regional Disparities and Economic Development* (Canberra A.N.U. Press 1981), pp. 81-98.
2. Cf. Benjamin Higgins, "National Development and Regional Policy," in Ed Prantilla, editor, *National Development and Regional Policy* (Nagoya United Nations Centre for Regional Development, 1981).
3. Donald J. Savoie, "The Toppling of DREE and Prospects for Regional Economic Development," *Canadian Public Policy*, vol. X, no. 3, Sept. 1984, p. 322.
4. This quotation is given from memory of the seminar, but I am sure that it is basically correct.
5. Benjamin Higgins, Fernand Martin and André Raynauld, *Les orientations du développement économique régional du Québec* (Ottawa: Department of Regional Economic Expansion, 1970).
6. Economic Council of Canada, *Living Together: A Study of Regional Disparities* (Ottawa, 1977), Chapter 7 and Appendix A.
7. The analysis behind these statements is presented in Chapter 4.

Chapter Two

1. Raoul Blanchard, *L'ouest du Canada français* (Montreal: Beauchemin 1953), pp. 207, 213.
2. Hugh MacLennan, "The Rivers that Made a Nation," reprinted in Elspeth Cameron, editor, *The Other Side of Hugh MacLennan* (Toronto: Macmillan, 1978), p. 196.

3. Raymond TANGHE, "La population," in Esdras Minville, editor, *Montréal écono-mique*: étude préparée à l'occasion du troisième centennaire de la ville, (Montréal: Université de Montréal) (IDES, 1943) p. 101.
4. BLANCHARD, *Canada français*, p. 224.
5. MACLENNAN, "Rivers that Made a Nation," p. 196.
6. I. WELD, *Travels through the States of North America and the Provinces of Upper and Lower Canada During the Years 1795, 1796, and 1797* (London: Stockdale, 4th edition, 1807), pp. 180, 183.
7. BLANCHARD, *Canada français*, p. 225.
8. William H. NICHOLLS, *Southern Traditions and Regional Progress* (Chapel Hill: University of North Carolina Press, 1959), pp. 34-35.
9. Ibid., p. 35.
10. Ibid., p. 29.
11. Ibid., pp. 31, 63.
12. Ibid., p. 48.
13. Louis Adolphe PAQUET, "La terre canadienne," *Études et appréciations*, vol. 1 (Québec: Imprimerie Fransciscaine Missionnaire, 1918) pp. 3-12; and "La vocation de la race française en Amérique,"*Discours et Allocutions*, vol. 1 (Québec: Imprimerie Franciscaine Missionnaire, 1915) p. 187.
14. Sir John BOURINET, *Canada* (New York: G.P. Putnam and Sons, 1898), pp. 438-39.
15. J.P. BEAULIEU, *Province of Quebec Industrial Expansion Publication* (Quebec: Office provincial de publicité pour le ministère du Commerce et de l'Industrie), September 1952.
16. Albert FAUCHER et Maurice LAMONTAGNE, "History of Industrial Development," in *Essays on Contemporary Quebec*, J.C. Falardeau ed. (Québec: Les Presses Universitaires Laval, 1953), p. 37.
17. Pierre Elliot TRUDEAU, "La Province au Moment de la Grève," in *La Grève de l'Amiante*, (ed. Pierre Elliot Trudeau) (Montréal: Les Éditions Cité Libre, 1956), p. 12.
18. BLANCHARD, *Canada français*, p. 236.
19. Stephen LEACOCK, *Montreal: Seaport and City* (New York: Doubleday, 1942).
20. Jean Delage cites, without giving a date, a survey undertaken by the Carnegie Institute of Canadian-American Industry. Of 168 replies from Canadian companies, the number mentioning each of the suggested reasons for choosing their location was as follows: proximity to markets 91; ease of communications 52; skilled or cheap labour 56; proximity to parent company 33; purchase of an existing enterprise 31; low rent of facilities 31; low cost of raw materials 22; proximity to complementary industries 21; low cost of energy 19; other favourable condition 14. Jean Delage, "Industrie Manufacturière," in Esdras Minville, ed., *Montréal économique*, p. 199.
21. Hans Peter GASSMANN, "Data Networks: New Information Infrastructure" *The OECD Observer*, no. 95, November 1978, pp. 12-13.

Chapter Three

1. Jean-Yves DUMONT, Économiste, District Montréal Métropolitain, Commission des Services Économiques Région du Québec, Emploi et Immigration Canada, *Rapport annuel — Première étape*, February 1978.

2. This figure, and a good many others in this section for the period prior to 1974, comes from André Ryba, *Le rôle du secteur financier dans le développement du Québec, un essai en finance régionale* (Montréal : Centre de recherche en développement régional, 1974).
3. Ibid., p. 4.
4. Ibid., p. 150.
5. Quoted by Ryba, ibid., p. 142.
6. These figures are from the I.N.R.S.-Urbanisation data bank. See Pierre Lamonde and Mario Polèse, "L'Évolution de la structure économique de Montréal, 1971-1981," (Montréal : I.N.R.S.-Urbanisation, June 1984).
7. Mario Polèse, "Montreal's Role as an International Business Centre : Cultural Images vs. Economic Realities," (Montreal : Institut national de la recherche scientifique-Urbanisation, October 1983).
8. Bernard Bonin, "La vocation internationale de Montréal : Mythes et réalités" (Montréal : Centre d'études en administration internationale. École des Hautes Études Commerciales, May 1982) pp. 21-23 (mimeograph).
9. Bonin, Ibid., p. 2.
10. Fernand Martin, "The Role of the Hinterland in the Performance of the Port of Montreal in Containerized Traffic" (Montreal : mimeographed, May 1983).
11. Fernand Martin, "Position Concurrentielle de Montréal dans les Transports et les Communications" (Montréal : Centre d'études en administration internationale, May 1982).
12. G. Norcliffe, *Industrial Development in Canadian Ports* (Toronto : Toronto-York University Joint Program in Transportation, September 1982).

Chapter Four

1. Benjamin Higgins, Fernand Martin et André Raynauld, *Les orientations du développement économique du Québec* (HMR Report), (Ottawa : Department of Regional Economic Expansion, 1970).
2. There were good reasons for this rivalry. A laker, built like a shoe box, is very efficient in any waters where it is safe. Nearly every inch can be used for cargo. An ocean vessel needs a deep keel, a long pointed prow, and a rounded stern ; the ratio of cargo weight to total weight is substantially lower for an ocean freighter.
3. Economic Council of Canada, *Living Together : a Study of Regional Disparities* Ottawa 1977, Table 7-2, p. 125.
4. Ibid., p. 127.
5. Ibid., p. 131.
6. Ibid., p. 128.
7. Ibid., p. 128.
8. Jacques Boudeville, "Les Régions de villes et l'Europe," Congrès de l'Association de sciences régionales de langue française (Rotterdam 1974, mimeographed).
9. André Raynauld, "Some Remarks on the New International Economic Order," Address to the Chicago Council on Foreign Relations, 24 Feb. 1976 (mimeographed).
10. F. Martin, N. Swan, I. Banks, G. Barker, R. Beaudry, *Comparaison interrégionale de la diffusion des innovations au Canada* (Ottawa : Economic Council of Canada, 1979).

11. N.L. Gill, "Croissance et asservissement," *Socialisme québécois*, no. 23 (Montréal, 1972): 11-32.
12. Ibid.
13. Gilles Paquet, "Les orientations du développement économique dans la province de Québec, *Débat, Actualité économique* vol. 47, no. 4: (April-June 1971): 110-15.
14. Gerald Fortin, "Les orientations du développement économique dans la province de Québec" *Débat, Actualité économique*, vol. 47, no. 4 (1971): 121-31.
15. David McClelland and David C. Winters, *Motivating Economic Achievement* (New York: The Free Press, 1973).
16. François Perroux, "Multinational Investments and the Analysis of Development and Integration Poles" *Économies et sociétés*, Cahiers de l'I.S.E.A., série F, no. 24, 1973, pp. 842-44.

Chapter Five

1. Everett C. Hughes, *French Canada in Transition* (Chicago: University of Chicago Press, 1943), pp. 1, 8.
2. Philippe Garigue, "St-Justin: A case study in Rural French-Canadian Social Organization," *The Canadian Journal of Economics and Political Science*, vol. XXII, no. 3, August 1956, pp. 317-18.
3. Ibid., p. 318.
4. O.J. Firestone, "Quebec and Ontario — is the Economic Gap Narrowing?" Address to the Chartered Institute of Secretaries, Ottawa, 16 January 1969, p. 1.
5. Kenneth Buckley, *Capital Formation in Canada 1896-1930* (Toronto: University of Toronto Press, 1955).
6. Mary Innis, *An Economic History of Canada* (Toronto: The Ryerson Press, 1954) p. 246.
7. Harold A. Innis, *Essays in Canadian Economic History* (Toronto: University of Toronto Press, 1962), pp. 74-75.
8. Hugh MacLennan, "Two Solitudes Thirty Three Years Later," in Elspeth Cameron, (ed.), *The Other Side of Hugh MacLennan* (Toronto: MacMillan, 1978), p. 296.
9. Ibid., p. 296.
10. Jean Delage, in Esdras Minville, ed., *Montréal économique*, p. 209.
11. Report of the Royal Commission on Bilingualism and Biculturalism, Book III, *The Work World* (Ottawa, 1969) p. 41.
12. Ibid., p. 42.
13. Forgive me for recounting a personal experience. Soon after World War II, I was working with Dr. O.J. Firestone, preparing documentation for a federal-provincial conference, a rather technical job. Even then efforts were made in Ottawa to recruit qualified French Canadians where possible. When a graduate from one of the better known Quebec classical colleges applied for a post as research assistant, stating that he had graduated with honours in economics, he was interviewed. Asked what courses he had taken in economics, he said, "Oh, economic theory, money and banking, public finance." "And what did you read in economic theory?" "Oh, Plato, and Aristotle, and St. Thomas Acquinas." "And in money and banking?" "Oh Plato, and Aristotle, St. Thomas Acquinas."

"Same thing for public finance ?" "Of course !" Needless to say, this situation has since changed drastically.

14. Jac André BOULET, *L'évolution des disparités linguistiques de revenu de travail dans la zone métropolitaine de Montréal de 1961 à 1977*, Ottawa, Economic Council of Canada, February 1979; and *La langue et le revenu de travail à Montreal* (Ottawa: Economic Council of Canada, 1980).
15. The 1961 study was based on a sample of 20% of the male population. The 1971 census sample was 33% of the male population. The 1978 study by Professors Paul Bernard and Jean Renaud of the University of Montreal sociology department covered a sample of 955 workers aged 17 and over.
16. N.W. TAYLOR, "The French Canadian Industrial Entrepreneur and his Environment," in M. Rioux and Y. Martin, eds, *Canadian Society*, vol. 1 (Toronto: McClelland Stuart French, 1974), pp. 271-95.
17. A.A. HUNTER, "A Comparative Analysis of Anglophone-Francophone Occupational Prestige Structures in Canada," *Cahiers canadiens de sociologie*, Vol. 2, No. 2, 1977, pp. 187, 190.
18. These figures are taken from Pierre FORTIN, "Economic Growth in Quebec (1973-80): "The Human Capital Connection" (Toronto: University of Toronto Institute of Policy Analysis, Sept. 1982). Fortin cites The Conference Board of Canada, *The Provincial Economies: 1961*-1980 Data (1981).
19. Ibid., p. 5.
20. Ibid., p. 6.

Chapter Six

1. Edgar RUST, "Development without Growth: Lessons from the U.S. Metropolitan Experience," in E.W. Hanten, M.J. Kasoff, and F.S. Redburn, eds, *New Directions for the Mature Metropolis: Policies and Strategies for Change* (Cambridge, Massachusetts: Schenkman, 1980) pp. 42-57.
2. Harry W. RICHARDSON, "Approaches to Regional Development Theory in Western Market Economies," in George Demko ed., *Regional Development: Problems and Policies in Eastern and Western Europe* (London and Sydney: Croom Helm, 1984) pp. 22-23.
3. Sir Roy HARROD, *Towards a Dynamic Economics* (London: Macmillan, 1948).
4. Evsey DOMAR, *Essays in the Theory of Economic Growth* (New York, Oxford, 1957).
5. John CORNWALL, *Growth and Stability in a Mature Economy* (London: Martin Robinson, 1972).
6. Gunnar MYRDAL, *Economic Theory and Underdeveloped Regions* (London: Duckworth, 1957).
7. See Benjamin HIGGINS, "Trade-Off Curves, Trends, and Regional Disparities: The Case of Quebec," *Économie appliquée*, Tome XXVIII, no. 2-3, 1975.
8. See Benjamin HIGGINS and N.T. DUNG, "Dualism, Dependency, and Continuing Underdevelopment," in R.P. Misra and Masahiko Honjo eds, *Changing Perceptions of Development Problems* (Nagoya: Maruzen for UNCRD, 1981).
9. See, for example, *Review of Radical Political Economics, Special Issue* on "Uneven Regional Development," vol. 10, no. 3, Fall 1978, especially J. Lovering, "The Theory of the 'Internal Colony' and the Political Economy of Wales," pp. 55-67. See also Stuart HOLLAND, *Capital vs. the Regions* (London: Macmillan, 1976). Despite the title, which might lead the reader to expect an

orthodox Marxist theory of exploitation, Holland's analysis runs more along the lines of uneven development and polarization, and his policy recommendations are directed towards harnessing and directing the activities of large corporations on the basis planning agreements rather than overthrow of the capitalist system altogether.

10. Neil SMITH, *Uneven Development* (Oxford: Basil Blackwell, 1984), p. 152.

11. Ibid., p. 136.

12. See, for example, Brian BERRY, "Cities as Systems Within Systems of Cities," in William H. Leahy, David L. McKee, and Robert D. Dean, eds, *Urban Economics* (New York: The Free Press, 1970),: 157-76.

13. Brian BERRY, "Hierarchical Diffusion: The Basis of Development Filtering and Spread in a System of Growth Centers," in Niles Hansen, ed., *Growth Centers in Regional Economic Development* (New York and London: The Free Press, 1972): 108-38.

14. J.R. LASUEN, "On Growth Poles," *Urban Studies*, June 1969, pp. 142-43, (Reprinted in Hansen, ed., *Urban Economics*, pp. 20-49.

15. William ALONZO and Elliott MEDRICH, "Spontaneous Growth Centers in Twentieth-Century American Urbanization", in Hansen, ed., *Urban Economics*, pp. 229-65.

16. J.R. LASUEN, *On Growth Poles*, pp. 146-47.

17. Gregory A. JACKSON and George S. MASNICK, "Take Another Look at Regional U.S. Growth," *Harvard Business Review*, vol. 61, no. 2, March-April 1983, p. 76.

18. A. FIELDING, "Counterurbanization in Western-Europe," *Progress in Planning*, 17 (part 1), pp. 1-52, 1982. Quoted in Daniel R. Vinning and Steven B. Cochrane, "Recent Trends in Migration Between Core and Peripheral Regions in Developed and Advanced Countries." Paper presented to the Canadian Regional Science Association, May 1985 (mimeographed).

19. Brian BERRY, "The Counterurbanization Process: How General?," in: Niles Hansen ed., *Human Settlement Systems* (Cambridge, Massachusetts: Ballinger, 1978), pp. 25-50.

20. Niles HANSEN, "Small and Medium-Size Cities in Development," paper presented to the International Symposium on Regional Development and National Economic Growth, Institut canadien de recherche sur le développement régional, Wolfville, Nova Scotia, 25-28 July 1985.

21. Daniel VINNING and Steven COCHRANE, "Recent Trends in Migration," May 1985.

22. Niles HANSEN, "Small and Medium-Size Cities."

23. Ibid., pp. 8-11.

24. Philippe AYDALOT, *Technologies nouvelles et espace: Rapport préliminaire de recherche* (Paris: Groupe technologies nouvelles et espace, October 1984). See also his *Crise et espace*, (Paris: Economica, 1984); and *Dynamique spatiale et développement spatial* (Paris: Economica, 1976).

25. Cf. Gunnar OLSSON, "Central Place Systems, Spatial Interaction, and Stochastic Processes," in Leahy, McKee, Dean, eds, *Urban Economics* (1970): 177-208.

26. Lloyd RODWIN, "Urban Growth Strategies Reconsidered," in Hansen, *Growth Centers*, pp. 1-19.

27. Walter CHRISTALLER, *Die Zentralen Orte in Suddeutschland*, 1933. English translation by C.W. Baskin, *Central Places in Southern Germany* (Englewood Cliffs, N.J.: Prentice Hall, 1966).

28. The treatment of development poles is brief here because I have published extensively on the subject elsewhere. Cf. Benjamin Higgins, "Development Poles: Do They Exist?," in A. Kuklinski, editor, *Polarized Development and Regional Policies* (The Hague and Paris: Mouton, 1981): 19-36; and "From

Growth Poles to Systems of Interactions in Space," *Growth and Change*, vol. 14, no. 4, (Oct. 1983) : 3-12. The latter article contains a brief bibliography of Perroux's work on growth poles.

29. Michael RAY, "Urban Growth and the Concept of Functional Region," in N.H. Lithwick and Gilles Paquet, eds, *Urban Studies: A Canadian Perspective* (Toronto: Methuen, 1960).
30. Martial FAUTEUX, "La Croissance de la Population dans la Région de Montréal," *Cahiers de géographie de Québec*, vol. 27, no. 1, (1983).
31. Australian economist Dr. Helen Hughes, at a recent international conference in Canberra, explained Singapore's spectacular growth of the past decade by saying, "Singapore is not cursed by rich natural resources and a vast hinterland." Her point, of course, is that such countries (one could add Switzerland, Holland, Sweden, Japan) have no choice but the human-resource-based route to development.
32. André RAYNAULD, "Towards an Economic Strategy for Canada," address to the 77th Annual General Meeting of the Canadian Institute of Mining Technology, Toronto, 5 May 1975.

Chapter Seven

1. There are many countries where the metropolitan centre generally regarded as being the most attractive is not the biggest: Rio de Janeiro vs. São Paulo in Brazil; Rome vs. Milan in Italy; Kyoto vs. Tokyo in Japan; Delhi vs. Calcutta in India; Leningrad vs. Moscow in Russia, etc.
2. For a more detailed account of the selection of Ste Scholastique, see Benjamin HIGGINS, "The Montreal International Airport Site," *Growth and Change: A Journal of Regional Development*, vol. 2, no. 1 (January 1971) pp. 3-13.
3. Fernand MARTIN, *Position concurrentielle de Montréal dans les transports et les communications* (Montréal: Centre d'étude en administration internationale, May 1982) p. 106 (mimeograph).
4. Ibid., p. 170.
5. Cf. Pierre-Paul Proulx, éd., *Vers une problématique globale du développement de la région de Montréal* (Montréal: Centre de recherche en développement régional, June 1976) : III-71.
6. Reported in *La Presse*, Montréal, 25 September 1984.
7. This section draws heavily on a Report for the Ontario Department of Treasury, Economics, and Intergovernmental Affairs by a University of Ottawa Team: Benjamin HIGGINS and Others, *A Strategy for the Development of the Eastern Ontario Region*, Ottawa, 1976.
8. Ibid., p. 2.
9. Mario POLÈSE, "Montréal's Role as an International Business Centre: Cultural Images versus Economic Realities" (Montreal: Institut national de recherche scientifique-Urbanisation, October, 1983) p. 4.
10. Ibid., p. 18.
11. For a more detailed analysis of the economic aspects of independence, see Government of Canada, *Sovereignty-Association — the Contradictions and Trade Realities in Canada and the Issue "Sovereignty-Association"* both Ottawa 1978. Henceforth cited as "Sovereignty" and "Trade Realities."
12. "Sovereignty," p. 32.
13. "Trade Realities," p. 13.
14. Ibid., p. 15.

APPENDIX

Presentation of Ben Higgins at
1983 McGill University Convocation by the
Chairman of the Department of Economics

Mr. Chancellor:

Nothing could give me more personal pleasure than to introduce Professor Benjamin Higgins as recipient of an honorary
Doctor of Laws degree at McGill University. It has been my good
fortune to know him as teacher — my teacher — friend and
colleague over the past forty-one years.

Even after four decades, one continues to learn something
new about Ben Higgins. Only two days ago, I discovered that his
parents, coming from distant places, first met on the McGill
campus. It is therefore literally true to say that he owes his very
existence to McGill. And it is at least as striking a fact that four
generations of Higginses, including his grandchildren, have distinguished themselves at this university.

Ben Higgins is one of a kind. The economics profession has
never produced his likeness before, and one can safely predict
that no way will be found to clone him in the years and decades
ahead. Whether it be walking up the steps of our old Arts Building
on his hands, or engaging in classroom bouts of snowball-throwing
with his students, or roaming the far corners of the earth to
savour its excitement and diversity — Ben Higgins has always had
that unique capacity for converting time-worn clichés into vivid

reality. "Living life to the fullest," "ever-young at heart," "citizen of the world" — for most of us, these are only the stuff of which dreams are made; for Ben Higgins, they are the dreams come true.

And yet this lighter side of the Higgins legend, however impressive, is no match for the record of solid achievement. Professor Higgins has devoted the last thirty-five years to the twin problems of development in Third World countries and urban and regional growth in rich and poor countries alike. He has served as economic adviser to the United Nations, the World Bank, UNESCO, the International Labour Organization, and the Canadian International Development Agency; and to a score of governments, including those of Brazil, Egypt, Haiti, Indonesia, Malaysia, Mexico, the Philippines, Sierra Leone and Sri Lanka. Here at home, he has been a consultant to the Economic Council of Canada and the federal Department of Regional Economic Expansion; also to the Quebec Office of Planning, and the governments of Manitoba, New Brunswick, Nova Scotia and Ontario.

Dr. Higgins has served as professor of economics at McGill, the Université de Montréal, the Massachusetts Institute of Technology, and the Universities of Ottawa, Melbourne and Texas. He has been a visiting professor at the Australian National University, Yale University and the University of California at Berkeley, as well as a senior fellow in the East-West Center at the University of Hawaii.

Professor Higgins is the author of no less than fifteen books, some two dozen major reports, and about 100 articles in professional journals and symposia. Perhaps best known of all is his massive *Economic Development: Problems, Principles, and Policies*, which has become a standard work in the field. He is a fellow of the Royal Society of Canada and holds an Honorary M.A. from the University of Melbourne.

The word "retirement" has no place in Ben Higgins' vocabulary. He has held four academic posts since leaving the University of Ottawa as Professor Emeritus in 1979. In 1981, he was appointed director of the Centre for Applied Studies in Development at the University of the South Pacific, in Fiji. This, his current position, represents only the latest phase of his so-called "retirement." He has produced about a dozen research reports and papers over the past four years. No professional end is in sight, or even remotely on the horizon. And for Ben Higgins, this is exactly as it should be.

In short, Mr. Chancellor, I present to you the one and only Professor Benjamin Higgins — teacher, scholar, man for all

252

seasons, major contributor to our understanding of world development problems, and inspiration for so many lesser mortals who
contemplate, but can never achieve, the fullness of life's experience
that he has lived. Even if only for a little while, Ben Higgins has
come home to McGill. I could find no better occasion for rejoicing
and taking pride.

The Eighth Day of June
Nineteen Hundred and
Eighty-Three

Irving BRECHER
Chairman of the Department
of Economics

Quo Vadis the McGill Class of '83 ?
Benjamin Higgins

Despite the two generation gap, you of the Class of '83 and I have
one thing in common : we both made a bad choice of graduating
year. I graduated in 1933, in the depths of the Great Depression.
You graduate half a century later, in the midst of the worst
recession since. The fact that 50 years have gone by without
another great depression is mark of our progress in economic
theory and policy. The fact that the world economy is now
functioning so badly is a measure of our continuing ignorance. We
economists are like the general who can tell you exactly how to
win the last war : we can tell you how to fight World War II
without inflation, and how to get through postwar reconstruction
without mass unemployment. But we have no palatable remedy
for reducing unemployment and inflation together, and no universal remedy for eliminating poverty in poor countries. As in 1933 so
in 1983 there are signs of recovery; but without marked improvement in economic theory and policy unemployment, inflation and
poverty will be with us for some time to come.

True to the grand tradition of "the dismal science," I expect
the next few years to be especially troublesome ones for Canada.
We have delayed far too long the quantum leap from natural-
resource-based to human-resource-based development that every

country must sooner or later make if it is to provide productive employment for its entire labour force and progressively raise standards of living. At a recent conference in Canberra we were discussing the "miracle" of Singapore's transition from poverty to affluence. An Australian economist broke in, rather impatiently, "That's no miracle! Singapore is not cursed with rich natural resources and a vast hinterland!" Countries that have those things tend to rely on them for their development, as Australia, New Zealand, Canada and even the U.S. have done. The real success stories of recent decades have been those of smaller countries with limited resources: Switzerland, Sweden, Holland, Singapore, Hong Kong, Taiwan, Japan. In such countries there is no choice but to go the human-resource route, developing on the basis of scientifically oriented industry, sophisticated services, and ever higher technology.

Nor can we stop the developing countries from increasing their share of industrial exports. The comparative advantage of most of them lies clearly in industry, just as ours lies clearly in agriculture. One of the disturbing features of our disorderly world economy is that in many countries the bulk of the labour force is engaged in just those sectors where comparative disadvantage is more pronounced. We should not prolong this state of affairs by protectionism.

Within Canada the Province of Quebec shows most clearly the reliance on natural resources and accompanying technological lag. Ever since Confederation Quebec has been nearly as industrialized as Ontario; but Quebec's industry has been lower-technology and lower-productivity, a fact which goes far to explain the lower incomes in Quebec. The further fact that the more advanced enterprises were under anglophone management, which preferred graduates of anglophone institutions in top scientific and managerial jobs, helps to explain the gap between French and English incomes within Quebec.

The technological lag in Quebec centres on Montreal, where most of the Hi-Tech industries and sophisticated services are. As you all know, these are precisely the enterprises that are leaving Montreal for Toronto: Behind this movement there are more fundamental forces at work than fear of Quebec independence. Montreal grew up in the days of water transport on the basis of the confluence of three rivers and the Lachine rapids, which compelled portage in the early days and trans-shipment later. But a barrier to transport is a rather shaky foundation for a thriving city. As Jean Delage says in a prescient passage written in 1943, "N'allons pas imprudemment nous en remettre trop exclusivement aux avantages de notre beau fleuve et des rapides de Lachine."

Cities grow and prosper mainly through interaction with other cities. Increasingly Montreal has become stranded in an industrial desert. Eastern Ontario, which was the industrial heartland of Ontario up to 1850, has stagnated since. There is nothing in northern New England and little in northern New Brunswick. Within Quebec itself there is no other major industrial and services centre with which to interact. The latest blow is the decay of the Great Lakes industrial region and the shift of Hi-Tech industry to the sunbelt, a move which hurts Toronto, but hurts Montreal more. The only solution for Montreal now is to operate in a world market, on the basis of Hi-Tech industries and services where transport costs don't matter.

A good model for Montreal is Boston. When I graduated in 1933 the New England economy, with Boston as its centre, was flat on its back. On top of the devastation of the Great Depression, the textile and pulp and paper industries had migrated to the south, the boot and shoe industry to the mid-west. As you graduate in 1983 Boston and New England are more dynamic and prosperous than ever, with a highly skilled financial sector and a galaxy of Hi-Tech industries. Behind this transformation are Boston's great universities: Harvard, MIT, BU, Brandeis, Tufts. Graduates of these institutions feel that not to see the Charles River every day is to be cast into outer darkness; and that attitude gives a comparative advantage to Hi-Tech enterprises settling in the Boston area.

And so, by what I hope were easy stages, we come back to McGill. In the process of transforming Montreal into a Canadian Boston, and thus strengthening the Quebec and Canadian economies, McGill, with its almost 2-centuries-old tradition of freedom of inquiry, freedom of speech and freedom of publication, has a unique role to play. When I asked our vice chancellor at U.S.P. for a few days off to collect an LL.D. at McGill, he replied, "Ah well, if you must have a Canadian LL.D., it's as well to have it from Canada's best university." But McGill is not alone. In the French-speaking world, the University of Montreal is as well known as McGill is in the English-speaking world. Two weeks ago at a brasserie in Noumea, capital of Nouvelle Calédonie, two French colonials drew me into conversation. When they learned that I had lectured at the U. of M. they said: "Ah bon! L'Université de

Montréal est fameuse dans le monde entier !" The "two solitudes" of McGill and the U. of M. have broken down since I was at McGill, but I would like to see still more cooperation between them. Concordia and the Université du Québec have their own characteristic contributions to make. Together the four universities can make Montreal, like Boston, a city whose graduates don't want to leave, thus giving Montreal a comparative advantage for Hi-Tech enterprises. And if we should not count too much on "our beautiful river and the Lachine rapids" for Montreal's future, surely the St. Lawrence is a better river to see every day than the Charles.

So my message to the Class of '83 is this: stay in Quebec. Help to reconstruct the Quebec and Montreal economies, thus making Canada more whole and more likely to hold together. The scenario I propose will not unfold if all graduates of anglophone universities go to anglophone institutions in anglophone areas and vice versa. You may feel that the picture I have painted of Quebec's future is hardly conducive to staying. But you are the very people whose commitment to that future can make it worthwhile to stay.

My colleagues at the U. of M. used to pay me the compliment of saying, "Il est Québécois par choix." And it was true, I was a Quebecer by choice, as I hope you will be. But I also recall Mayor Drapeau's speech at Montreal's reception for General de Gaulle, after the famous "vive le Québec libre" statement. Near the end, he said: "D'ailleurs, nous les Québécois aimons notre vaste pays." A Quebec, a Montreal, a McGill, which were not part of this vast country of ours could never be the same to me, much as I love them too. So — vive le Canada, vive le Québec, vive Montréal, vive le McGill — vive le McGill libre.